James M. Gavin after his promotion to major general and command of the 82nd Airborne Division, one year after the Sicily campaign. At 37, he became the youngest American two-star general since the Civil War.

DROP ZONE SICILY

Allied Airborne Strike
July 1943

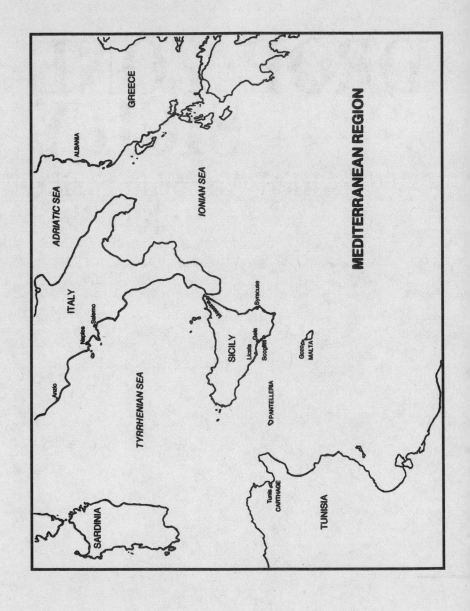

MEDITERRANEAN REGION

DROP ZONE
SICILY

Allied Airborne Strike
July 1943

WILLIAM B. BREUER

★
PRESIDIO

This book is dedicated to those gallant young warriors, the All-Americans of the 82nd Airborne Division and the Red Devils of the British 1st Airborne Division, and to the valiant pilots and air crews who took them into battle.

CONTENTS

List of Maps   vii

Foreword   ix

Prologue   xi

Chapter One
The Plan for the Parachute Drop   1

Chapter Two
Sicily: Top Secret   12

Chapter Three
D-Day Minus One   24

Chapter Four
Mission Ladbroke   40

Chapter Five
Husky One   55

Chapter Six
The Enemy   76

Chapter Seven
√ Assault by Sea   93

Chapter Eight
Heroes of Piano Lupo   108

Chapter Nine
Pillbox Resistance   124

Chapter Ten
Biazza Ridge   135

Chapter Eleven
The "Friendly Fire" Disaster   150

Chapter Twelve
Shoot-out on Hill 41   173

Chapter Thirteen
Attack on Primosole Bridge   189

Chapter Fourteen
Charge at Tumminello Pass   201

Chapter Fifteen
Expedition in a Leaking Fishing Boat   211

Epilogue   222

Personal Interviews and Contacts   227

Bibliography   229

Index   233

MAPS

Mediterranean Region	Frontispiece
Route of Ladbroke Mission	44
Vicinity of Landing Zone for Ladbroke Mission	49
Route of Husky One Mission	62
Planned Drop Zones Near Gela	69
Seaborne Assault	105
Route of Fustian Mission	192
Vicinity of Drop and Landing Zones for Fustian Mission	196

FOREWORD

Drop Zone Sicily, which reports the airborne attack on that island during World War II, is a significant and thoughtful book. It is significant because it was America's very first effort at committing troops to combat by air on a regimental scale and because the airborne assault cracked open Hitler's Festung Europa for the first time. This book is thoughtful because the author has gone to great lengths in digging out the facts behind that airborne operation.

The parachute operation itself faced unusual odds. Two German panzer divisions were on Sicily, a fact known to General Eisenhower and the Allied high command in advance through ULTRA (the top secret device that intercepted and deciphered German messages). But to protect the secret of ULTRA for use in future campaigns, the invading troops were not informed of this. On the contrary, they were told that only a few German technicians were on Sicily.

In addition, our parachute troops were trained to jump with winds up to about 12–15 miles per hour at the most. Just before takeoff for Sicily there was a gale, a 35-mile-per-hour wind, blowing across the Mediterranean that night. Undaunted, our paratroopers jumped on schedule, landing in small packets by battalions miles apart instead of together. They were at once met by the elite Hermann Goering Panzer Division with its colossal Tiger tanks, against which the lightly armed American paratroopers had no effective weapons.

Despite this, our young paratroopers, in combat for the first time, stood up to the panzers, fought them to a standstill, and drove them from the battlefield.

Drop Zone Sicily is a story of the courage of young Americans in their baptism of fire against an experienced and skilled foe. I am glad that their story is being told.

In his fast-moving style, the author describes events as they happened, warts and all. This fine book relates a story that will live in our history for years to come.

Lt. Gen. James M. Gavin (Ret.)
World War II Commander, 82nd Airborne Division

PROLOGUE

As the new year 1943 burst forth over a world engulfed by the holocaust known as World War II, round two of the deadly struggle between the Grand Alliance (the United States, Great Britain and Russia) and the Axis Powers (Germany, Italy, Japan and their satellites) was about to erupt.

Round one had opened on September 1, 1939, when the powerful Wehrmacht (armed forces) of Adolph Hitler's Nazi Germany invaded Poland and crushed that weak country in a few weeks. From that point on, until mid-1942, one European nation after the other had fallen to the mighty legions of the German fuehrer. Adolph Hitler reigned as absolute master of Festung Europa (Fortress Europe).

As 1942 wore on, the fortunes of war changed for Hitler and his principal partner, the bombastic, strutting premier of Fascist Italy, Benito Mussolini. German armies on the frozen Russian front suffered a military catastrophe at Stalingrad, and Generalfeldmarschall Erwin Rommel, the famed Desert Fox, was steadily retreating westward across North Africa with British Gen. Bernard L. Montgomery nipping at his heels every mile of the way.

In November, Anglo-American armies under Gen. Dwight D. Eisenhower had invaded North Africa and were steadily pushing eastward to link up with Montgomery's Eighth Army in Tunisia to corner the Desert Fox, Rommel, and his Afrika Korps.

The war in the air was also going badly for Hitler and Mussolini. The United States Army Air Corps and the British Royal Air Force were growing increasingly stronger, while the once mighty German Luftwaffe, due to a shortage of oil and the combat attrition of its pilots and air crews, was growing steadily weaker, although still a force to be reckoned with.

Taking off from scores of airfields that dotted England, U.S. Army Air Corps and British RAF heavy-bomber fleets were accelerating the pounding of cities, factories and communication lines in the Third Reich, reducing massive areas to rubble.

Wehrmacht casualties, after nearly three and one-half years of fighting, had passed the two million mark. Nearly every home in Germany had one or more loved ones who paid the ultimate price on the far-flung battlefields, in the bitterly contested skies or on the high seas.

On the home front in the Third Reich, more than one million civilians had been killed or wounded and hundreds of thousands of homes and buildings destroyed as Allied air armadas sought to cripple the German war machine. Except for Nazi Party functionaries and their families, there were acute shortages of food, fuel, clothing and other necessities. As 1942 drew to a close, symptoms of war weariness were prevalent among the German *herrenvolk*.

Balanced against these increasing Axis military reversals on land was a calamity being suffered by the United States and Great Britain that nearly brought these two war partners to their knees. German U-boats (submarines) had been inflicting enormous losses on crucial Allied shipping, principally in North Atlantic waters, the supply lifeline for American and British forces in Europe and North Africa.

Since the war began, the German U-boat fleet under Grand Adm. Karl Doenitz had become increasingly more powerful, and in 1942 German submarines sent five Allied merchant vessels (plus many crews) to watery graves every 24 hours. This resulted in more than 1,800 American and British merchant ships being destroyed in that one year.

So daring had become the U-boat campaign that hundreds of Allied vessels were being sunk within minutes of leaving ports along the eastern seaboard of the United States. Looking through periscopes on clear days, captains of U-boats lying in wait just below the surface could see the skylines of New York, Norfolk, Boston, Miami and other bustling ports.

Allied government and military leaders at the highest levels were deeply worried over these catastrophic shipping losses and the increasing boldness of U-boat packs. To the more pessimistic, it appeared that the U-boat onslaught could result in the loss of the war by the Allies.

The American home front and armed forces were being kept in the dark concerning the U-boat success, but not so the German people and Wehrmacht. Dr. Josef Goebbels, the propaganda genius of Nazi Germany, trumpeted over the airwaves of the Third Reich, "German heroism conquers even the wildest oceans!"

As 1943 opened, Admiral Doenitz had 400 submarines in his fleet, compared to 57 when the war began. Now the U-boat commander was poised to crush the United States and Great Britain by launching the mightiest U-boat onslaught in history.

Adolph Hitler, supreme warlord of the Third Reich and master of most of Europe, had suffered reversals on land and in the sky, but his Kriegsmarine (navy) had brought Allied leaders to the brink of panic with relentless submarine blows. Round one had ended in a draw, with the ultimate survivor in the war between the Grand Alliance and the Axis Powers still in doubt.

At this point, on January 13, 1943, an Allied summit conference was convened at Hotel Anfa, near Casablanca. Headed by Franklin D. Roosevelt, president of the United States, and Winston S. Churchill, prime minister of Great Britain, top government and military leaders sought to answer the question: where would the next Anglo-American blow fall?

Hardly had the participants settled in their chairs than heated debate erupted between the English-speaking partners. Gen. George C. Marshall, the low-key, silver-thatched United States Army Chief of Staff, spoke strongly in favor of a massive Anglo-American assault later that same year (1943) across the English Channel against German-occupied northwest France. Marshall argued that such an operation was the quickest way to knife into the heart of the Third Reich and bring the war to a successful conclusion.

The British, with Chief of the Imperial General Staff Gen. Alan Brooke as spokesman, disagreed vehemently with the concept of a cross-Channel attack in 1943. "We are not strong enough yet for such an ambitious venture," Brooke argued. "It could only result in disaster for us if we tried."

General Brooke proposed offensive operations in the Mediterranean to force Hitler to reinforce his armies there, which would require the fuehrer to pull out divisions facing the Russians.

As the conference droned on, the American delegation found itself on the losing end of the verbal dueling and, after four days, capitulated.

"I think the Mediterranean is a kind of dark hole into which one enters at one's own peril," General Marshall observed, aware that his side had been outgunned and outmaneuvered. "But under the present circumstances, I'll support operations against southern Europe, and I'm opposed as much as ever to interminable operations in the Mediterranean."

Before departing for home, President Roosevelt and Prime Minister Churchill agreed to meet with the press of the free world. There Roosevelt, in an off-the-cuff manner, loosed a thunderclap that would dismay other Allied leaders and furnish a gleeful Adolph Hitler with a monumentally damaging propaganda tool.

With scores of journalists avidly taking down notes, the American president casually observed, "Prime Minister Churchill and I have determined that we will accept nothing less than unconditional surrender of Germany, Italy and Japan."

Seated next to the president, Winston Churchill was stunned. That was the first time the British prime minister had heard the phrase "unconditional surrender" used with regard to the war with the Axis.

Churchill was deeply alarmed. With the Third Reich and its Wehrmacht still a powerful force to be reckoned with, the prime minister held the opinion that the posture to be assumed by Allied leadership was one of defiance. He felt it was a blunder of the first magnitude to be dictating harsh terms to the Axis Powers at a time victory or defeat teetered in the balance.

But the damage was done; Churchill could not publicly take issue with his war partner. He assured reporters that he concurred with the unconditional surrender proclamation which he had only moments before heard for the first time. The ultimatum was flashed around the world.

Later, a high official in Churchill's government told him, "Unless those terms are softened, the German army will fight with the ferocity of cornered rats." Already on public record, the prime minister simply shrugged his shoulders.

Gen. Dwight Eisenhower confided to an aide, "If you are given the choice of mounting the scaffold or charging 20 bayonets, you might as well charge the bayonets."

In Berlin, top Nazis rejoiced. The eloquent Dr. Goebbels trumpeted to a gathering of Nazi leaders, "Since the enemies of Germany are determined to enslave the German nation, the war has become an urgent struggle for national preservation in which no sacrifice is too great!"

In Junkers bombers over England and in Messerschmitt fighters above the Fatherland, in U-boats beneath the cold, murky waters of the North Atlantic, in snow-covered foxholes in the frozen tundra of Russia, at dispersed outposts along the underbelly of Europe, the German military man inwardly reaffirmed his vow to fight to the end—with courage, tenacity and a growing feeling of desperation.

A few weeks after the Casablanca conference, General Eisenhower, who had been appointed to command operations in the Mediterranean, received a message from the Combined Chiefs of Staff: "You are to launch an assault against enemy-held Sicily in 1943, with the target date to be the period of the favorable July moon."

The impending Allied invasion of mountainous Sicily was code-named Operation Husky and would be the largest combined maneuver in history involving the land, sea and air forces of two nations. Spearheading the sledgehammer blow to crack open Hitler's Festung Europa, for the first time, would be paratroopers of the U.S. 82nd Airborne Division and glidermen and parachutists of Britain's 1st Airborne Division.

The Allied airborne fighting men would pounce on the enemy at midnight.

CHAPTER ONE

THE PLAN FOR
THE PARACHUTE DROP

A merciless sun, hanging like a huge ball of fire high in the cloudless heavens, beat down on the desolate, rock-hard desert around Oujda, French Morocco, as a tall, thin army officer strolled briskly into the old quonset hut that served as headquarters of the U.S. 82nd Airborne Division. Eagles on his shoulders, a crossed-rifles emblem on his shirt collar, and a round patch depicting a blossoming parachute on his cap identified him as a colonel in the paratroops.

James M. Gavin, commanding officer of the 505th Parachute Infantry Regiment during the nearly two years of its existence, had been ordered to report to Maj. Gen. Matthew B. Ridgway only two days after the division had arrived in the Oujda area. Traveling in rickety old boxcars that had signs in French painted on them reading "40 Men or 8 Horses," the 82nd Airborne had completed a tedious eight-day trek by rail in stifling heat and blinding sandstorms from the port of debarkation at Casablanca.

Now the paratroopers and glidermen of the division were bivouacked in long rows of pup tents outside Oujda and in the vicinity of Marnia, 12 miles to the east. It was May 24, 1943.

Gavin, known as "Slim Jim" to members of the division, knocked on a door with the sign Commanding General crudely lettered on it. Responding to a call to enter, Gavin passed through the doorway as General Ridgway rose from his desk to greet him. As was his custom, the leader of the division pumped Gavin's hand vigorously. Ridgway had a reputation as a great handshaker among the officers of his command.

Colonel Gavin took a seat and Ridgway promptly got to the point of the conference. Speaking in almost conspiratorial tones, barely able to conceal his own excitement, General Ridgway cautioned Gavin that the information he was about to relate was "top secret."

With Gavin's interest mounting, Ridgway continued: "I've been notified by Seventh Army that we're going to parachute into Sicily the night of July 9."

This was the first Gavin knew of the next blow to be struck by the Allies following the destruction of Axis forces in North Africa only 12 days previously. Along with all officers and men in the 82nd Airborne, Gavin had engaged in extensive speculation as to the locale to be invaded by the Anglo-American forces on the road to Berlin.

Gavin felt a surge of elation over Ridgway's revelation. The dynamic young colonel had been highly regarded in the peacetime army as one of its most promising officers, but in 18 years of service he had never heard a shot fired in anger.

Inwardly, Gavin felt he had much to prove. He had washed out of flying school after his 1929 graduation from the U.S. Military Academy at West Point. And while teaching military tactics at that institution in 1941 and seeking a transfer to join the fledgling paratroops, Gavin's commandant wrote on the request: "This officer does not seem peculiarly fitted to be a paratrooper."

Ridgway continued outlining airborne plans for the invasion of Sicily. Gavin's excitement reached a peak when the general stated, "There are not enough C-47s to drop the entire parachute element in the initial assault, so I have decided to give the mission to your 505th as a regimental combat team."

Gavin's first test in the crucible of combat was in the offing.

"The jump will be made around midnight under a full moon," Ridgway continued. "I don't have to remind you that you and your men will be the first armed Americans to set foot on Hitler's Europe, or that you will be making history by participating in the first nighttime mass parachute drop." He added, "As you know, not even the Germans in the Low Countries or in Crete dared to conduct large-scale airborne landings at night."

Both Ridgway and Gavin were fully aware that in a broader context, the forthcoming massive seaborne-airborne assault on Sicily would have the deepest significance. It would be the first true test of combined operations by a military coalition, the United States and Great Britain, and if Sicily were seized, it could conceivably knock Italy out of the war.

At the conclusion of the discussion, Gavin saluted, the men shook hands, and an exhilarated colonel departed the building.

Walking back to his quarters from his conference with General Ridgway, Gavin's elation was tempered by the knowledge that his parachute combat team would include a battalion of Col. Reuben H. Tucker's 504th Parachute Infantry Regiment. Colonels Gavin and Tucker had long been firm friends and mutual admirers, but there had been intense rivalry between the 505s of Gavin and the 504s of Tucker. In weak moments, the 504s would admit the 505s of Gavin were "a pretty good outfit, but they can't even compare with the 504th." For their part, Gavin's men would confess under duress that the 504th was a good outfit to have beside them in a scrap, but "they can't measure up to 'Slim Jim's' boys."

Later that night after his talk with General Ridgway, Colonel Gavin strolled outside his quarters into the muggy silence of the barren desert. He gazed at the full moon posing majestically in the dark blue sky and reflected that the next time that same moon was full, he'd be parachuting into Sicily with his men. Now that he knew the mission and the precise date, he would plunge into relentless training exercises with even more than his customary enthusiasm and drive.

Meanwhile, elsewhere in the sweltering bivouac area near Oujda, Col. Reuben Tucker, the forceful leader of the other parachute regiment in the 82nd Airborne Division, was furious. He had just learned that he and the main body of his 504th regiment would be left behind in Tunisia while Jim Gavin's 505th would "get all the glory."

The commander of the 504th, known to some as Tommy Tucker after the popular big-band leader of the time but to most fellow officers as Rube, was aware that there were insufficient C-47 troop carrier airplanes to drop both of the 82nd Airborne parachute regiments at one time in the initial assault. But Colonel Tucker's fighting heart revolted over the unthinkable —he and the bulk of his regiment would play a follow-up role in the historic first parachute strike to crack open Nazi Europe.

"To make the situation worse," Tucker fumed to his aides, "Ridgway had to steal one of my battalions and give it to Jim for the jump."

Colonel Tucker understood. But it still hurt.

The tough, superbly trained paratroopers and glidermen of the 82nd

Airborne Division had left Fort Bragg, North Carolina, a month previously for an undisclosed destination overseas. They were intensely proud of belonging to an exclusive fraternity, one in which memberships could not be purchased, nor bestowed due to wealth, influence or social standing, but had to be earned by measuring up through one of the most grueling training programs.

At the time the All-Americans, as they were known, were notified at Fort Bragg that they were going overseas, a solemn-faced officer, with a trace of deep remorse in his voice, told them that they would make the entire trek by train and ship, disguised as ordinary soldiers. They would wear leggings instead of their prized jump boots, and their coveted parachute wings, exclusive jump suits and cap patches would be hidden from public view.

"The first time Adolph Hitler is going to learn that the toughest fighting men in the world have arrived overseas is when we kick the bastard right square in his Nazi ass!" the officer bellowed to the assembled All-Americans.

It was a painful experience for the proud paratroopers to remove their badges of honor and conceal them in duffel bags. Smarting from being shorn of his distinctive items, a trooper disgustedly ranted to his comrades, "Why don't they order us to put on leotards, and we can go overseas disguised as a division of USO ballet dancers?"

On the same night that Colonel Gavin had learned from General Ridgway that 82nd Airborne Division paratroopers would spearhead the assault on Axis-held Sicily, Adolph Hitler was presiding at a conference in Berlin. Present were leading functionaries of the Nazi Party. It was 2 A.M., and in the Reich Chancellory the fuehrer was rambling at length on two subjects dear to his heart—the eradication of the Jews and the domination of the world.

Hitler was a night person. He conducted meetings with his field marshals and generals until midnight, then gathered together his Nazi leaders to harangue them until nearly dawn. Others at these feverish and exhaustive conferences were allowed to inject little more than monosyllabic remarks.

Satisfied that much had been accomplished, Hitler adjourned the meeting as dawn was about to break over the war-torn German capital. Later that afternoon, after a refreshing sleep, Dr. Josef Goebbels, minister of propaganda for the Third Reich, wrote in his personal diary:

The Fuhrer argued last night that the anti-Semitism which formerly ani-mated the Nazi Party must again become the focal point of our spiritual struggle.

The Fuhrer gave expression to his unshakable conviction that the Reich will be master of all Europe. From then on the way to world domination is practically certain.

As Adolph Hitler was proceeding with his plans, paratroopers and glidermen of the 82nd Airborne were engaged in intensive around-the-clock training on the desert of North Africa. "You've got to be tough 'cause the German you meet will be goddamned tough!" General Ridgway said repeatedly to his perspiring fighting men.

Paratroopers, a cocky and exclusive breed of fighting men, regarded the human race as divided into two categories—those who leapt out of air-planes and those who did not. The parachutists had little respect (if any) for those in the latter classification.

Due to the nature of the parachute business, there was a unique and close-knit relationship between officers and men, one of mutual respect and confidence in each other. Chaplains, cooks, surgeons, generals, riflemen, clerks and medics faced identical dangers when jumping into combat. Bod-ies hurtling from airplanes and floating down under billowing white parachutes all looked alike to hostile gunners on the ground. A general or colonel or chaplain was just as likely to plunge to his death with a "streamer" (a chute that failed to open) as was the most humble private.

Unlike members of the 82nd Airborne Division's two parachute regi-ments who were volunteers, men in the 325th Glider Infantry Regiment had been assigned to that military occupation because they had been deemed outstanding soldiers.

Although the glider riders, as the paratroopers called them, were out-numbered by parachutists, three to one, the airborne soldiers, who would enter battle by crash-landing behind enemy lines in flimsy, motorless air-craft, had an esprit of their own. But long ago the glidermen began to regard themselves as the poor relations of the airborne division, to be condoned but recognized only when it was absolutely necessary.

Glidermen were especially outraged over the disparity of pay. For per-forming hazardous duty, parachute officers received an additional $100 per month and enlisted men had $50 attached to their monthly pay. Glidermen received no hazardous duty pay.

"I would give a year's pay if the desk-bound son of a bitch in Washington who decided crash landing in one of these canvas coffins isn't hazardous duty would go up with us just once," a gliderman raged.

It was more than pay inequity that bothered the 82nd Airborne glidermen. Unlike the paratroopers, the men who rode into battle in gliders were not authorized to wear distinctive cap patches, wing insignias or ankle-high boots. Other than the word airborne on the shoulder patches worn by each All-American, glidermen of the division looked much like regular soldiers.

Bivouacked adjacent to the main body of the 82nd Airborne outside Oujda was the 509th Parachute Infantry Battalion, whose members were the first American paratroopers to go overseas and the first to jump into combat. Commanded by Lt. Col. Doyle R. Yardley, a former schoolteacher from Texas, the independent 509th Battalion was attached to the newly arrived 82nd Airborne Division.

The 509th Parachute Infantry Battalion had made three combat jumps in North Africa in 1942 and had fought as straight infantry against Rommel's vaunted Afrika Korps in Tunisia. Now the troopers of the battalion were chagrined to be attached to the 82nd Airborne, whose members the veterans of the 509th considered greenhorns at the fighting business.

Soon the men of the 509th Parachute Infantry Battalion were loudly announcing in sleazy bars that the 82nd Airborne Division, 12 times larger numerically, was attached to the 509th. Although few of the All-Americans had been under fire, their ranks included some of the toughest soldiers in the U.S. Army.

It was not long before fists, with bottles and chairs in supporting roles, were flying in the native saloons in and around Oujda as the battle-tested men of the 509th and the green but rugged troopers of the 82nd Airborne engaged in free-for-all brawls. A few hours later the participants would be engaging in rigorous training exercises or long hikes under a scorching sun across the concrete-hard desert.

As these arduous combat preparations continued night and day, few members of the airborne division were aware that a target and a firm date for the next Anglo-American blow had been set—Sicily, with D-Day July 9. The impending assault on Hitler's Fortress Europe was cloaked in a shroud of deep secrecy.

Only General Ridgway, Brig. Gen. Charles L. Keerans, the assistant division commander, Brig. Gen. Maxwell D. Taylor, the artillery commander, the three regimental colonels and a few staff members knew the secret.

Unaware that their immediate destiny had been decided at the highest levels of command, the paratroopers and glidermen had little relief from training.

Off-duty hours were boring, tedious and uncomfortable. The pup tents were stifling. When the sun made its appearance, the men trying to sleep in the tiny canvas tents were nearly boiled alive. Sleep was impossible. Yet at night it was back to the desert for more combat training.

Returning exhausted from the night jaunts across the desolate terrain, the All-Americans would invariably be told by General Ridgway, "You've got to be tough! The Kraut you tangle with will sure as hell be tough!"

Flies nearly blackened the sky around the long line of pup tents—millions of flies. The food dished up by hard-working cooks, who did the best they could under the conditions in which they labored, was suspect. Seldom could a meal be eaten without a fly being discovered in it. Sand blowing into the food had long before been accepted by the airborne men as a fact of life in the deserts of North Africa.

Most of the All-Americans were racked with dysentery, and those going on guard duty found it necessary to take along entrenching shovels for emergency use. Tempers under these brutal climatic conditions, already frayed, often exploded, and rollicking brawls, even among good friends, broke out along the rows of pup tents.

May moved into June. The bronzed parachutists and glidermen were not only keen, lean and mean—they were angry.

Alternately, and with equal fervor, they cursed North Africa, the German Wehrmacht, sand, the food, generals, the U.S. Army, Arabs, Adolph Hitler, the Italian army, cactus needles, pup tents, and whatever other target presented itself.

"I don't give a goddamn if I get a bullet right between the eyes in my first minute of combat," a paratrooper griped to comrades. "I've got my belly full of this stinking A-rab hell hole. Bring on those goddamned Krauts and Spaghetti Benders!"

Although the 82nd Airborne was headed for battle, experiments to develop new techniques continued. General Ridgway ordered the 505th Parachute Infantry Regiment to conduct trial and error tests on parachuting mules into combat. The sturdy, surefooted beasts of burden could prove useful in supplying troops in the mountainous terrain of Sicily, someone at a high level of command had decided.

Col. James Gavin turned the mule-dropping assignment over to Maj. Mark J. Alexander, executive officer of the 2nd Battalion. As was his custom, the young officer energetically plunged into the mission. He rounded up two sergeants and a corporal, having purchased two mules from an Arab after a considerable amount of haggling over the price.

The pair of mules were fitted with 48-foot parachutes, taken to an airfield and, through an all-out effort by the paratroopers, corralled into a C-47. Once inside, the mules were blindfolded, the airplane took off, and the reluctant, long-eared animals were shoved through the cargo door in the vicinity of Oujda.

Both mules received broken legs on crashing into the ground and had to be destroyed. The mule-dropping project was promptly abandoned. It would be six weeks before the All-Americans would learn firsthand that Sicily had more mules per square foot than nearly any other country in the world.

While Anglo-American forces were coiling to spring onto Axis-held Sicily, Adolph Hitler, his Oberkommando der Wehrmacht (armed forces high command), and German and Italian field commanders in the Mediterranean held divided opinions as to where the Allies would strike next. The German fuehrer, who had personally assumed control of the Wehrmacht more than two years earlier, believed that the powerful Anglo-American war machine in North Africa would invade Sardinia or Greece. The Oberkommando der Wehrmacht (OKW), not unexpectedly, had agreed with the commander in chief's point of view. But the fuehrer's thinking had been infected by his being the victim of a major deception.

When Axis armies in Tunisia surrendered to the Allies in May, it was obvious to the high command on both sides that Sicily was the next logical target. Sicily, the mountainous, triangular-shaped island the size of the state of New Hampshire, was long regarded as a stepping-stone to continental Europe.

Now the problem facing the Anglo-Americans was: what could be done to deceive Hitler into believing that the impending Allied blow would hit elsewhere than the *obvious* target, Sicily?

It was decided that the stratagem to play upon Adolph Hitler should be that Sicily was too obvious a target and that the Anglo-Americans would strike instead at either the island of Sardinia, as a stepping-stone for a thrust into southern France, or Greece as a base to attack through the Balkans. Such a stratagem, if successful, would cloak the true target of Husky—Sicily.

A plan aptly code-named Operation Trojan Horse was developed by MI-6, Great Britain's intelligence branch, under the guidance of Stewart Menzies, a 53-year-old aristocrat. Menzies and a number of associates constituted a top secret organization known as the XX-Committee (double cross committee), a highly creative and resourceful panel of experts in a variety of fields.

As ingenious as was the plan to cloak Allied intentions, its thrust was an improvisation of a ploy as old as warfare—planting false papers where the enemy would "accidentally" discover them and cause him to take an action to his own disadvantage. The main ingredient of Trojan Horse was Operation Mincemeat, which was sprung on the Germans April 30, 1943, after eight weeks of the most tedious and painstaking preparation by the XX-Committee.

On that morning the body of a Royal Marine officer, whose papers identified him as Capt. (Acting Maj.) William Martin, 09560, floated ashore at Huelva, Spain, in the Gulf of Cadiz. He apparently had died in an airplane crash at sea. The Royal Marine officer obviously was a courier, for a dispatch case was fastened to one arm. In the case were top-secret documents from the highest level of British government, which indicated conclusively that the Anglo-Americans would invade Greece or Sardinia—not Sicily.

In Huelva was an Abwehr (the German counterintelligence branch) agent who, through collusion with pro-German Spanish authorities, made copies of the documents and rushed the prints to his chief, Adm. Wilhelm Canaris, in Berlin. There the documents were meticulously tested as to authenticity. Canaris promptly informed Adolph Hitler that the papers were genuine, that indeed the Allies planned to invade Greece or Sardinia.

Hitler was exuberant over the intelligence coup by his Abwehr and promptly began shifting his forces to strengthen the Balkans and Sardinia for the impending Allied invasion.

Actually, the unidentified man in the British officer's uniform was a civilian who had died of pneumonia. He had been packed in dry ice and taken offshore from Huelva, Spain, in a submarine where he was cast adrift. Other ingenious and subtle devices were implemented by the XX-Committee to reinforce Hitler's belief that the Anglo-Americans would hit at Sardinia or Greece, and the fuehrer's conviction that the Allied blow would come at one of the two locales grew stronger with the passing of time.

Not all of Hitler's field marshals and generals agreed with him, but those in the minority were careful to conceal their views. Generalfeldmarschall Albert Kesselring, known to the Allies as "Smiling Al," was one of those. Kesselring, Oberbefehlshaber Sued (Commander in Chief, South), was in charge of Wehrmacht forces in the Mediterranean region. Late in May, as indications continued to multiply that the Anglo-Americans in North Africa would strike soon, Field Marshal Kesselring flew from his headquarters at Frascati, 10 miles south of Rome, to Enna, in central Sicily, to confer with Generale d'Armata Alfredo Guzzoni, commander of Sixth Army. The purpose of Kesselring's visit was to determine firsthand the state of readiness of German and Italian forces in Sixth Army.

General Guzzoni had been called out of retirement in April to take charge of Axis defenses in Sicily. Despite his 66 years, the Italian general was vigorous and a competent tactician. Unlike Hitler and the OKW in Berlin, Guzzoni was convinced that the impending Allied assault would hit Sicily.

When the energetic Guzzoni arrived at Enna early in May, he was appalled by the condition of its defenses. The 230,000 Italian soldiers on Sicily were poorly equipped, inadequately trained, and lacked mobility. Morale was at rock bottom. Guzzoni knew his greatest difficulty would be to get his men to fight when the Anglo-American blow struck the island.

Though distressed over the situation he inherited, Guzzoni did not despair. He knew that two crack German panzer divisions and other Wehrmacht troops were being rushed to Sicily. These first-rate German fighters, Guzzoni was convinced, would stiffen the backbone of his less than enthusiastic Italian divisions.

Now, in late May, Field Marshal Kesselring was conferring with General Guzzoni and German and Italian commanders on Sicily. Kesselring stressed, "It makes no difference whether or not you receive orders from Sixth Army in Enna. There will be no time to wait if the enemy strikes. You must go into immediate action against the enemy the moment you determine his intentions."

Guzzoni nodded his head in firm agreement.

Generalleutnant Paul Conrath, the tough-talking, aggressive commander of the elite Hermann Goering Division, impulsively blurted out, "If you mean go for them, Feldmarschall, then I'm your man!"

While General Guzzoni was in command of all Axis forces on Sicily, a highly regarded German general would be at his elbow at all times as an "advisor." Generalmajor Fridolin von Senger und Etterlin had distinguished himself as a leader of a panzer corps in Russia. An ex-Rhodes Scholar and graduate of England's prestigious Oxford University, von Senger und Etterlin was a member of an aristocratic German family and a Benedictine lay brother, curious qualifications for a general so highly regarded by Hitler and other top Nazis.

Hitler had a good reason for sending the aggressive von Senger to Sicily. His mission: prod the Italians to fight. In General Guzzoni, von Senger soon discovered that he had a first-class scrapper to "advise."

CHAPTER TWO

SICILY: TOP SECRET

F ive sleek Mosquito fighter-bombers of the British Royal Air Force were speeding through the sky on a lovely spring night in the Mediterranean. The craft had lifted off from an airfield on the tiny island of Malta, 70 miles due south of Sicily, and set a course for the American parachute drop zone north and northeast of Gela. It was June 10—one month before D-Day in Sicily.

In the lead plane with a pilot was Col. James Gavin, who would jump with his reinforced 505th Parachute Infantry Regiment. Passengers in the other Mosquitoes were two of Gavin's battalion commanders and two pilots of the 52nd Trooper Carrier Wing, the C-47 outfit which would lift Gavin's paratroopers to Sicily.

Gavin and the other passengers were reconnoitering the flight route and the drop zone. This night had been selected for the reconnaissance because the moon was in the same phase as it would be the night of the parachute assault.

The recon had started that afternoon at Kairouan, Tunisia, when Colonel Gavin and the other four American officers took off for Homs, where they had tea with a Royal Air Force unit and then flew on to Malta in time for dinner.

After dining, two British intelligence officers escorted the three American parachute leaders and two Troop Carrier Command pilots to an airfield hangar. There the five men going on the recon flight were asked to place the contents from pockets onto a table. The experienced British officers knew one or more of the Mosquitoes could be shot down over Sicily, and the contents in the American officers' pockets might help Axis intelligence piece together Allied plans for the impending assault on the island.

Climbing into the Mosquitoes, fast, highly maneuverable aircraft, the Americans and their British pilots took off in the darkness, heading due north, knifing across the shore of southern Sicily at almost the precise sector over which the sky armada carrying Colonel Gavin's men the night of July 8 would fly. The little formation then flew on inland and came under heavy antiaircraft fire in the vicinity of Ponte Olivio airfield, at the western edge of the DZ (drop zone).

Violent explosions rocked the five Mosquitoes, and pilots began taking intense evasive action, weaving and bobbing their aircraft to avoid the heavy concentration of enemy flak. The five planes quickly headed for the open sea, then high-tailed it back to Malta.

Climbing out of his Mosquito after landing and heading for the hangar to recover his personal possessions, Colonel Gavin expressed disappointment in the reconnaissance flight. He felt that he was no better informed than when he took off, due to the high speed and the evasive action taken over the DZ.

Earlier that day at Algiers, North Africa, Gen. Dwight Eisenhower stood before a roomful of reporters at his Allied Force Headquarters. Knowing that the Anglo-American war machine had been lying relatively dormant since the capitulation of Axis forces in Tunisia the previous month, the correspondents were expecting a routine announcement—perhaps an appointment or two to key posts in the Allied coalition.

What the reporters received instead was a bombshell.

Eisenhower, far too heavily committed to engage in preliminary prattle, got right to the heart of his announcement. "We will assault Sicily early in July, with the British Eighth Army under General Montgomery attacking the eastern beaches north of Syracuse and the U.S. Seventh Army under General Patton attacking the southern beaches," he stated.

Mouths fell open. An eerie hush pervaded the conference room. An official announcement to scores of news reporters one month in advance of a major military operation, including the target and time, stunned the correspondents.

Eisenhower held back virtually nothing. Reporters ceased to scribble notes because the top secret information they were receiving could not be transmitted to their newspapers, magazines and radio stations back home. Each correspondent realized that thousands of Allied lives and a crucial campaign would be the price paid for any inadvertent leakage of this awesome top secret briefing.

As the supreme commander neared the conclusion of his presentation, he stated, "We will use airborne troops on a much larger scale than has yet been attempted in warfare."

Eisenhower left the room. Several score of war reporters sat in place—dazed and silent. Then, individually and in little knots, the correspondents drifted away. Many resisted impulses to glance back over their shoulders to see if anyone was following them—Abwehr agents.

The supreme commander's thunderclap had not been loosed impulsively. It had been extensively debated with key staff officers. Curiously, the purpose of briefing reporters a month in advance was to maintain secrecy. During periods when no major operation was in progress, reporters had to continue to send back regular reports to their newspapers, magazines or radio stations. Most of these stories were speculative in nature as the reporter sought a new "angle." Eisenhower feared that a flood of conjectural reports in United States media could be pieced together by crafty German intelligence agencies to pinpoint Sicily as the target for invasion.

While Eisenhower was briefing reporters on the Allies' forthcoming offensive, impeccably groomed German staff officers were sitting down to breakfast in the dining room of the beautiful San Dominico Hotel at Taormina. Perched on a high cliff with a breathless view of the sea, the hotel was the forward headquarters in Sicily for Field Marshal Kesselring.

As the Wehrmacht officers were sipping coffee, the familiar sound of airplane motors was heard. Unseen to the Germans in the dining room, a small flight of Royal Air Force bombers was opening bomb-bay doors. Moments later a whining noise—the sound of falling bombs—caused the diners to scramble under the tables. A bomb crashed through the ceiling and exploded in the center of the dining room, killing several German officers and seriously wounding others.

ULTRA, an ingenious British decoding device that had long been intercepting German radio messages, had pinpointed the San Dominico Hotel. But the chief quarry in the bombing, Kesselring, escaped the vengeance of the hunters in the sky. He was in Rome at the time.

Meanwhile, outside searing, fly-infested Oujda, French Morocco, men of the 82nd Airborne Division fell out one morning to receive welcome news —the division was moving out. As troopers listened avidly, officers explained that the 82nd would make a 1,000-mile trek eastward, by airplane, glider, truck, jeep and "40 and 8" boxcars.

Most All-Americans were elated to be leaving. A few cynics saw the trek as a move to "another goddamned A-rab hellhole."

"Troopers, I'll let you in on a secret I learned from General Eisenhower," one skeptical parachutist confided. "The mission of the 82nd Airborne in this war is to travel constantly up and down this goddamned North Africa desert to confuse the Krauts."

Shortly after dawn on June 16, a detail of officers and men, most burdened with full field packs, climbed into trucks and drove off in a swirl of sandy gusts for their destination in far-off Tunisia. In the days ahead other elements departed Oujda, and in two weeks' time all of the 82nd Airborne Division was established in a complex of tent camps in a 30-mile arc around the Moslem holy city of Kairouan.

Unlike the barren wasteland outside Oujda, there were olive groves and high cactus hedges around the new campsites, which provided shade in which to pitch pup tents and avoid the direct rays of the fireball sun.

The tents at Oujda had been set up in neat rows, as the area was outside the range of Axis bombers. But around Kairouan, less than 250 miles from enemy air bases, tent encampments had to be dispersed and camouflaged.

Unknown to the All-Americans, other young warriors from the sky— the Red Devils of Britain's 1st Airborne Division—were assembling in North Africa to join in the impending airborne operation. The Red Devils were commanded by Maj. Gen. G. F. "Hoppy" Hopkinson, a wiry and energetic leader who had replaced the "father" of the British airborne service, Maj. Gen. Frederick A. M. "Boy" Browning. The latter had been assigned as airborne advisor to General Eisenhower for Operation Husky.

The battle-tested 1st Parachute Brigade, commanded by Brig. Gerald Lathbury, was posted near Mascara, in Algeria. It was joined by the 2nd Parachute Brigade, led by Brig. Eric Down, and the 1st Air Landing Brigade (gliders), commanded by Brig. P. H. W. "Pip" Hicks. Arriving from Palestine was the 4th Parachute Brigade, whose leader was Brig. H. W. Hackett.

Now General Hopkinson had his entire 1st Airborne Division together and, like most of his men, was straining for early action. Unlike the All-

Americans, whose homeland had not been sullied by a single Axis bomb, the Red Devils had a tangible and compelling motive for battling Axis forces—vengeance. The men, who wore an emblem on each sleeve depicting Bellerophon astride the winged horse Pegasus, knew firsthand the enormous destruction and heavy death toll that the Luftwaffe had inflicted on England.

Outside Kairouan in late June, elements of the 82nd Airborne Division held a night practice parachute drop. Among those participating were two recent arrivals from the United States. As the pair of young paratroopers descended to earth under blossoming white parachutes, unseen in the darkness loomed a cluster of giant cacti trees which grew in abundance in the desert around Kairouan.

The two parachutists crashed into a pair of the cacti trees, and several one- to two-foot spines, which could have penetrated a thick board, knifed into their bodies. Screaming in excruciating agony, the troopers remained suspended in the trees and impaled on the spines. As the sounds of the horrible screaming echoed across the bleak, dark desert, other All-Americans rushed to the site but were unable to aid the victims. The pair of youths, who had not been in camp long enough for comrades to learn their names, died in anguish.

Eventually removed from the trees in death, the unlucky troopers were buried soon afterward. So many cactus spines had entered their bodies that they were interred with the sharp-pointed needles still in them.

Across the Mediterranean from where the American and British airborne divisions were preparing for imminent battle, Col. Emilio Fadella, the bright, youthful Italian Chief of Staff of Sixth Army, was having a convivial conversation with Adolph Hitler's advisor to the Sicily garrison, Gen. Fridolin von Senger und Etterlin. The two military leaders were exchanging candid views on the ultimate outcome of the war.

Colonel Fadella was far from optimistic. "General von Senger," he said, "your famous Clausewitz has written that when it becomes evident a war can no longer be won, you should, with the aid of the politicians, try to obtain an honorable end to the affair."

"I entirely agree," the suave von Senger replied. "But the trouble is, Hitler has never read Clausewitz."

Meanwhile, at Allied Force Headquarters in Algiers, Gen. Dwight Eisenhower and his staff had given final approval to the plan for Operation

Husky. Parachute and glider elements would strike the first blow, landing just before midnight, under a full moon, on July 8. The U.S. 505th Regimental combat team, commanded by Col. James Gavin, was to drop north and northeast of the coastal town of Gela and seize the commanding high ground known as Piano Lupo, block enemy efforts to reach landing seaborne forces, disrupt enemy communications, and create general havoc.

Brigadier Hicks and his British 1st Air Landing Brigade were to crash-land in gliders near Syracuse, on the east coast of Sicily, at about the same time that Colonel Gavin's paratroopers were bailing out. The Red Devil glidermen were to seize and hold the key Ponte Grande bridge to allow British seaborne forces to pour across the river span into the port of Syracuse.

A few hours after the airborne elements had landed and under cover of darkness, seaborne assault troops would storm ashore at eight points along a 100-mile sector which reached from Syracuse on the east coast to Licata, along the southern shoreline.

Under flamboyant Lt. Gen. George S. Patton, the U.S. Seventh Army, which had been organized in North Africa under a cloak of secrecy only a few weeks before, would land along the southern coast. At the same time, the veteran British Eighth Army, commanded by wiry, energetic Gen. Bernard L. Montgomery, would assault the east coast of the island, south of the large city of Syracuse. Once the Allies established a foothold on Sicily, other Anglo-American divisions would pour onto the island.

The combined airborne-amphibious assault would be a mammoth undertaking. Forces had to be collected, trained, equipped and eventually embarked from widely dispersed bases in the Mediterranean, England and the United States, the latter more than 4,000 miles from Sicily. In the initial assault there would be 160,000 men, nearly 3,000 ships and landing craft, 14,000 vehicles, 600 tanks and 1,800 guns.

General Eisenhower, the supreme commander, would establish his headquarters at the tiny island of Malta, 70 miles south of Sicily, just before D-Day in order to be nearby if an immediate crucial decision were required. Under Eisenhower in the chain of command would be British Gen. Harold R. L. G. Alexander, who would lead Fifteenth Army Group. Patton's and Montgomery's field armies would be under Alexander.

The airborne phase of Husky called for four separate missions—all at night. The darkness would help protect the lumbering, unarmed C-47 troop carrier planes from ground antiaircraft fire and Luftwaffe night interceptors and aid in attaining tactical surprise for the paratroopers and glidermen.

Britain's 1st Air Landing Brigade under Brigadier Hicks would lead off the assault. Hicks's 1,600 men would travel to battle in 144 Horsa and Waco gliders pulled by C-47s of the U.S. 51st Troop Carrier Group and by English Albemarle bombers. This initial British glider operation was code-named Ladbroke.

Hard on the winged heels of Brigadier Hicks's glidermen, Colonel Gavin and his U.S. 505th Parachute Regimental Combat Team, which included a battalion of Col. Reuben Tucker's 504th Regiment, would lift off in 266 C-47s, bound for drop zones near Gela. Gavin's mission was code-named Husky Number One.

Colonel Tucker and his remaining two battalions and support elements were to take off the following night in Husky Number Two. Tucker and his troopers were to land on a DZ west of Gela already secured by Gavin's men.

The final airborne mission, code-named Fustian, would take place five days later. On the night of July 13, battle-tested men of Brigadier Lathbury's British 1st Parachute Brigade would bail out and seize the key Primasole bridge over the Simento River, which would allow Gen. Bernard Montgomery's seaborne Eighth Army to pour over the span. The Desert Rats would then attack northward to the Catania plain and push on to the invasion's ultimate objective, the port of Messina, at the northeast tip of Sicily.

If Montgomery's army, with its path cleared by the 1st Parachute Brigade, could reach Messina at an early date, German and Italian forces on Sicily would be cut off from their only route of escape—the two-mile-wide Strait of Messina which flowed between the island and the toe of mainland Italy.

In the scorching heat in tented bivouac areas around the holy city of Kairouan, word that the veteran U.S. 509th Parachute Infantry Battalion was not included in plans for the airborne assault on Nazi Europe angered most members of the outfit that had made three combat jumps in North Africa and had fought Rommel's Afrika Korps there.

"That's what happens when you're a bastard battalion," a 509er fumed to his comrades. "We don't have the brass to go to bat for us with the big shots."

Rage was equally rife in the encampment of the 82nd Airborne's 325th

Glider Infantry Regiment. As their parachute comrades tangled with the Germans and Italians in Sicily, the glidermen would remain in reserve in Tunisia. "We've always been the poor relations of this outfit," a gliderman observed resignedly. "Nothing's changed."

There was ample reason for leaving the All-American glidermen among the cacti trees of Tunisia: all available Allied gliders had been turned over to the British for the mission to secure Ponte Grande bridge in front of General Montgomery's Eighth Army.

At headquarters of the British 1st Airborne Division, Gen. Hoppy Hopkinson, leader of the unit, was engaged in animated discussion with Col. George Chatterton, commander of British glider pilots in North Africa. The feisty Hopkinson had been eager to get his division involved in the Sicily invasion. Without the knowledge of the senior airborne advisor to General Eisenhower, General Browning, Hopkinson had convinced Bernard Montgomery of the wisdom of a night glider assault to seize Ponte Grande at Syracuse in front of the advancing Eighth Army.

As a result of General Hopkinson's persuasive salesmanship, Montgomery had insisted that the glider mission at Syracuse and a later parachute drop just south of the Catania plain be included in Operation Husky.

Now Hopkinson was briefing Colonel Chatterton in glowing terms on the forthcoming British glider assault. The colonel commanding the glider pilots became increasingly disturbed, then totally dismayed. General Hopkinson made it all sound so routine, Chatterton mused to himself, but he was convinced the night glider assault as planned would result in disaster.

Chatterton inquired as to where sufficient gliders and tugs would be obtained. Hopkinson replied that the American Army Air Corps would provide additional C-47 tugs and Waco gliders to supplement the British airlift.

The colonel continued to raise objections. He pointed out that his pilots had had minimal training in British-built Horsa gliders and none at all in America Wacos, and that they would have to crash-land at night under enemy fire and on terrain of an unknown nature.

General Hopkinson had grown increasingly irritable and now lost his temper. "Now listen to me, Colonel. I'm going to leave this room for a half hour. When I'm gone, you think this over and study the photographs of the landing zone. When I return, if you still think this mission is too difficult, you can consider yourself relieved of your command and I'll send you back to England."

Hopkinson, anger deeply etched into his red face, stomped out of the room.

Colonel Chatterton began sifting through aerial photographs of the landing zone south of Syracuse. He was appalled, convinced that it would be difficult to locate a worse site in Europe for a mass glider landing. Huge boulders dotted the fields which sloped sharply on the sides of the mountains. Some fields in the landing zone were surrounded by thick stone walls and others were patterned with olive groves.

In the few minutes remaining before General Hopkinson returned to the room, Chatterton reached an agonizing decision: he would proceed with preparations for the glider mission wholeheartedly and without further protest. He concluded that the commander of the 1st Airborne Division was determined to go through with the glider mission as planned, and should Chatterton be relieved, there was no experienced officer in North Africa to take his place.

Hopkinson, grim and unsmiling, stalked back into the room. Advised by Chatterton of his decision, the general's stern visage broke out in a wide smile. "I knew you'd see it my way when you thought it over," Hopkinson beamed, patting the worried colonel on the back.

As D-Day for Sicily rapidly drew closer, a long-simmering dispute between two Allied airborne generals spilled over into the open. Gen. Matthew Ridgway, commander of the U.S. 82nd Airborne Division, and British Gen. Frederick Browning, airborne advisor to the supreme commander, had for weeks been feuding over tactics to be employed and the allocation of military resources. This antagonism had grown steadily due to divergent national interests, and a personality clash between the two strong-willed airborne generals had added fuel to the bickering.

Ridgway and other top American airborne officers were constantly irritated over what they considered subtle remarks and actions by Browning which conveyed the suave British general's view of the 82nd Airborne and its commanders as newcomers to the art of war, particularly with regard to parachute and glider operations.

The hackles would rise on the back of General Ridgway's neck when Browning would reply to the American's comment by saying, "Now, my dear Ridgway, what you Americans don't understand is . . ."

On the other side of the coin, Matt Ridgway, a brusque, no-nonsense commander, would hardly qualify for the striped pants and top hat of the diplomatic corps. Ridgway, likewise, had an inborn talent for rousing the ire of General Browning, even in matters of minimal significance.

Personality clashes aside, the hard, indisputable fact at the core of the ongoing dispute was that American C-47 troop carrier and glider-tug airplanes were steadily being taken away from allocation to the 82nd Airborne Division and turned over to the British for their use in the Sicily assault. As orders for the transfer of these invaluable aircraft emanated from Allied Force Headquarters in Algiers, where General Browning was senior airborne advisor, Ridgway and his commanders were convinced that the British general was the culprit.

Meanwhile, in the tent encampments of the 82nd Airborne Division scattered in a wide arc around the holy city of Kairouan, Tunisia, rumors abounded as to the locale of the forthcoming Anglo-American operation. There were numerous 82nd men of Greek descent who were enthusiastic over the possibility that they would land in Greece to help liberate their ancestors' homeland from its Nazi oppressors.

One of these, Lt. Anthony J. Pappas, whose father operated a popular restaurant in Chicago, sought out his regimental commander. "Colonel Gavin," Pappas began with a trace of a pleading smile on his face, "can't you give us just a little hint that we sure as hell are going to jump into Greece like the rumor says we are?"

Gavin, who had known for several weeks that the target for the impending invasion would be Sicily, merely grinned and replied, "Tony, that's a damned good question."

Reflecting later on the eagerness of Lieutenant Pappas to learn if the All-Americans were going to parachute into Greece, Colonel Gavin thought to himself: What a great addition that would have been to add to our cover plan on the Sicily assault if I had hinted to Tony that yes, indeed, we would parachute into Greece. The GI grapevine, being what it is, would have it all over North Africa by morning that our target was Greece, and Axis agents would surely pick up the false rumor.

As the month of June dwindled to a few days and Allied D-Day in Sicily was rapidly approaching, Field Marshal Kesselring, at his headquarters at Frascati, south of Rome, was growing increasingly uneasy over the wide expanse of southern Europe and the Balkans that was his responsibility to defend. Unlike his fuehrer and the OKW in Berlin, Kesselring held the view that the Anglo-Americans would make their primary strike at Sicily, with the possibility of diversionary attacks at Greece, Sardinia or else-where.

Should Allied forces succeed in surprising the Wehrmacht, Adolph Hitler would require a scapegoat among the military. Kesselring was too cagy an old warrior to allow that title to be bestowed upon him. Conse-quently, the commander in chief-south deemed it prudent to inform OKW in Berlin as to the complete disposition of German and Italian forces in Sicily and elsewhere in the Mediterranean. If there were blame to be at-tached to some future military disaster, Kesselring wanted to make certain that the German high command was aware of circumstances in advance so that the fuehrer's wrath could be distributed among many.

The lengthy message containing Axis troop dispositions was transmitted in the German ENIGMA code, considered by Hitler and others in the Wehrmacht as "unbreakable." The detailed report was intercepted by the ingenious British decoding machine, ULTRA, translated and placed on the desk of Allied Supreme Commander General Eisenhower almost at the same time it reached the intended recipient, Feldmarschall Wilhelm Kei-tel, in Berlin.

The Kesselring troop-disposition report produced a stunning bombshell for Eisenhower and his staff. Instead of meeting only the demoralized, ill-equipped and poorly led Italian army in Sicily, the Germans had secretly slipped two first-rate armored divisions across the Strait of Messina. The most alarming aspect of the intercepted enemy report was that the elite, battle-tested Hermann Goering Panzer Fallschirmjaeger (tank, para-trooper) Division was in position a short distance inland from where the lightly armed U.S. 82nd Airborne Division was to jump. Eisenhower had ample reason for concern.

The American paratroopers would be highly vulnerable to armored as-sault in the early hours of their mission. Carrying only the personal weap-ons with which they bailed out, Colonel Gavin's parachutists would be without artillery support, antitank guns or tanks. Their only weapon against enemy panzers would be the 2.36-inch rocket fired from bazookas, which had often bounced off German tanks in North Africa fighting.

A determined attack against Gavin's 3,400 paratroopers by tanks of the Hermann Goering Division could wipe out the parachute force and allow enemy panzers to rush onward to the beaches to rake American seaborne troops at point-blank range as they came ashore and were vulnerable. In such an eventuality, the entire invasion of Sicily could meet with catastrophe.

Interception of Kesselring's top-secret report on Axis troop dispositions once again brought to the forefront an anguished question for high-level Allied military and governmental leaders: who should share in enemy secrets uncovered by the ingenious ULTRA? It was vital to the Allied war effort that the existence of ULTRA be concealed from the enemy, regardless of the price to be paid.

Colonel Gavin's paratroopers could certainly be better prepared to handle a confrontation with German panzers were they to know in advance of the thick-plated monsters in the vicinity of the drop zone. But lightly armed parachutists behind enemy lines were likely candidates for capture, and German interrogators would soon learn that the American invaders from the sky had full knowledge of the presence of the Hermann Goering Division in Sicily.

This top-secret information, Wehrmacht intelligence would conclude, could have been obtained by the Anglo-Americans from two sources: a traitor in the German chain of command or the interception and deciphering of German messages by the Allies. Either way, the Third Reich most assuredly would abandon its sophisticated ENIGMA device, and for a while at least the Allies would be deprived of the enormous military advantage of knowing enemy intentions in advance.

Weighing all factors after consultation with key staff officers and high-ranking field commanders who had access to the ULTRA secret, General Eisenhower arrived at an agonizing decision. Even if withholding information on the presence of the Hermann Goering Division near the drop zone resulted in Colonel Gavin and his 505th Parachute Infantry Regimental Combat Team being wiped out to a man, the precious secret of ULTRA had to be protected.

Jim Gavin and his parachutists would leap into Sicily at midnight on July 8, totally unaware that scores of German panzers were lurking just inland in the darkness.

CHAPTER THREE

D-DAY MINUS ONE

June faded into July. Along the vast sweep of the North African coast, German and Italian reconnaissance flights had been increasing in number. Scores of ports were bustling and crammed with Allied ships. Noting the increase in Anglo-American activity, Axis commanders in the Mediterranean knew that the Allies were preparing to launch the long-awaited offensive.

Despite the nearness of D-Day, a formal parade was held at Allied Force Headquarters in Algiers on the Fourth of July, America's Independence Day. Taking the review were General Eisenhower, American Adm. H. Kent Hewitt and British Adm. Bertram Ramsey, all of whom would play key roles in Operation Husky.

At Bizerte on the same day, hard-fighting, tough-talking Maj. Gen. Lucien K. Truscott, commander of the U.S. 3rd Infantry Division, bellowed over a loudspeaker to his assembled troops, "You are going to meet the Boche soon. Carve your name in his goddamned face!"

Among the cactus trees and olive groves around Kairouan, Tunisia, tension was growing increasingly thick among men of the 82nd Airborne Division. They sensed that the Big Day—their baptism of fire—was nearing, but only top officers were aware of the target and the date. The uncertainties as to their immediate destiny stoked the fires of speculation. They argued for hours as to whether the target of their mass drop would be Sardinia, Greece, Sicily, Italy, southern France, or elsewhere. A few troopers insisted the 82nd Airborne's mission would be to drop on Berlin and kill Adolph Hitler.

On July 5, the massive invasion of Sicily got under way. Hundreds of American and English vessels, loaded with assault troops, tanks, artillery, trucks and other rolling stock, huge stores of supplies, and a wide assortment of the accoutrements of war, began edging out of the harbors along hundreds of miles of North African coastline.

Gen. George S. Patton's "secret" U.S. Seventh Army departed from Algiers, Bizerte and Oran in a huge convoy commanded by Vice Adm. Hewitt. Casting off from Benghazi, Tripoli, Port Said, Alexandria, and distant Beirut and Haifa were scores of ships carrying Gen. Bernard L. Montgomery's British Eighth Army. In a few days the two gigantic convoys would converge and set a course for southeast Sicily.

Meanwhile, tension was gripping members of the German and Italian armed forces in the Mediterranean as indications became more evident that the Anglo-Americans would strike soon.

Apprehension also was heavy among poverty-stricken civilians in Sicily, the closest target to the massing Allied forces in North Africa. Taking advantage of civilian fears, the Germans sought to discourage the natives from giving aid to the invaders should Sicily be the target. A Wehrmacht officer in the inland town of Vittoria told a gathering of wide-eyed citizens, "American paratroopers are cutthroats. You had better beware of them if they should land. All of the paratroopers are former convicts of the worst type—murderers, rapists and thugs. They were released from prison to join the paratroops."

Word of the murdering rapists—American paratroopers—swept through the civilian population of the mountainous island. Before going to bed, most Sicilian families checked the locks on their doors in the event American parachutists descended among them during the night.

As midnight approached on July 6, an urgent message was handed to Gen. Alfredo Guzzoni at his Sixth Army headquarters in the ancient walled town of Enna, in central Sicily. The commander responsible for defending the island had put in his customary 17-hour day, when he started reading: "You are to defend Sicily at all costs." It was signed Benito Mussolini.

At 82nd Airborne headquarters in Tunisia, as D-Day neared, Gen. Matt Ridgway was growing increasingly concerned that the C-47 armada carrying the 505th Parachute Infantry Regiment and attached units would be flying at night over hundreds of Allied ships. Most of the sailors had not been in combat before and would be nervous, with jittery trigger fingers.

Ridgway and his commanders knew that if a single jumpy navy man opened fire on the low-flying, lumbering C-47s crammed with paratroopers, it was likely that other "friendly" guns would join in. The result would be a catastrophe.

The airborne general fired off letters to General Eisenhower and to General Patton, commander of the assaulting Seventh Army, expressing his deep concern over the possibility of disastrous friendly fire on his paratroop-laden C-47s. Ridgway received "assurances" from ground and sea commanders that the flight of paratroopers would not be fired on. The assurances did nothing to relieve Ridgway's worries. How does one assure that a jittery sailor or soldier will not open fire?

As dawn burst over Tunisia on July 7, men of the 82nd Airborne, expecting yet another grueling training day, were electrified—they were to be briefed on an imminent parachute mission: the All-Americans learned that they would pounce on the enemy in Sicily in just over 48 hours. Most of the troopers were elated and relieved. Whatever Dame Fate held in store for them, the endless waiting, boredom and relentless training were finished.

At the conclusion of the briefings, the excited paratroopers returned to their tents in animated conversation. "Goddamn, I knew all along it would be Sicily" was heard from hundreds of voices. Not a trooper in the 82nd Airborne confessed to surprise at the target.

Elsewhere in their encampments, the Red Devils of the British 1st Airborne Division heard the news of their glider and parachute assaults with similar sentiments to those of their American cousins—relief that the endless suspense and boredom were over.

At the same time the paratroopers and glidermen were being briefed, British glider pilots were learning of their roles in the airborne strike. Seated with them were 19 Americans who had volunteered to fly into Sicily in Wacos as copilots.

The British and American glider pilots had much in common—they were a breed unto themselves. And they constituted a mixed bag of backgrounds. There were those who had flunked out of flight school as cadets, those bored with routine army life in some other branch, and officers who fled desk jobs to fly and fight (for once on the ground, the glider pilot became an infantryman).

These men were lured by the risk involved in combat glider flying, the smell and the sight of danger. Some were barroom brawlers who held a deep aversion to military discipline and lived only to fight. Many were attracted to adventure much as a moth was attracted to the light of a candle. Now their moment of truth was at hand. There were few occupations in war more hazardous than that of a glider pilot in combat.

Elsewhere, excited American C-47 pilots who would fly the U.S. 505th Parachute Infantry Regimental Combat Team into battle were sitting in hot tents, listening intently to details of their flight. The 52nd Troop Carrier Wing heard with a degree of uneasiness that in order to avoid the huge Allied fleet steaming toward Sicily they would have to fly a lengthy, circuitous route to reach the paratroopers' drop zone. Relatively inexperienced in night formation flying, the pilots were aware that the mission would be fraught with peril in excess of the normal hazards of a daytime combat operation.

Lifting off from airfields in Tunisia in the waning hours of daylight, the flight would assemble and fly southeast to Chergui Island. From there it would steer eastward to Malta, 70 miles south of Sicily, the first major checkpoint.

"You should have no trouble locating Malta," a confident briefing officer assured the C-47 pilots. "Bright searchlights will be turned on at regular intervals to assist you in finding the island."

On spotting the lights at Malta, the armada of C-47s was to dogleg to the left and fly almost directly north to the second checkpoint—the southeast tip of Sicily.

"There will be a full moon that night," the pilots were told. "You should be able easily to recognize the Sicily coastline and orient yourselves."

Reaching the southeast shore of Sicily, the troop carrier formation was to turn left, remaining a considerable distance from land to avoid enemy antiaircraft fire. When the flight reached the point where the Acate River flowed into the Mediterranean, the paratrooper convoy was to make a right turn and head for the drop zones a short distance inland, north and northeast of Gela. Seaborne forces were to storm ashore near Gela a few hours after the 505s jumped.

"In order to avoid detection by enemy radio directional finders, virtually the entire mission will be flown at 200 feet," the briefing officer pointed out.

This unexpected disclosure caused more inner concern among the C-47 pilots. A slight human miscalculation or a sudden downward gust of wind while skimming along over the water in the darkness could send an airplane plunging to a watery grave.

As the C-47 flight made its final turn at the mouth of the Acate River, it was to climb to 600 feet for the mass parachute drop. A prominent terrain feature known as Biviere Pond, just south of the DZ, would serve as a checkpoint.

At the conclusion of the informational sessions, the C-47 pilots emerged with feelings of deep concern. Instead of the 250-mile trek from Tunisian airfields to the drop zones in Sicily, the paratrooper flight would fly in excess of 420 miles, on a twisting and turning course while in tight formation at night and only 200 feet from sudden death in the dark waters of the Mediterranean. Early exhilaration over taking part in the first assault on Hitler's Festung Europa was tempered by the knowledge that the largely inexperienced pilots were being asked to perform a navigational feat that might be beyond their capabilities.*

Meanwhile, on July 8, Supreme Commander Eisenhower and his key staff aides flew to Malta. There the Anglo-American commanders responsible for the invasion established headquarters in deep underground chambers laboriously carved out of solid stone a few years previously. Eisenhower felt it was vital that he be relatively close to the action in the event a major decision was required of him.

It was a curious temporary command setup. American and British airborne troops were 250 miles from enemy-held Sicily, in Tunisia, and seaborne assault forces were still more than 100 miles from the beaches. Eisenhower and his top ground, sea and air commanders were, in effect, the "point" in the Allied amphibious operation.

As Allied pilots and airborne men were being briefed in North Africa on July 9, hundreds of Anglo-American vessels, carrying tens of thousands of assault troops and huge quantities of guns and supplies, were rendezvousing south of Sicily to prepare for the final run to the convoy's destination, some 10 miles offshore from the targeted island.

Sailing out of the port of Algiers early that morning was the large

---

* Pilots were inexperienced for good reason. Parachute and glider operations were new to the Army Air Corps. The United States had never conducted a glider operation before (in fact, the first one was in Normandy nearly a year later). Only two small-sized (relatively speaking) parachute operations had been made by the U.S. Army previously, which involved a total of perhaps only 115 pilots.

communications transport *Monrovia* which would serve as the floating headquarters for Gen. George Patton, commander of the U.S. Seventh Army, until he could move ashore. The French civilian navigational pilot who had boarded the *Monrovia* to guide it out to the open sea was ready to leave the ship and return by tugboat to the harbor. As the Frenchman departed, he waved to the bridge and called out cheerfully, "A pleasant trip to Sicily!"

Those who heard the call were stunned. How many more civilians in Algiers—and elsewhere in North Africa—knew that the Allies were on the way to assault Sicily? Ten? A hundred? A thousand? It was one more worry for commanders on their way to battle, but nothing could be done about it. Perhaps, they thought, the Frenchman had just taken a lucky guess. But, then again . . .

One factor was certain: if the "secret" of Sicily had become a matter of common knowledge, it would have been picked up by Axis spies who abounded in the teeming cities of North Africa.

Early in the afternoon of July 9, while General Eisenhower was settling into his new advanced headquarters on Malta, a German staff officer rushed into the office of Field Marshal Kesselring at his Mediterranean headquarters at Frascati, south of Rome. The aide handed the Wehrmacht commander an urgent message. It reported that Luftwaffe reconnaissance planes had spotted a powerful Allied invasion fleet steaming in the Mediterranean—destination unknown. Kesselring promptly alerted all German forces from Greece and the Balkans at the eastern tip of the Mediterranean Sea hundreds of miles west to Sardinia, Sicily and mainland Italy.

On Malta, General Eisenhower awakened early that morning of D-Day minus one. The previous day the supreme commander had moved in as the house guest of British Gen. Lord Gort, governor of the island. Eisenhower immediately opened his bedroom window and thrust his head out the opening. To the man responsible for the success or failure of Operation Husky, the single most important factor in the world at that moment was climatic conditions in the Mediterranean on the eve of the massive invasion. At this time of year the weather was customarily serene, and Eisenhower breathed an inner sigh of relief to note firsthand that D-Day minus one was a normal, tranquil summer day with only a trace of a mild breeze. Good weather was vital to the success of both the airborne and seaborne operations.

Despite the favorable climatic conditions early that morning, as noon approached Allied commanders on Malta became deeply alarmed. The weather had deteriorated badly and heavy winds began gusting. In only seven hours American paratroopers and British glider forces were to lift off from North Africa to spearhead the invasion.

Faces in the deep subterranean chambers at Malta turned from cheerful to stern to grim.

General Eisenhower, who had been nervously pacing his office, went to the chambers occupied by British Adm. Andrew B. Cunningham, commander of naval forces for the invasion. Meteorologists were entering the admiral's office at frequent intervals to report on forecasts. Each talked in terms of "force" when discussing the rising winds. One would enter and merely say, "Force IV, sir." The next man would report, "Force V, Admiral."

Army man Eisenhower did not grasp this naval meteorological term. "What in the hell does that mean in miles per hour?" the supreme commander would rasp.

Soon Eisenhower had no need to know the precise miles per hour. As each meteorologist entered the admiral's office, the supreme commander could tell by the look on Cunningham's face that Force V was worse than Force IV and that each forebode danger for the assault on Sicily, now but a few hours away.

There was still time to call off the invasion, which would mean a delay of many weeks before it could be mounted again. Even then Allied plans might have to be totally altered and another locale selected for the invasion. With thousands of fighting men disembarked in North Africa, knowing that Sicily had been the invasion target, it would be almost a certainty that Axis spies would pick up this information within a few hours.

As General Eisenhower was mulling over the unthinkable thought—he might have to cancel the invasion of Sicily at the final hour and order the mighty Allied fleet to return to North African ports—a meteorologist hurried into the room with news that, for the first time since early morning, brought flickering smiles to the faces of the supreme commander and Admiral Cunningham.

"Sir, we believe the wind velocities will fall considerably by sundown and may continue to drop in succeeding hours," the navy weatherman reported.

As the minutes ticked on and the weather question remained uncertain, tension thick enough to be cut with a knife built up in the subterranean invasion headquarters. "Hell's bells!" Eisenhower exclaimed, using his favorite expression. "I'm going outside for a short walk." He pushed back his chair, got to his feet and left the room.

The supreme commander and a few aides strolled along in the open air, but none could shake the overriding concern—weather—from his mind. The hour was fast approaching when it would no longer be possible to turn back the Anglo-American airborne and seaborne forces from assaulting Sicily.

As Eisenhower and his aides continued their walk, an officer hurried up to the supreme commander and handed him an urgent message. It was from Ike's boss, Army Chief of Staff George C. Marshall in Washington. Tension, it appeared, had wafted across the Atlantic Ocean and reached the U.S. War Department.

Marshall's message read: "Is the attack on or off?"

Eisenhower handed the decoded inquiry back to the staff officer and observed to his aides in a low voice, "This probably should be answered by saying, 'I wish I knew.' "

As early evening approached, predictions were for a slight improvement in wind velocity. A short time later, seated alone in his office, General Eisenhower turned over in his mind all factors involved in Operation Husky. The self-styled farm boy within minutes would have to make his most crucial decision of the war to date: should he cancel the invasion of Sicily or risk disaster for his airborne and seaborne fighting men?

At the final moment for calling off the assault on Hitler's Europe, Eisenhower dictated a wire to General Marshall in Washington: "Invasion on as planned."

The die was cast. Control of the mammoth amphibious-airborne operation was no longer in any one man's hand. Now The Plan took over.

Earlier that morning of D-Day minus one, members of the 82nd Airborne Division who would jump into Axis-held Sicily late that night were awakened in their pup tents around Kairouan, Tunisia, by the customary fiery blasts of an angry red sun rising boldly over the eastern horizon. After an early breakfast, members of the 505th Parachute Infantry Regimental Combat Team began drawing ammunition and rations. Half-hearted attempts were made to joke over the assortment of pills each trooper was issued—atabrine pills to prevent malaria, water-purifying pills and antifatigue pills.

"They should have given me these antifatigue pills a hell of a lot sooner," a young trooper remarked in feigned anger. "I've been tired ever since I joined up with the goddamned army." The comment received only a few subdued snickers. Already tension was starting to build.

The combat team Col. Jim Gavin would lead into hostile Sicily that night included his own 505th Parachute Infantry Regiment, the 3rd Battalion of Col. Reuben Tucker's 504th Parachute Infantry Regiment, the 456th Parachute Field Artillery Battalion, Company B of the 307th Airborne Engineer Battalion, plus Signal, Medical and Naval support units.

Colonel Tucker and the remainder of his 504s were to jump the next night on a DZ near Gela already secured by Gavin's paratroopers. That was the plan.

Early in the afternoon, chilling shouts rang out in the scattered bivouac areas of the 505th Regimental Combat Team: "Load up the trucks! We're moving out!"

Despite the scorching heat of a typical Tunisian summer day, this summons to battle sent shivers up spines. War was no longer an abstract affair to be discussed, trained for, and viewed in movie theater newsreels. Suddenly war in all its violence had become real and immediate—and personal.

The grim-faced parachutists began loading themselves with a wide assortment of the accoutrements of war. Each trooper would carry a Garand rifle, tommy gun, carbine or BAR (Browning automatic rifle), and many would have .45 Colt pistols in hip holsters. Pockets were crammed with grenades with extras in canvas bags. Each would carry a long, razor-sharp knife with brass knucks on the handle so that an enemy could be dispatched with either end of the instrument.

Bandoleers of small arms bullets crisscrossed bodies, and extra tommy gun ammunition hung from belts. Switchblades were hidden in secret pockets to be utilized to free parachutes caught in high trees or, if captured, to slit the throat of an unsuspecting enemy soldier.

There was more—much more. Along with heavy steel helmets and jump boots, entrenching tools, first-aid kits, compasses and maps, and musette bags, some troopers were burdened with even heavier loads: communication radios, rocket launchers (bazookas) and rockets, mine detectors, light machine guns, .60- and .81-millimeter mortars, mortar shells, steel cases of machine gun ammunition.

The paratrooper in the early hours on the ground fought a lonely war. Whatever the military specialty of a parachutist—cook, mechanic, clerk, demolitions man or other occupation—he was first a fighting man. So he jumped into combat burdened with 100 pounds of weapons and equipment to cope with any eventuality. For many hours paratroopers behind enemy lines would not be reinforced, resupplied or have available armored, artillery or antitank gun support.

Arriving at scattered airports around Kairouan, the troopers dismounted from trucks and, struggling under their heavy combat burdens, waddled to the C-47s which would soon wing them into battle. Weapons and equipment were piled beneath the wings or alongside the fusilage. Most of the men sat on the dusty, sun-baked ground and checked and rechecked their personal weapons. Then they checked them again, making sure mechanisms were in perfect working order.

As the troopers huddled in small knots, they idly gazed out over the forbidding landscape, at the ugly cactus trees and hedges with their hostile sharp-pointed needles which for weeks had infiltrated into the men's jump boots. Their eyes viewed the barren desert and the old Arab stone huts off in the distance being baked relentlessly by the Mediterranean sun.

For many weeks the All-Americans had violently cursed every aspect of this inhospitable, arid, scorching desert wasteland. Now, on the eve of battle, when many troopers might never see this view again, the object of countless curses seemed as beautiful as the lush greenery of the mystical enchanted islands they had read about in fairy tales as children.

Time moved on and shouts rang out across the barren airfields: "Chow!" The men cast quick glances at watches; it was only 4 P.M. The evening meal was early on this July 9, as the diners had an appointment across the Mediterranean Sea in a few hours. A sumptuous meal was served—turkey, dressing, mashed potatoes and ice cream. Most troopers had little appetite, simply pecking at their food.

Seated on the sand with a knot of comrades and eating from his mess kit, a trooper observed to no one in particular, "This is the United States Army's version of the Last Supper."

A couple of men snickered softly. That was all. Somehow, matters no longer seemed as humorous as they once did.

Many of Colonel Gavin's men had shaved their heads completely, while others left only a narrow strip of hair running from the nape of the neck to the forehead, giving them the appearance of Red Indians of the Old West on the warpath. To add to their ferocious looks, the men with the Indian hair styles daubed warpaint on their faces. These troopers had no way of knowing that the whimsical affectations would later add fuel to the rumors spread among Sicilian civilians by the Wehrmacht that American para- troopers were ex-convicts, let out of prison to join the notorious airborne service.

As Gavin's men nervously bided their time around several airfields crammed with squat, low-winged C-47s, Capt. Carlos C. Alden, the 33- year-old surgeon of the attached 509th Parachute Infantry Battalion, was prowling among the aircraft at one facility. He was conspicuous by the red beret he habitually wore. Several months previously, back in North Africa, Gen. "Boy" Browning, the "father" of the British airborne, had spontane- ously removed the beret of the Red Devils from his own head and pre- sented it to Alden as a mark of respect.

Known to generals and privates alike as "Doc," Alden had distin- guished himself in two combat jumps and ground action against Rommel's Afrika Korps in North Africa. Alden's independent battalion had for many weeks been attached to the 82nd Airborne Division, but the surgeon was unhappy that he and his unit were going to be left behind in the initial assault against Hitler's Europe.

"Sounds like fun," Alden mused to his 509th comrades when he learned of the Sicily parachute mission. "Only trouble is, we're going to sit here on our asses."

Alden said he was going to try to go along anyhow by stowing away on one of the C-47s.

"Hell, Doc," cautioned a comrade, "you'll be court-martialed for being absent without leave."

"So what?" was the reply. "I have to go to Sicily on official business— reconnoitering for aid station sites in the event our battalion jumps there later."

Doc Alden was not the stereotyped combat doctor. He had seen his unarmed medics, wearing large Red Cross arm bands, shot down in North Africa combat. From that point on, Alden and his medics refused to wear medical identification in combat, and most went into action fully armed.

Alden himself carried a tommy gun or rifle, two pistols, pockets full of grenades, extra ammunition hanging from his belt, and a trench knife. He was an expert in the use of all of these weapons and had used them repeat- edly in North African fighting.

Now, only a few hours before swarms of C-47s would take off for the drop zone in Sicily, Alden stalked from plane to plane, trying to locate an empty seat. He could find none and had to admit defeat and return to his battalion's nearby bivouac area.

Elsewhere, at an airfield in the vicinity of Kairouan, an excited officer dashed up to Col. George Chatterton, commander of British glider pilots in North Africa, and said he had discovered evidence of tampering with the motorless craft on the verge of lifting off for Sicily. The officer took Chatterton to a Horsa glider parked on the field and pointed to the intercom wires between the glider and its tug.

The intercom wires were wrapped around the tow rope of each glider and its airplane to furnish communications between the tandem. Chatterton stooped for a closer inspection and saw that black tape had been wrapped around the tow rope close to one of the fittings.

Slightly alarmed, the British colonel unwrapped the tape and saw that the wire had been cut. Sabotage—in broad daylight, directly in the center of an airfield swarming with Allied military personnel.

With time running out and takeoff near, hurried inspections were held of other gliders on the field. Soon reports reached the colonel that several other intercom wires had been similarly sabotaged. But there was no time for thorough inspections, and feverish last-minute preparations for the mission to seize Ponte Grande bridge near Syracuse continued.

Worries were piling upon the head of Colonel Chatterton. Already convinced that he and his men were embarking upon a suicidal mission and beset with evidence that one or more saboteurs were at work on the airfield, the glider-pilot commander now had a compelling new concern—the wind. Nearing gale-force velocity, gusts of dusty wind were sweeping along the ground at the Tunisian airstrips. So intense were these wind blasts that Chatterton feared the fragile gliders would crack open in flight or the entire air armada would be blown far off course.

Colonel Chatterton was by no means alone in his deep concern over climatic conditions. Last-minute reports from meteorologists stated the winds were 40 miles per hour aloft and 15 to 20 miles per hour on the surface. The howling gale could swamp seaborne landing craft and wreak havoc with C-47 troop carriers and gliders.

Among the Allied battle commanders intently monitoring weather reports was the officer who would be among the first to know if the gale velocity winds would inflict catastrophe upon the Anglo-Americans—Col. Jim Gavin, leader of the American parachute assault. Going into battle for the first time, Gavin revealed no outward sign of the tremendous burden he carried on his shoulders. In addition to the personal danger he would share in equal measure with his 3,405 paratroopers, the 36-year-old colonel had the awesome responsibility for a mission which, if a failure, could result in disaster for the entire invasion of Sicily.

Despite the personal and professional challenge he was facing, Gavin drew strength from his firm belief that he would jump into battle for the first time at the head of the finest group of fighting men in the world. For their part, the colonel's troopers held their commander in almost worshipful awe.

"I'd follow Slim Jim to hell—and pay for the coal to keep the fires going," a trooper mused to his comrades while waiting to board a C-47.

While American parachute Col. James Gavin, British glider Col. George Chatterton and other Allied battle commanders were intently monitoring wind conditions in Tunisia prior to takeoff, Lord Gort, British governor of Malta, was hosting a small dinner gathering at his palace.

Lord Gort's dinner guests, a few hours before the initial airborne assault on Axis-held Sicily, were Supreme Commander Eisenhower; Lord Louis Mountbatten, the tall, handsome British chief of combined operations and a member of the Royal Family; Adm. Andrew Cunningham; and a few other top Allied officers.

It was a gloomy gathering. A pall of apprehension hung over the room as thick as the steaks the high brass were picking at. The gale velocity wind pervaded the dining chamber.

Conversation was varied and subdued. Inevitably the topic returned time and again to the heavy gales blowing gustily outside the palace. Lord Mountbatten, in his precise English diction, finally summed up what each diner had been thinking, "I must say, to be perfectly honest, it doesn't look too good."

There was no response. Each officer resumed picking at his food.

Out on the dark Mediterranean Sea, a message was handed to Gen. Bernard Montgomery, commander of the British Eighth Army. He was aboard his headquarters ship steaming toward the beaches at the southeast tip of Sicily. Donning his spectacles, Montgomery read:

Every good wish and all our confidence goes with you and your splendid Eighth Army. Churchill.

That was all from the customarily loquacious British prime minister.

In London as H-hour in Sicily drew near, Gen. Alan Brooke, the suave British Chief of the Imperial General Staff, held a particular anxiety over the outcome of Operation Husky. Brooke, the previous January in a summit meeting at Casablanca between President Roosevelt and Prime Minister Churchill, had argued strenuously for an Anglo-American invasion along the underbelly of Europe. The highest-ranking British soldier won out in a heated debate with American Chief of Staff General Marshall, who championed an attack across the English Channel against German-occupied northwest France in 1943.

General Brooke now picked up his pen and wrote in his diary:

> Thank goodness the terrible tension is about over. I have full confidence our attack will succeed.

Meanwhile, late that afternoon, a tall, thin, bespectacled man was walking briskly along the main street of Algiers, rue Michelet. Richard Tregaskis, who had won fame as a war correspondent the previous year while covering from the front lines the U.S. Marines' invasion of Japanese-held Guadalcanal, saw a familiar figure approaching. It was an old friend, Pete Huss, the bureau chief for International News Service at Allied Forces headquarters in Algiers.

The two men greeted each other warmly, shook hands, and then went to Huss's third-floor room at the Aletti Hotel.

As Huss closed the door behind them, Tregaskis said, "I've just flown in from Morocco and have cut a hell of a lot of red tape to rush here in time for the big excursion into Europe. I want to go along." The lanky war reporter anxiously inquired, "Is it Sicily or Sardinia?" He added that "from indications in London I would guess it would be one or the other."

"Right," replied Huss. "It's Sicily."

"When's D-Day?"

"Probably tomorrow."

Tregaskis moved out onto the balcony which offered a sweeping view of the harbor panorama. Gazing over the blue water of the Bay of Algiers, he counted 12 drab gray vessels crammed with American soldiers, edging out to the open sea.

"That'll give you an idea of the magnitude of this operation," Huss observed. "It's the biggest invasion in history. Those 12 ships full of GIs you see out there, those are only the reserves. The main force sailed for Sicily several days ago."

A solemn Tregaskis stood silently for several minutes and watched the convoy of troop-laden transports knifing through the white-capped, gentle waves of the bay. He knew that within a few hours many of the young Americans lining the rails would be dead or maimed. A tear crept into the eye of the battle-hardened reporter.

As the time for launching the airborne phase of Husky drew ever closer, at scattered airfields in Tunisia Col. Jim Gavin's paratroopers grew more grim and introspective. Only a handful of 505s had ever been under fire; now, before midnight, they would leap out of low-flying, slow-moving transport planes into the darkness of hostile Sicily. Each man, in his own way, was quietly steeling his spirit for the ordeal he was about to face.

One silent fear each trooper on the eve of battle carried in his heart was more profound than any of his other deep apprehensions. It was the fear that he would, by some action or inaction, conduct himself in the ordeal ahead in such a manner so as to bring disfavor upon himself in the eyes of his comrades. That was the greatest fear of all.

As the glowing orange of the sun began to dip below the western landscape, troopers gazed at it sentimentally. This was the same North African sun they had so roundly cursed for many weeks. Now it was beautiful. It would be the last sunset many troopers would see.

As the paratroopers of the 505th Regiment were awaiting the order to load onto transport planes, messengers circulated among the fighting men with slips of paper containing a prebattle exhortation from the commanding officer, Col. James Gavin:

Soldiers of the 505th Combat Team:

Tonight you embark upon a combat mission for which our people and the free people of the world have been waiting for two years.

You will spearhead the landing of an American force upon the island of Sicily. Every preparation has been made to eliminate the element of chance. You have been given the means to do the job and you are backed by the largest assemblage of air power in the world's history.

The term American Parachutist has become synonymous with courage of a high order. Let us carry the fight to the enemy and make American Parachutists feared and respected through all his ranks.

I know you will do your job. Good landing, good fight, and good luck.

Many All-Americans read "Slim Jim's" message a second and a third time, then carefully folded the slip of paper and inserted it into their jump suit pocket. They made mental notes to mail it home at the first opportunity. The home folks would be proud of them and the 82nd Airborne Division. Some had no way of knowing that they soon would be buried with Colonel Gavin's prized message still resting in their jump-suit pockets.

Minutes before lift off, a young parachutist confided to a close comrade, "You know, I've made nine practice jumps. But right now is the first time I realized that when I go out that door tonight only God is going to jump with me."

"Yeah," responded the other, "it'll be pretty lonely over there."

CHAPTER FOUR

MISSION LADBROKE

A t sunset, solemn-faced Red Devils of Britain's crack 1st Airborne Division started climbing into their gliders at six airfields around Kairouan. The 1st Landing Brigade, under Brigadier Hicks, was preparing to launch Operation Ladbroke, the glider strike to seize the crucial high-arched Ponte Grande bridge outside Syracuse in front of General Montgomery's seaborne Eighth Army.

Gusty swirls of wind and dust whipped across the Tunisian airfields, buffeting the hordes of flimsy gliders and their tow planes. From the six fields 144 airplanes would tow 136 American-made Waco and 8 larger British Horsa gliders to their release points.

American pilots of the 51st Troop Carrier Wing would fly 109 C-47s, each tugging a glider loaded with Red Devils. British pilots of the 38th Wing would tow motorless aircraft in 28 Albemarle and 7 Halifax four-engine bombers. All the glider pilots were British, but 19 Americans had volunteered to make the mission as copilots.

The American volunteers, although totally inexperienced in combat operations and formation flying at night, were aware that the British glider pilots had had less than five hours' practice in flying American Wacos, only one hour of the five at night. Seated alongside the Britains, the Americans felt that they could contribute their much longer experience in Wacos to the success of the glider mission.

There was another reason for these 19 American glider pilots to volunteer: they were eager to taste the zing of battle, to plunge into the unknown dangers that lay ahead. These were men born to fight.

The glider mission had been planned in painstaking detail. Each Waco and Horsa had been assigned a specific task. Six of the Horsas, each carrying 28 fully equipped Red Devils, were to land almost upon the principal objective, the stone Ponte Grande bridge, one and a half miles southwest of Syracuse, and seize the span from the enemy. The other gliders, mainly the smaller Wacos carrying 13 glidermen each, would crash-land at several landing zones one-half to three miles from the Ponte Grande bridge. The glidermen then were to rush to the river span and assist comrades in holding the key objective.

Loading into the gliders at the Tunisian fields were 1,200 men, plus 7 jeeps, 6 artillery pieces and 10 three-inch mortars. As with parachutists, the British glidermen would have to take along all weapons and equipment needed to do the job, as they could expect no immediate resupply or reinforcement.

Going along with the glidermen would be the top brass of the 1st Airborne Division who would take their chances in direct proportion to those of their men. The diminutive, pugnacious leader of the division, Major General Hopkinson, who had conceived the mission and "sold" it to his boss, Eighth Army commander, General Montgomery, was racing from glider to glider, shouting words of encouragement as his men climbed into their fragile craft.

When the signal was given to "go," Hoppy Hopkinson would squeeze into the narrow confines of a copilot's seat, and the sky armada would lift off.

General Hopkinson was in his element. Since taking over command of the 1st Airborne Division two months previously, Hopkinson had been itching to prove to the Allied high command—and to the Germans—what his finely honed division could achieve on the field of battle. Now he was getting that chance—and he would personally lead the assault.

If Hopkinson was concerned by the view held by some of his officers, that the Red Devil glider force was embarking upon a suicidal mission, he had carefully concealed his apprehension.

Elsewhere on the same field, a glider pilot was overseeing last-minute loading of his aircraft. He saw a large trailer, covered by canvas, being maneuvered into his glider. Curious as to its contents, he raised the canvas cover slightly, and what he viewed caused his blood to chill. The trailer was loaded with canvas bags, tags and wooden crosses—enough to bury and mark the graves of scores of Red Devils in Sicily.

Hurriedly relashing the cover, the pilot made no mention to others of his gruesome discovery. But he wished his curiosity hadn't got the better of him only minutes before takeoff. And he found it difficult to shake from his mind a recurring thought: Would any of the canvas bags, tags and crosses be earmarked for *him?*

Nearby, British glider pilot H. N. Andrews had many concerns on his mind, as did all those preparing to fly the motorless craft. Not the least of Andy Andrews's worries was the overloading of his Waco glider. Instead of the Waco's recommended load of 2 pilots and 13 glidermen, planners of the mission had assigned two extra riders—a colonel and a chaplain.

"Well, I guess we ought to be happy to have a chaplain in the glider with us," Andrews observed to his American copilot, Flight Officer Morris Kyle. "But they could have weighted down someone else's glider with the colonel, as far as I'm concerned."

Kyle nodded in agreement. Two extra bodies in a motorless airplane, which most assuredly would be buffeted about by the heavy gales, would drastically increase the possibility of the glider being blown into other craft in the air or plunging into the sea.

The 144 combinations of tow plane and glider would make the entire flight at 250 to 500 feet above the Mediterranean in order to remain under the level of detection by enemy radar.

Suddenly the tranquillity at the six Tunisian airfields was shattered. With an ear-piercing roar that echoed and re-echoed across the dusty surface, the powerful tow planes—C-47s, Albemarles and Halifaxes—revved motors, and at 6:42 P.M. a ground crew expertly hitched the first tug to its glider. One by one, the tug-glider combinations roared down the runways. The gale-force winds had whipped up thick clouds of dust, and pilot visibility was zero as the aircraft lifted into the sky.

At intervals of less than a minute, the tugs, with their gliders the prescribed 300 feet behind, were airborne and circling into flight formation over a wide expanse of the inhospitable North African landscape. Down below, pilots could hardly make out the runways which were blanketed with swirling clouds of thick dust and sand.

By 8:20 P.M. all tug-glider combinations had maneuvered into position, and the winged armada set a course for the landing zones near Syracuse. The battle for Sicily was about to be joined.

A few minutes out over the sea, trouble first reared its ugly head. A tug-glider combination was forced to turn back for an emergency landing when a jeep in the glider broke its lashings and nearly shook the motorless craft apart. Five tow planes, flown by British pilots, turned and headed back for Tunisia, reporting that their gliders were acting in a peculiar manner and they feared the motorless craft and their occupants would plunge into the Mediterranean.

Heading due east to the first checkpoint, tiny Malta 200 miles away, the other tugs and gliders skimmed over the water at such low altitudes that some pilots had to turn on the electric wipers to keep spray off the windshields.

Blown off course by the heavy winds, a few tug-glider combinations missed Malta altogether, but they soon recognized their error and altered course to dogleg to the left and head for the Syracuse landing zones. Most pilots had spotted the beacon on Malta, which was lighted at intervals to guide the glider formation.

As General Hopkinson's Red Devils flew over Malta, a few hundred feet below, several shadowy figures were intently gazing upward from their vantage point atop a rocky, barren hillock. One of those squinting his eyes in an effort to part the haze of night and gain a glimpse of the silhouettes of the passing flight was Gen. Dwight Eisenhower, the man responsible for the entire operation against Sicily.

Eisenhower was disappointed. He could hardly make out the horde of tow planes and gliders even though the moon was full. But he could hear the roar of tow plane motors and knew that up there in the darkness the airborne soldiers he was sending into battle were on course and on time.

Ike reached into his pocket and took out his seven lucky coins which he had long carried for use in crucial situations. As was his habit, he vigorously rubbed the coins. But as with any competent military leader, Eisenhower was covering all bets. He bowed his head in silent prayer to the Ultimate Commander in Chief and asked for protection for the men passing overhead in the darkness who, in less than one hour, would be locked in violent combat with a strong and battle-tested foe. Only two aides who had known General Eisenhower intimately recognized that he was offering a brief prayer for the well-being of his fighting men.

As tugs and gliders began the final 70-mile run to landfall at Cape Passero at the southeast tip of Sicily, the heavy winds began to gust with increasing violence and reached a velocity of 45 miles per hour. Down

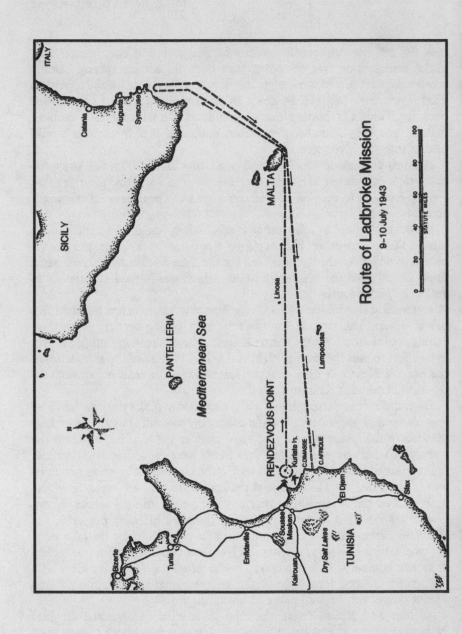

Route of Ladbroke Mission
9–10 July 1943

below, the mighty gale whipped the sea into tall, white-capped waves, and the scores of gliders winging through the night were finding it nearly impossible to hold prescribed positions 300 feet behind tow planes. The air blasts were causing the light, flimsy gliders to pitch and heave. Col. George Chatterton, the commander of the British glider pilots in the Mediterranean, was at the controls of his motorless craft when he noticed the outline of a C-47 flying dangerously close alongside him. He feared a midair collision.

Seconds later Chatterton was startled to realize the identity of the C-47 that was flying alongside his glider. It was his own tow plane. The caprices of the gale had caused his motorless craft to close the 300-foot gap between tow plane and glider. In effect, Chatterton's craft was flying along on its own.

Halfway between Malta and the landing zones on Sicily, the gale claimed its first victims. The tow rope on a Horsa glider broke, the craft pitched and lurched out of control, and 28 Red Devils and 2 pilots plunged to watery graves. Minutes later a Waco broke loose from its tug, and 13 British glidermen and the two-man crew crashed into the sea.

After skimming over the water for most of the flight from Tunisia, the tow planes, on sighting Cape Passero, began climbing to 1,500 feet in preparation for the release of the gliders. As the tug-glider combinations struggled to gain altitude, pilots and Red Devils, peering nervously out of windows, spotted a frightening scene below—the sky armada was passing directly over a huge convoy which was carrying General Montgomery's British Eighth Army to the beaches.

It was a moment fraught with peril. Should a lone jittery gunner on one of the dark vessels open fire on the slow-moving flight, scores of weapons in the ship convoy could join in raking the sky armada. The tug-glider combinations droned onward; not a shot was fired from the ships down below. In each of the aircraft, audible sighs of relief were heard.

Minutes later, as the tow planes and gliders began the 18-mile-stretch run up the east coast to Sicily to the glider-release point near Syracuse, land-based searchlights suddenly flashed on, sending brilliant fingers of white jabbing into the dark sky. The radiant light bathing the sky armada sent chills up the spines of Red Devils and pilots. Enemy antiaircraft batteries in the darkness far below went into action, and flak began exploding around the gliders and tow planes, leaving the sky dotted with wispy puffs of black smoke.

Shrapnel showered the thin skins of the aircraft. Grotesque patterns of machine gun tracers crisscrossed the sky. The stricken faces of Red Devils and pilots were ghostlike in the relentless glare of the searchlights. The flight formation, already disrupted by the heavy gale, disintegrated.

The shoreline and the glider-release point were shrouded by huge, billowing clouds of thick dust and sand whipped up by the high-velocity winds. Smoke from fires set by Allied bombers helped to obscure landmarks. Unnerved by their first taste of enemy gunfire, blinded by searchlights, unable to see checkpoints due to the heavy ground smog, the inexperienced pilots became confused.

Some aircraft turned inland to skirt the pervasive accumulations of blowing dust, sand and smoke, dodging and weaving to avoid midair collisions. Some pilots dipped closer to the ground to escape the fixed glare of the searchlights and to get their bearings. Others gained altitude. Pilots turned to the left. Others banked to the right.

In the mass aerial confusion above the bleak landscape of southeast Sicily, a few tug-glider combinations performed the impossible. They turned 180 degrees and flew back through the oncoming flight stream, miraculously passing the entire column of aircraft without a collision.

At this crucial point, with the flight formation in total disarray, the intercom system in nearly half the tug-glider combinations failed, which prevented tow-plane pilots from giving the gliders verbal orders to cut loose. So the tandems flew on past the glider-release point.

In the chaos, a number of tow planes climbed to 3,000 feet, and their gliders released high above the other tug-glider combinations. The released gliders then drifted down through the wildly gyrating aircraft flying at a lower level.

Most gliders were cut loose at random, and soon the moonlit sky was awash with motorless craft moving inexorably toward crash landings somewhere in Sicily. Few pilots knew which part of Sicily.

The airborne invaders were unaware that they were flying over and crash-landing onto one of the most heavily fortified regions in the vast sweep of southern Europe—the Piazzi Maritime Augusta-Syracusa (coastal strongpoint between the cities of Augusta and Syracuse). The strongpoint included the two ancient cities and 18 miles of coast, and was counted on by the Axis to repel any invader from the air or sea. Clustered in the strongpoint were 24 coast defense batteries, 5 anti-paratroop-glider batteries, and hundreds of machine guns.

In the aerial melee, five gliders landed near Cape Passero, 15 miles south of the landing zones, and seven or eight others, mistakenly cast loose, plunged into the water in the Cape Passero region. A lone glider crash-landed near Augusta, more than 18 miles north of the targeted Ponte Grande bridge just outside Syracuse.

Sixty-seven Waco gliders plunged into the sea during the chaos in the sky, drowning some 200 Red Devils and pilots. Others dunked in the water managed to reach shore, while some glidermen and air crewmen clung to floating pieces of wreckage until picked up by passing vessels.

Along the coastal waters of Sicily, now alight with the violent flames of war, Col. George Chatterton was clinging for his life on the wing of his crashed glider. A Red Devil had pulled Chatterton from the submerged cabin and helped the stunned officer onto the wing. On shore, Italian defenders fired at the invaders clinging desperately to the wreckage bobbing about on the angry waves whipped up by gale-velocity winds.

The Italians' aim was poor and soon the men began swimming for shore. Some time later the exhausted survivors pulled themselves up onto the sandy beach. They were safe—at least for the moment.

A glider in which American Flight Officer Robert Wilson was copilot released two miles offshore and crashed into the sea. As Red Devils and the two pilots scrambled from the cabin, the glider steadily submerged until only a wing remained above water. The men climbed onto the wing, but a head count quickly revealed two Red Devils were missing. Flight Officer Wilson, at great personal peril because the glider could sink deeply into the Mediterranean at any moment, worked his way inside the cabin in the total darkness and tried to locate the two missing Red Devils. They had vanished.

Searchlights were sweeping the water around the desperate men on the wing, and parachute flares lighted the area as though it were daylight instead of midnight. They expected a burst of direct fire from shore-based guns only two miles away to knock them off the floating wing. But no fire came. There were simply too many other juicy targets for the gunners along the Piazzi Maritime Augusta-Syracusa to concentrate on one group of refugees from the angry water of the Mediterranean.

Over seven hours later, these Red Devils and pilots, weak from lack of food and the tension and exhaustion of the ordeal of clinging for life on a fragile glider wing for interminable hours, were picked up by a passing British warship and eventually returned to Algiers.

Elsewhere along the coastal waters of southeast Sicily, a diminutive Red Devil was being dragged out of the water where his glider had skidded to a crash landing some hours before. Along with other surviving passengers in his glider, the Red Devil had clung to the floating wreckage. His insignia identified him as a major general in the British Army—Hoppy Hopkinson, commander of the 1st Airborne Division.

Helped onto the beach, coughing up sea water, gasping for breath and sputtering in rage, General Hopkinson was roundly cursing American tow plane pilots and blaming them for all his ills and what appeared to be a failure for his division. Only that morning Hopkinson had been praising the ability and cooperation of Americans of the 51st Troop Carrier Wing.

A British Horsa glider, carrying 28 Red Devils and 2 pilots, had just been cut loose near its landing zone. On board was Maj. Thomas Ballinger, a battalion commander in the glider mission. Stored in the craft was a large number of bangalore torpedoes, long, thin tubes filled with explosives whose purpose was to blow up enemy wire entanglements.

Gliding toward a landing, Major Ballinger's craft was taken under fire, and machine gun bullets punctured the midnight sky around it. Suddenly there was a tremendous midair explosion. An enemy tracer had found its mark and detonated the bangalore torpedoes. Glider and 30 occupants were scattered to the four winds.

Crashed gliders, lying silently in grotesque, twisted masses or burned to a crisp, were scattered about the landscape over a wide expanse of southeast Sicily. The mutilated bodies of Red Devils and pilots were entwined in the wreckage or lay mutely on the ground nearby. A pilot was crushed to death in his glider after an antitank gun broke loose from its mooring on landing and pinned the luckless flier in the wreckage. A glider struck the edge of a canal and blew up after explosives inside were detonated by the impact. Yet another motorless craft came to rest high in a huge tree, its pilot dead inside and a jeep still moored in place.

One glider flew into the face of a cliff. The mangled bodies of the pilot and copilot were still strapped to their seats, but the 13 Red Devils aboard had escaped death. Some were injured, a few seriously, but the remainder shouldered their weapons and headed for the objective—the Ponte Grande bridge.

Other gliders smashed into orchards and vineyards which checkered the area, while some crashed into stone walls that bounded the fields. In many

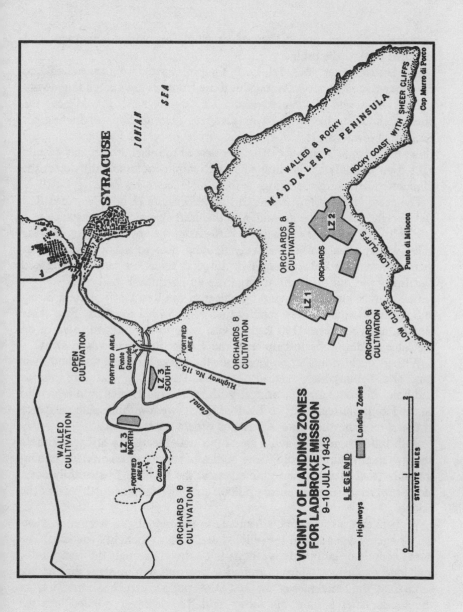

**VICINITY OF LANDING ZONES
FOR LADBROKE MISSION**
9-10 JULY 1943

LEGEND

—— Highways

▨ Landing Zones

STATUTE MILES
0 — 2

SYRACUSE

IONIAN SEA

WALLED & ROCKY
MADDALENA PENINSULA

ROCKY COAST WITH SHEER CLIFFS

Cap Murro di Porco

ORCHARDS &
CULTIVATION

ORCHARDS

LZ 2

LOW CLIFFS

Punta di Milocca

LZ 1

LOW CLIFFS

ORCHARDS &
CULTIVATION

OPEN
CULTIVATION

FORTIFIED AREA

Ponte Grande

FORTIFIED
AREA

Highway No. 115

ORCHARDS &
CULTIVATION

LZ 3
SOUTH

Canal

WALLED
CULTIVATION

LZ 3
NORTH

FORTIFIED
AREA

Canal

ORCHARDS &
CULTIVATION

instances, survivors pulled themselves from the twisted wreckages and marched toward the bridge.

One British glider pilot, Sgt. D. P. Galpin, murmured a brief thanks to the enemy searchlight operators. Cut loose from his tug and gliding downward, Galpin was frantically seeking his landing zone, a field near the Ponte Grande bridge. As he was about to give up hope of finding his designated locale, an Italian spotlight zeroed in on his craft, catching the glider in its bright beams. As the glider neared the earth, the enemy beacon lighted up not only the landing zone but Galpin could actually detect the silhouette of the targeted bridge a short distance to his front.

The enemy light followed Galpin's glider with its 28 heavily armed Red Devils right down to the ground, and the craft skidded some distance to a safe halt, only a couple of hundred yards from the key river span. Having unknowingly shepherded 30 enemy fighting men to a safe landing near their objective, the Italian searchlight lifted its relentless gaze, and the Red Devils hopped out hurriedly to organize an assault on the bridge.

Lt. Louis Withers, commanding officer of the Red Devil platoon riding in Sergeant Galpin's glider, rapidly took stock of his situation. Five other Horsas, carrying nearly 150 Red Devils, were to have glided to earth on the same landing zone to help seize the bridge. But none was in sight.

Withers decided to wait no longer for the arrival of the Horsas and their cargoes of fighting men. Instead of the 200 Red Devils who were to seize and hold the Ponte Grande bridge, Withers and his 27 men would have to do the job. In hushed tones, as the Red Devils were within a short distance of the river span, the lieutenant issued orders for the attack.

Both the Apana River and a canal ran underneath the bridge. Withers and five men swam the cold, deep bodies of water, and, shivering uncontrollably from their dips into the streams, the Red Devils stealthily crept along toward a menacing enemy pillbox guarding the far (north) end of the bridge.

Withers and his five men, advancing in the moonlight, were soon spotted by enemy defenders in the pillbox, and a sharp firefight broke out. The harsh sounds of automatic weapons fire echoed through the rocky hills, and loud explosions of hand grenades rang out in the night air. At the same time, the remainder of the Red Devil platoon struck the bridge from the south. After a short but bitter fight, the defenders melted into the darkness. Lieutenant Withers and his glidermen took possession of the primary objective of Operation Ladbroke.

Twenty-eight Red Devils had achieved what 1,200 had set out to do. But the British fighting men knew this had merely been the opening round. The enemy would be back in force—and soon.

Under the stone arches and at the base of the pillars supporting the river span, Withers's men located demolition charges which were ripped loose and tossed into the water. The Italian defenders, taken by surprise, had not had time to detonate the charges and bring the arching, stone bridge tumbling into a heap of masonry, which would have held up seaborne forces of Eighth Army in their rush for the major port of Syracuse.

During the night Withers and his men were reinforced by a detachment of Red Devils who had landed in a Horsa half a mile to the south. A nervous vigil was kept at the river span, but there had been no indication of an impending enemy attack to recapture the structure. As the ominous night began to dissolve into the dawn of July 10, 8 Red Devil officers and 65 enlisted men held Ponte Grande bridge.

Earlier about 150 Red Devils had landed in Wacos on Maddalena Peninsula, four miles southeast of Ponte Grande bridge. Rapidly organizing under the light of a bright moon, the glidermen attacked and captured the Cape Murro de Porco radio station, but not before the excited staff had broadcast to the island that swarms of Allied gliders were circling southeastern Sicily and landing at many locales.

One of those receiving the radio warning was Generale Enrico Rossi, commander of the Italian XVI Corps and responsible for the defense of southeast Sicily. Rossi promptly ordered four combat groups to rush toward the invaders in the heavily fortified Piazzi Maritime Augusta-Syracusa. Any of these combat teams had the strength and the weapons to drive the tiny Red Devil band from Ponte Grande bridge, but none reached the site. Rossi's orders never arrived.

Although scattered about the island like chaff in a windstorm, the British glidermen had not been idle. Hundreds of Red Devils, in tiny groups and individually, went to work cutting telephone wires and creating confusion among Axis defenders. These actions had disrupted Italian army communications to the point that General Rossi could not coordinate a major assault on Ponte Grande bridge.

Shortly after dawn, Brig. P. H. "Pip" Hicks, commander of the 1st Air Landing Brigade, opened a functioning headquarters on the island. Hicks almost did not make it ashore—or survive.

The brigadier's glider had released too soon while still over water and was struck by a shell, crashing into the sea a mile from shore. The occupants managed to escape from the submerged cabin and climb onto a floating wing. Only one man was injured in the crash landing.

Suddenly a searchlight on shore flashed, and the desperate and shivering Red Devils on the wing were illuminated as though it were midday. Immediately machine guns on shore opened fire, and tracers began hissing past the men's heads and skipping along the water beside them.

For nearly two hours the Red Devils and two pilots laboriously struggled to cling tightly to the life-saving wing and not fall off to a ghastly death in the deep waters of the Mediterranean. In constant danger of being drowned or picked off by periodic machine gun fire from the beach, Hicks and his men slipped into the water and began fighting the hostile, frothy waves kicked up by the gale in a desperate bid to swim ashore.

After what seemed to them an eternity, the Red Devils and the two pilots, one by one, crawled onto the sandy beaches of Sicily. Each was totally exhausted. Most knew that they were at the end of their stamina, that they could not have swum another 10 yards. Gasping, coughing up water, too weak to stand, Brigadier Hicks lay motionless on the sand for nearly 10 minutes, then pulled himself to his feet and moved off unsteadily in search of his fighting men.

Despite the failure of General Rossi, commander of the Italian XVI Corps, to get any of his strong combat teams to the Ponte Grande bridge site to wrest the span back from the Red Devils, local commanders in Syracuse finally took action and sent a force against the small band of lightly armed British defenders. Led by several armored cars, the Italian infantrymen deployed and began working their way toward the bridge, firing wildly as they advanced. The Red Devils, vastly outnumbered, blazed away at the darting attackers. Thousands of bullets whistled through the area, and the sound of gunfire echoed through the valleys and bounced off the rock croppings of the high cliffs that checkered the area.

Soon there were the harsh cracks of explosions on the bridge. The attackers had opened a deadly mortar barrage while continuing to rake the dwindling ranks of Red Devils with heavy bursts of automatic weapons and rifle fire. Piercing screams and shrieks rang out above the din of battle as bullets and shells ripped into the flesh of the British soldiers defending the bridge.

Now the Italians had wheeled up a field gun and were sending out flat-trajectory fire. Through sheer numbers and overwhelming firepower, the

Italians, by the middle of the afternoon, overran the handful of Red Devils on the north bank of the canal. Several glidermen tried to swim the body of water but were cut down halfway across by bursts from automatic weapons.

Having fired their final round and tossed their last grenade, the little knot of Red Devils on the north bank of the canal surrendered.

The Italians next directed their attention to 13 Red Devils holding out in a ditch on the south bank of the canal, raking the glidermen at point-blank range with machine gun bursts. The airborne men returned the fire but where soon out of ammunition. They tossed away empty weapons and, with arms raised, emerged from the ditch.

Only a handful of Red Devils, three British and one American glider pilots had held the bridge for nearly 12 hours but had been virtually wiped out. Over a third of their number had been killed and another third wounded or captured. Still a few Red Devils on the south bank of the Apana River fought on as their ammunition dwindled and the enemy force was closing in from three sides.

At 3:15 P.M. the last of the small airborne force, several wounded and swathed in blood-stained bandages, ran out of ammunition. They pitched weapons into the Apana River and surrendered. Ponte Grande bridge was back in the hands of the Axis.

Standing defiantly, the knot of surviving Red Devils were searched by Italian infantrymen, who removed watches, pens, and assorted belongings. The British prisoners were then marched a mile and a half under guard to Syracuse.

Nearing the outskirts of the large city, the glidermen and their Italian captors abruptly bumped into a Red Devil captain and a gliderman with an automatic weapon. Quickly sizing up the situation, the captain and his companion opened fire on the handful of Italian guards, being careful not to hit the prisoners. The brief encounter was over in a matter of seconds. Those Italians not killed in the initial burst of fire surrendered. After less than one hour in captivity, the Red Devils of Ponte Grande bridge were free men once again.

Late that afternoon, advanced elements of the seaborne British 5th Division reached the bridge, launched an attack, and sent the Italian force holding the river span reeling back toward Syracuse. As night closed in, the primary objective of Operation Ladbroke was again back in British hands.

Supporting British infantry and tanks poured across the bridge which the small band of Red Devils had seized, saved from destruction by ripping out explosives planted on the span, then paid a fearful price in blood and lives until seaborne Tommies arrived. Only 19 glidermen and 2 pilots survived unscathed.

The stand by the British airborne men at Ponte Grande bridge set off a chain reaction among Axis forces in the heavily fortified Piazzi Maritime Augusta-Syracusa. German antiaircraft batteries in Syracuse and Augusta hurriedly retreated to the north. Nervous Italian flak batteries in the region followed. As British Eighth Army elements crossed over the bridge, Italian commanders ordered the remaining defensive points in Syracuse destroyed and the large city abandoned.

Within 36 hours after the first Waco and Horsa crash-landed, Syracuse became a vitally needed Allied port.

CHAPTER FIVE

HUSKY ONE

The heavy winds were rocking the squat, low-winged troop carrier C-47s on the dusty airfield near Kairouan as Col. James Gavin, commander of the American parachute force to spearhead Gen. George Patton's seaborne assault of Sicily, conferred earnestly with his boss, Maj. Gen. Matt Ridgway.

Nearly shouting to be heard above the collective roar of powerful airplane motors warming up for imminent takeoff, Ridgway was offering words of encouragement to his young regimental colonel who was soon going into battle for the first time. There was little of substance to be said by either man. Tedious preparation for the mission—Husky One—had been completed. Now The Plan would take over.

"We're counting on you and your men," Ridgway assured Gavin. "We know damned well you can get the job done. Now give 'em hell over there!"

The glidermen of the British 1st Airborne Division had only a short time before taken off from other airfields around Kairouan for the longer flight to southeast Sicily. Now Slim Jim Gavin's paratroopers would climb into 266 transport planes and set a circuitous course for the drop zones north and northeast of Gela, some 60 miles west of the British landing zones near Syracuse.

Colonel Gavin and 17 other paratroopers would ride to battle in the lead C-47 carrying headquarters personnel of the 505th Parachute Infantry

Regiment. Exchanging idle remarks with Gavin as he stood near his C-47, struggling to put on his parachute harness and other equipment, were two aides, Maj. Benjamin H. Vandervoort and Capt. Alfred W. Ireland. Both would fly with the colonel in the lead plane.

Also laboring to get his parachute harness and 100 pounds of weapons and gear onto, over and around his perspiring body was a young staff sergeant who would be Number 7 man in Colonel Gavin's stick (an indefinite number of men bailing out of an airplane). His name was Jack E. Gavin—no relation to the regiment's commanding officer.

Since being a member of the 505s, Sergeant Gavin had been the butt of endless jokes which he accepted good-naturedly. "How's Uncle Jim today?" a comrade would needle. "Have you asked Uncle Jim when he's going to give you another goddamned stripe?" another would interject.

As time moved closer to boarding the aircraft, a tall, heavyset man with a black, bushy beard was having a difficult time slipping into his parachute harness. Somehow he seemed out of place among the paratroopers. Perhaps it was his beard, the only facial adornment on the field, that set him apart. Or it might have been the clumsy manner in which he was going about what should have been a routine task.

He was 34-year-old John Hall Thompson, a correspondent of the *Chicago Tribune*, who had been the first civilian reporter in history to jump in a combat operation. The previous November he had bailed out onto Youks les Bains airfield in North Africa with the 509th Parachute Infantry Battalion. Seventeen troopers received broken legs or ankles on that jump, but Thompson, who had never had a day of formal parachute training, landed lightly and without difficulty.

Now General Ridgway and Colonel Gavin of the 82nd Airborne Division had invited the parachuting reporter to leap into Sicily with the 505s.

"I ought to have my head examined," Thompson confided to a friend. "But I'm going along."

"You certainly should," the friend agreed. "Have your head examined, that is."

As Thompson, who had promptly been dubbed "Beaver" by members of the 82nd Airborne, wrestled with his paraphernalia, Colonel Gavin slipped over to Lt. Col. William T. Ryder, who had been the U.S. Army's first official paratrooper and was going to Sicily as an observer.

Nodding his head toward the civilian reporter, Gavin said to Ryder,

"Bill, keep an eye on old Beaver over there. He's going in armed only with a typewriter."

Thompson, loaded down with musette bag, web belt and web suspenders, first-aid pouch, canteen, trench knife for cutting his harness if caught in a tree, dispatch case and assorted personal items, waddled over to where Colonel Gavin and Ryder were conferring. He said matter-of-factly, "You know, I thought I was really weighted down until I started looking around at what these other guys are toting." The two parachute officers grinned.

Now there were only five minutes remaining until the order to board the transport planes. As Beaver Thompson was giving his equipment some last-minute tugs, a man with one star on his garrison cap sidled up to the correspondent. He was Brig. Gen. Charles L. Keerans, assistant commander of the 82nd Airborne Division. Keerans, who as a young man had been a daredevil motorcyclist, was a nonjumper who would remain in Tunisia for the next few days to expedite moving other elements of the division to Sicily after Colonel Gavin's initial strike.

"Say, Beaver, I don't see any weapon on you," General Keerans observed. "You're going to be jumping behind enemy lines and you'll need something to defend yourself with."

Keerans unhooked his web belt with its .45 automatic. "Here, take this," the general said, holding out the weapon to Thompson. "Thanks, but no thanks, General," the correspondent replied. "I don't know anything about guns. I'd end up shooting either myself or one of our own guys."

"Well, suit yourself," Keerans replied with a shrug. "But I still think you should take a weapon with you."

As an afterthought, the general inquired, "By the way, Beaver, where are you jumping in your stick?"

"Number 18—last man out."

"How come they put you Number 18?"

"I guess because I'm a civilian, and they wanted to make sure all the fighting men got out of the plane before I screwed things up."

As the two men exchanged remarks, Thompson had no way of knowing that the nonjumping General Keerans would be dead in 52 hours—the first airborne general to be killed in a combat operation.

Suddenly shouts rang out around the airfield: "All right, load 'em up!" The strident calls sent a shiver down the spine of most troopers despite the intense heat. They had heard this order many times before—only this time it was the real thing. For the first time, the rugged troopers of the 82nd Airborne were going into combat.

Lining up in single file at the doors of the various C-47s, the heavily laden paratroopers waddled up the short ladder, then on inside the cabin and to their assigned bucket seats.

When the 17 fighting men and 1 bearded correspondent had wiggled their way, shoulder to shoulder, into their seats in Colonel Gavin's plane, there were brief efforts at levity. Beaver Thompson, who was seated directly across from Colonel Ryder, asked with a straight face, "Out of curiosity, Colonel, what is a paratrooper 'observer' supposed to be observing?"

Came back the quick reply: "I'll be goddamned if I know!"

Actually, Ryder and another lieutenant colonel in the flight, Charles Billingslea, were being taken along as "spare" battalion commanders, immediate replacements should assigned leaders become casualties—a likely possibility.

As the troopers in the lead headquarters plane awaited imminent takeoff, their Air Corps copilot stuck his head into the cabin from the cockpit. "Forgot to tell you," the flier called out, "if we are forced down at sea, be sure to inflate those Mae Wests you're wearing. We'll try to land near a sea rescue service and the plane will probably float for awhile, unless it's badly damaged." With that the copilot pulled his head back into the cockpit.

There was a brief silence and then a trooper called out, "Is there any more cheery news before we take off?"

There were still a few minutes to wait. The heavy winds shook the thin skins of the C-47s, a fact that would have resulted in postponement had this been a practice drop. But this was not practice—this was the payoff. If troopers were bashed against the side of a tree or a rocky outcropping due to the severe gale, then that was part of the price to be paid in combat situations. There would be no turning back now, come what may.

Suddenly a mighty roar echoed across the bleak landscape as powerful engines were revved and pilots of the 52nd Troop Carrier Wing began to roll the C-47s onto runways for takeoff. The initial movement of the aircraft created queasy sensations in the pits of many troopers' stomachs. It was 8:35 P.M.

Colonel Gavin was wedged into his bucket seat, shoulder to shoulder with the man on each side, when he heard an urgent call above the din of the roaring engines. "Colonel Gavin! Colonel Gavin!" a voice was shouting. "Where is Colonel Gavin? I've got to find him!" There was desperation in the tone.

Sticking his head out the door, the colonel called, "Here I am."

A young Air Corps lieutenant from the airfield's weather station blurted out excitedly, "The wind is 35 miles per hour, west to east." He added apologetically, "They told me to tell you that."

Gavin took his seat and said quietly, "Well, I don't know what I'm supposed to do about it."

As the weather station soldier disappeared from view, to add to Gavin's considerable worries yet another base man appeared at the cargo door, weighted down with a bulging duffel bag over his shoulder. "I was told to give this to Colonel Gavin or the S-1," he stated, hoping someone would tell him to set his burden down. The S-1, Captain Ireland, was personnel officer and as such was responsible for prisoner-of-war record keeping.

Frowning, Captain Ireland stonily eyed the bulging canvas container, mumbling something about "rear area red tape."

Gavin, with an equally intent scowl on his face, sharply asked, "What in the hell's in it?"

"They are prisoner-of-war tags, sir. You or your S-1 is to fill out each tag properly and place it on each prisoner you capture."

With his C-47 virtually moving down the runway to roar into space, the colonel merely said resignedly, "Okay." He knew the duffel bag could be tossed in the Mediterranean when the flight was out to sea.

Gavin took his seat once again. Ireland, sitting next to him, merely grumbled under his breath.

One by one the bulky C-47s at scattered airports around Kairouan roared down runways and lifted off. At some fields dust clouds were so thick pilots had to take off on instruments. America's first major nighttime airborne operation had been launched. The troop-laden aircraft flew below 1,000 feet while circling to assemble over Tunisia, then set out on a circuitous course for Sicily.

The trek to battle would require three and one-half hours. If all went well, Slim Jim Gavin's parachutists would be on the ground in Sicily at midnight, with several hours before the moon set and daylight arrived in which to assemble and set up defensive positions. That is what The Plan called for.

Droning on into the gathering darkness, the paratrooper flight reached what should have been the checkpoint of the tiny island of Linosa. Linosa could not be seen. Even though the air armada had been skimming along just above the wind-whipped waves of the Mediterranean to escape enemy radar detection, neither the navigators nor the paratroopers could sight the landfall they were so intently watching for. It was obvious to most on board the C-47s: the flight was off course.

When the flight reached the next checkpoint, Malta, farther to the east, the powerful beacon that was to light the way could not be seen, even though it was a clear summer night. Flying on past Malta, navigators soon became aware that the flight had missed the tiny island, and on the basis of time calculation the entire sky armada wheeled to the left. Sicily, it was reckoned, was some 80 miles to the north.

Tension mounted in the cabins of scores of C-47s as the paratroopers, straining their necks to look out of the tiny windows, saw large numbers of ships below. They were plowing through the choppy, froth-capped waters on the way to Sicily. But the fighting men in the air were not to have seen any ships. The Plan called for them to pass between the British convoys on the right and the American fleet on the left to avoid the looming possibility of Allied gunners on the sea opening fire on the C-47s.

Colonel Gavin, who held the ultimate responsibility for the American parachute strike, carefully concealed his deep concerns. He was almost relieved to see the flash of gunfire in the night a considerable distance to his front; that would mean that the paratrooper flight was heading in the right direction. At least that was what Gavin assured his inner anxieties. He knew that the shimmering glow on the distant horizon could be a reflection from explosives being dropped on some island or country other than Sicily.

Sitting solemn and silent in his bucket seat, each paratrooper in Gavin's C-47 was deeply engrossed in his own thoughts. Several cast curious glances at the colonel standing in the door, as though expecting an announcement of major significance. Only the bearded civilian correspondent, Beaver Thompson, had ever heard a shot fired in battle.

Suddenly the paratroopers were jolted from their inner reflections—a stream of angry white tracer bullets hissed past the aircraft. Other enemy machine gunners in the darkness below joined in, and the sky around the C-47 was almost light enough by which to read a newspaper.

Moments later sharp cracks were heard outside the aircraft as ack-ack gunners sought out the intruders from the sky. Soon the night air was filled with crisscross patterns of white tracers and black puffs of smoke left in the wake of exploding antiaircraft shells. The C-47 pitched and heaved from the force of the nearby explosions and the gale-velocity winds. For the first time in their lives, Slim Jim Gavin and his men were under fire.

The men knew the C-47 gasoline tanks were not self-sealing and even a lone bullet striking the vulnerable fuel container could ignite the whole airplane into a ball of orange flame and send it spinning crazily into the murky waters of the Mediterranean. There would be no time for the parachutists to bail out.

An angry tearing noise pierced the ears of the troopers—machine gun bullets ripping through the wings of the aircraft. Anxious senses detected what sounded like a small boy tossing a handful of rocks at a wooden wall. "Shrapnel!" someone called out. The troopers fought off a gnawing urge to rush for the open door and leap out before the C-47 became a flaming torch. Palms sweated. Stomachs churned. Some felt like vomiting.

Suddenly the red light by the door flashed on. Its ominous, penetrating glow sent a new chill shooting through the blood of each trooper. There were four minutes to go until bail-out into battle.

Above the roar of the engines and the howling of wind rushing through the open door, the firm voice of Col. Jim Gavin called out, "Stand up and hook up!"

There was a rustling of gear in the dark cabin as troopers struggled to their feet. Each trooper hooked his anchor-line snap fastener to the overhead cable stretching the length of the cabin.

Gavin took his place in the door and scanned the terrain below. He could see no landmark he recognized in the moon-bathed terrain. He was convinced his entire flight had been blown far off course—possibly his 3,405 paratroopers were preparing to bail out over the wrong island or country in southern Europe.

Whichever the case, there was nothing Gavin could do about it. The field order for the mission, which the colonel had helped draw up, stated specifically that each paratrooper would jump regardless of the situation.

Nerves taut as kettledrums and stomachs twisting into knots, the standing troopers stared as though mesmerized at the ominous red light. Somehow, to men about to leap out into the unknown and hostile night, the red light signified danger.

Colonel Gavin, gripping the opening tightly on each side, crouched in the door with his head and shoulders protruding outside. He could not see the green light when it flashed on but would rely on the man behind him to

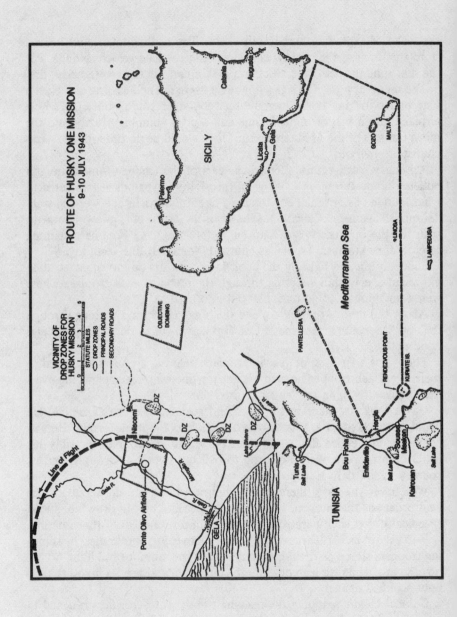

tap him sharply on the leg when it was the moment to hurtle into space. Are we over Sicily? whirled through Gavin's mind repeatedly.

Over Sicily or not, the green light flashed on, the trooper behind the colonel rapped him on the leg, and with a shout "Let's go!" Gavin leaped into space, followed at split-second intervals by the others.

As first man out of his C-47, Colonel Gavin was the first to hit the ground, which he did with terrific impact. The heavy gale was causing parachutes to oscillate and gyrate wildly. Many troopers were slammed to earth violently, then dragged across the rock-strewn landscape.

Shaking the cobwebs from his spinning head, Gavin checked his carbine and looked around. He was alone. Marching off along the route flown by his C-47 in approved fashion for "rolling up the stick," the colonel had gone but a short distance when he spotted two shadowy forms moving stealthily toward him. Comrades? Or scouts for an approaching enemy unit? Holding his carbine at the ready, Gavin called out in a low voice, "Halt! George!" Came the countersign: "Marshall."

The password and countersign for the night was the name of the U.S. Army Chief of Staff George Marshall.

The silhouetted figures emerged from the shadows and walked toward the regimental commander. Gavin recognized Major Vandervoort, the combat team's operations officer, and Captain Ireland, personnel officer.

"We'd better take off cross-country toward the DZ," the colonel stated, not certain of his own location or that of the drop zone or even if he was in Sicily.

As Gavin and the others crept onward in the moonlight, they gathered in other All-Americans. Some of the new men had been badly injured on landing. Now Gavin, commander of 3,405 paratroopers, had a force of 19.

Nearly an hour later, the column was marching quietly along a gravel road. Colonel Gavin and Vandervoort, at the head of the file, suddenly froze in place. The sound of foreign voices had penetrated their ears. They motioned for the troopers to conceal themselves along the side of the road, and Gavin and Vandervoort leaped behind a low stone wall.

As the troopers, weapons clutched tightly, crouched tensely, they heard the sound of a man whistling a tune, the off-key notes carrying loudly through the night air. The tune sounded like "O Sole Mio" to Colonel Gavin, but the whistling was of such poor quality he could not tell for sure.

Signaling for his men to stay down, Gavin edged up to the wall running parallel to the road and carefully peered over the top. He promptly saw the shadowy figure of the whistler—a lone man walking down the middle of the road, directly toward the concealed paratroopers. In the bright rays of the moon, it appeared that the man was an Italian soldier.

Colonel Gavin felt a surge of inner excitement on the approach of the whistler: after 20 years of military service, from private to colonel, he was about to have his first confrontation with The Enemy.

Leveling his carbine at the whistler, Gavin shouted, *"Alto!"* ("Halt!") The man froze as if made of stone.

Major Vandervoort rushed from his hiding place with a 45-caliber pistol in one hand and a razor-sharp trench knife in the other. "I'll take care of the bastard!"

Gavin was not sure what Vandervoort meant by "taking care" of the terrified captive but said, "Let's get out of the middle of the road and see what info we can get out of him." The colonel was particularly anxious to learn if he was in Sicily, Italy, the Balkans, Sardinia or elsewhere.

Moving into the shadows, Gavin asked the man in his high-school Italian the direction of Palermo. Either the captive did not understand or was too petrified to speak. "Which way to Syracuse?" the colonel inquired. Again the quaking Italian did not reply.

Gavin, selecting a large city on the east and west of Sicily, hoped that he could gain an indication of his location if the prisoner pointed in the direction of Palermo or Syracuse.

The troopers realized the captive was extremely frightened. Looking at the baggy pants distinctive to American paratroopers, the Italian may well have thought that fate had dealt him into the hands of a band of ex-convicts and murderers which he had been hearing about so much in recent weeks. It was also evident that the whistler was roaring drunk.

Gavin knew his band would have to move on and take their prisoner with them. If turned loose, he most certainly would notify Axis forces of the American paratroopers' presence.

"Let's make damned sure he doesn't get away from us," the colonel cautioned the others.

"I know how to handle a POW in a case like this," Major Vandervoort stated. He intended to make it difficult for the Italian to flee by causing him to use both hands to hold up his trousers.

Replacing his pistol in the holster, Vandervoort pressed the point of his trench knife against the chest of the quaking Italian to convince him of the consequence should he attempt to escape during the march. The drunk, terrified, began to mutter, *"Mama mia, mama mia!"*

Vandervoort next removed the man's belt and dropped it to the ground. Then, with the moon's rays flashing off the steel blade, the parachute officer reached down with his trench knife to snip the buttons off the prisoner's pants fly.

Believing atrocity-minded American paratroopers were going to castrate him, the intoxicated whistler let loose a scream that echoed across the landscape, grabbed the knife blade with one hand, his trousers with the other, and fell to the ground, still shouting and shrieking.

In his desperation the frantic Italian pulled Vandervoort and Gavin down on top of him, and the three grappled in a mass of tangled bodies and flailing arms and legs. Muffled Italian and American curses emerged from the gyrating pile of bodies.

Spurred on by the cold fear that surged through his being, the prisoner somehow disentangled himself, scrambled to his feet, and bolted off into the darkness, praising the saints in heaven that his private parts were still intact.

Rising to his feet, brushing the dust and leaves from his jump suit, and picking up his carbine, Colonel Gavin was thoroughly angry at his operations officer, Ben Vandervoort. The colonel was also a little embarrassed; in his first confrontation with The Enemy—a single drunken, terrified Italian soldier—the unarmed captive managed to flee some of the toughest armed fighting men in the U.S. Army.

"What in the hell did you think you were trying to do?" Gavin asked Vandervoort testily. Vandervoort did not reply. In his first meeting with an antagonist, the regimental operations officer may not have been too sure of the answer.

"Well, we'd better get the hell out of here," Gavin told the others. "With all that damned screaming, every enemy soldier for miles around has probably been alerted."

Forming into a column, the 20 All-Americans trudged off into the night. Far off in the distance to their front, the troopers could see the sky lighting on occasion from exploding bombs or bursting shells. That was reassuring to Gavin and his men; it furnished the best proof yet that they were, indeed, on the island of Sicily.

Seconds after Beaver Thompson jumped, following the last of Gavin's men, the sky around him broke out in a white brilliance. As he floated down, he was startled and dismayed to see the cause of the iridescence: a C-47 had been struck by shellfire and crashed to the ground, bursting into a flaming ball of fire. The sight gave the correspondent a sickening feeling; he uttered an instant prayer that the paratroopers had bailed out before the transport was struck.

Thompson had no time remaining to dwell on his sadness at the sight before his eyes. By now the ground was rushing up to meet him, and he saw by the light of the moon that he was going to crash into a grove of olive trees. He heard branches cracking and snapping as his frame hurtled through the trees before striking the ground with tremendous impact. The newsman felt a surge of sharp pain race through his body.

As he lay on the ground briefly to gain his bearings, he knew that he had been painfully injured in the landing but had no way of knowing at the time that he had suffered two broken ribs, a severely wrenched knee, an ugly gash on one leg, and cuts and scrapes on his knuckles.

Thompson peered into the darkness on all sides but could see no one. Nor did he hear a sound in the vicinity. He became convinced that he had made a one-man assault on enemy-held Sicily—a feeling hundreds of American paratroopers felt that night in isolated landings.

The *Chicago Tribune* correspondent got to his feet and began stumbling around in the darkness. Soon he knew he was no longer alone in Sicily—he located a medical sergeant. Thompson had carried only a trench knife on the jump; so after joining up with the medic, their total armament consisted of two trench knives and a hypodermic needle. Minutes later the pair ran onto a medical captain, and now the combined armament increased to three trench knives and two hypodermic needles.

"I'm glad to see you, Captain," Thompson said to the combat surgeon. "But I sure as hell wouldn't mind running onto one of our guys with a gun."

Hardly had he gotten the words out of his mouth than he heard someone calling softly in the darkness nearby. "Beaver. Beaver." A relieved Thompson recognized the voice. It was that of Lt. Col. William Ryder, the correspondent's friend who had made the jump as an observer and talked with Thompson on most of the plane ride to Sicily.

"Here I am," Thompson replied. Ryder had taken Colonel Gavin's orders seriously—"Keep your eye on Beaver."

Colonel Ryder, the army's official observer, emerged from the bushes.

Thompson, despite the dangerous situation, could not resist a quip: "Say, Colonel, have you found anything to observe yet?"

The group soon discovered a road sign stating the distance to Gela and, by using Ryder's military map of Sicily, determined that they were some 25 miles southeast of the drop zone. They began moving in what they hoped was the right direction. Along the way five more troopers joined the column. Then another All-American edged out of the darkness, and by the light of the moon Thompson recognized him as S. Sgt. Robert W. Gillette, who had been Number 3 man in Colonel Gavin's plane.

Much to his astonishment, Beaver Thompson saw that Gillette, in addition to the normal heavy combat load of a paratrooper, was carrying the newsman's secondhand, 15-pound portable typewriter. The machine had been packed in one of the equipment bundles tossed out of the C-47 by the airplane crew after the parachutists had jumped.

"Where in the hell did you get my typewriter?" Thompson asked in amazement.

"Well, I thought it was an equipment bundle lying on the ground," Sergeant Gillette replied. "So I ripped the bundle open and there was your damned old beat-up typewriter."

He said he had been toting the heavy typewriter for the past two hours because he thought he might run onto Thompson and knew the reporter would need the equipment. Thompson warmly thanked Gillette, then took over the task of lugging the ancient Remington.

As the nine-plane flights of Colonel Gavin's 505th Parachute Regimental Combat Team continued to approach the southern coast of Sicily, standing in the open door of one of the C-47s was Maj. Mark J. Alexander, commander of the 2nd Battalion of the 505th. Alexander had enlisted in the army as a private three years previously, had been commissioned, and had risen steadily in rank. Only two weeks before the Sicily mission, Alexander had been promoted from executive officer to battalion commander.

Now, as the C-47s carrying his battalion neared the hazy shoreline, the major was searching frantically for familiar landmarks along the coast. He could locate none. Up ahead he could see fountains of machine gun tracers searching the sky for paratroop-laden C-47s and the pyrotechnics given off by exploding antiaircraft shells.

While still out over the turquoise Mediterranean and unknown to Alexander in the door, the C-47's red warning light flashed on in the cabin. The troopers, aware of the curtain of enemy fire they were running into, struggled to their feet, hooked up static lines, and were ready to jump. The transport plane was not yet over land when the green light came on, and through instinct and training the parachutists began trying to get out the door, not aware that they were over water. In the process, they tried to push Major Alexander out through the opening.

Knowing that he and the entire stick would drown if they leaped out at this point, the major succeeded, through shouts and physical strength, in calming down his anxious paratroopers. Thoroughly angry, Alexander bolted into the cockpit. "Just what in the hell do you think you're doing turning on that green light?" the major demanded of the young pilot.

"The copilot here got in too much of a hurry," was the reply.

"He sure as hell did!" the parachute major shouted as he stalked back to his place in the door.

Minutes later Alexander's C-47 crossed the coastline where it was taken under heavy fire. A short distance inland the major and his battalion bailed out. As he had feared, Alexander and his men had been blown far off course. They would land near the small town of Santa Croce Camerina, more than 18 miles southeast of the DZ.

At about the same time Major Alexander was engaged in the grim wrestling match in the door of his C-47 to prevent his excited troopers from bailing out over water, Capt. Robert G. Kaufman was standing in the door of another transport plane. The young captain's C-47 was a minute or two from land, and his nervous men had already hooked up and were waiting for the imminent green light. Suddenly shells started bursting around Kaufman's aircraft, and a white-hot, jagged piece of shrapnel struck the captain in the neck. At that precise time the green light flashed on, even though the C-47 was still over water.

Either killed instantly or critically wounded, Captain Kaufman, operations officer of his battalion, fell forward and plunged into the sea 600 feet below. Seeing the jumpmaster bail out and the green light glowing, the remaining paratroopers leaped out the door after their leader. The Number 2 and Number 3 men came down in the water and were dragged under to watery graves. The balance of the stick, having the advantage of a few more seconds for the C-47 to get over land, came down on dry ground. They dropped onto an enemy pillbox complex and were taken under heavy fire.

Elsewhere in the ominous darkness many miles east of the DZ, Sgt. Buffalo Boy Canoe, a full-blooded Oglala Sioux Indian from South Dakota

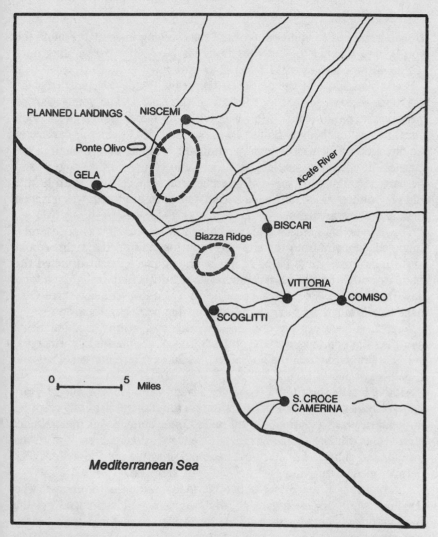

Planned landings northeast and east of Gela by 505th Parachute Regimental Combat Team. Actual landings were dispersed from Nicemi to S. Croce Camerina, with 23 planeloads dropped east of S. Croce Camerina in the British sector.

(from a family of 15 children, 6 of the sons serving in combat around the world), was shaking the cobwebs from his head after parachuting onto boulder-strewn terrain with tremendous impact.

Peering around into the blackness, Sergeant Canoe concluded that he was alone—except for enemy soldiers on three sides. The young warrior was spotted only seconds after landing, and tracer bullets were soon whistling past his body lying flat on the ground. He leveled his carbine in the direction of the nearest enemy automatic weapon, even though in the darkness he could not see the gun crew. Canoe squeezed the trigger—and the carbine jammed. A surge of apprehension gripped him. With hostile soldiers on three sides, all Canoe had to defend himself with was a trench knife and a few grenades.

Crawling on his stomach and crouching low to present a smaller target, Canoe edged away from the site and soon melted into the night. About half a mile from where he had landed, the young sergeant detected the shadowy outline of a small farmhouse, its windows illuminated by a faint glow from within. He silently crept up to a window and saw three Germans inside, laughing, talking and lifting wine bottles to their lips.

Sergeant Canoe concealed himself in shadows nearby, and moments later the front door opened. One of the Germans, reeling slightly, emerged, walked a few yards from the house, and began to relieve himself. That was to be his last act on earth.

Although suffering from a leg injury sustained on landing, the 21-year-old parachutist, in the manner of his Indian forefathers, stealthily crept up on the unsuspecting German. In his hand Canoe clutched his trench knife. With a loud whoop, Canoe charged the enemy soldier, threw him to the ground, and plunged his sharp-pointed knife into the unlucky fellow. The German made a gurgling noise, rolled over and died.

The ruckus was heard by the two Germans inside the farmhouse, who came out warily to investigate. Slowly the enemy soldiers edged out the door, automatic weapons in hand, as the American watched from nearby shadows.

One of the Germans called out in a low voice, *"Ludwig, kommen Sie hier!"* ("Come here at once!") There was no reply. In a slightly alarmed tone the other German called out, *"Lugwig! Kommen Sie!"* The only sound was the gentle rustle of tree leaves shimmering in the light breeze. Suddenly the stillness was shattered. A loud explosion and a brilliant orange flame engulfed the two Germans. Sergeant Canoe had tossed a gre-

nade which found its mark. The pair crumpled to the ground like rag dolls
—dead.

Knowing that the grenade blast might attract more Germans to the
farmhouse, Canoe hurried off into the darkness. Hit-and-run battle tactics
inherited from his Indian antecedents and refined through months of paratrooper training told him the wisest course of action was to move on.
Walking alertly through the darkness, eyes constantly attuned for possible
enemy ambushes, Canoe eventually encountered three fellow members of
Colonel Gavin's 505th Parachute Infantry Regiment. Huddled in the shadows of a clump of olive trees, two of the troopers were seriously wounded
and the third was slightly injured.

Tired from his recent endeavors and not knowing his location, Sergeant
Canoe sat down next to a baby-faced young trooper of Italian extraction
who appeared to be still in his teens. The youth's jump suit was saturated
with blood and he lay motionless. By the light of moon rays seeping
through the branches, Canoe could see that the badly wounded youth's
face was ashen. He obviously was dying.

Sergeant Canoe, the tough paratrooper, gently took the young trooper
into his arms and cradled his head with the tenderness a mother would
bestow upon her infant child. The sergeant could detect the youth's lips
moving almost imperceptibly and hear the almost inaudible words, "Our
Father, Who art in heaven, hallowed be Thy Name. . . ."

"Joe's from New Jersey," the lightly wounded companion of the dying
trooper whispered to Canoe. It was as though the other man did not want
the youth to die without someone else knowing his home state.

"Thy kingdom come, Thy will be done . . ."

Silence. The teenaged All-American died cuddled in Sergeant Canoe's
protective arms. Despite his excruciating pain, not once had the youth
whimpered or cried out in anguish.

Meanwhile, a group of 80 paratroopers of G Company, 505th Parachute
Infantry, was engaged in a bitter firefight with enemy defenders of Ponte
Dirillo, a two-lane concrete slab stretching for 200 yards across the bone-
dry Acate River.

Ponte Dirillo lay in the zone of advance of the seaborne 45th Infantry
Division, which would have to cross the span to capture two key airfields
inland. Maj. Gen. Troy Middleton, commanding the 45th Division, considered the Ponte Dirillo crossing so vital to his push inland that he assigned an entire battalion to seize it.

The 80 paratroopers under Capt. James McGinity drove the German defenders from pillboxes guarding the site and took control of the objective of a battalion of straight infantry still at sea.

Capturing the key bridge was not without its auxiliary rewards for Captain McGinity and his troopers. The dry riverbed was covered with tomato plants, many of which had just started to ripen. After two months of C rations in North Africa, the parachutists found the tomatoes delicious. Some comrades did not enjoy the treat. They were sprawled in death about the river span.

Elsewhere, Pvt. Billy J. Tackett, an 18-year-old trooper from Mississippi with a drawl his comrades said was thick enough to cut with a dull trench knife, had landed with terrific force after leaping out of a C-47. A member of the 376th Pack Field Artillery Battalion, Tackett had quit his formal studies at 17 and joined the paratroopers.

Tackett had been fortunate to get out the door of his C-47. The craft had been taken under fire from the ground as soon as it crossed the coastline. Several men in the plane had been struck by shrapnel and machine gun bullets and slumped to the floor in death.

As Tackett and the others in his C-47 floated earthward under billowing white parachutes, an enemy machine gun positioned in an olive grove began sending tracer bursts toward the descending paratroopers. Bullets ripped through Tackett's chute. One man screamed as a slug penetrated his body.

Tackett tugged at his risers to avoid landing on the machine gun nest and seconds later crashed into the ground. Clearing his head, dazed by the impact with the concrete-hard terrain, Tackett became aware that the enemy machine gun that had been firing at him and his comrades as they floated helplessly to earth was in a grove of trees just to his front.

Angered by this spitting tormentor that tried to kill him when he was unable to fight back, the teenager said to himself, I'm going to get the bastards! He sprang to his feet and dashed toward the now-silent machine gun position, his rifle clutched tightly in one hand.

Tackett had run only a few steps when a shadowy figure hurtled out of the darkness and crashed the trooper to the ground. Tackett thought he was in the iron grip of an enemy soldier and struggled to whip out his trench knife. Just then the unknown figure rasped, "Lay still, goddamn it!" The voice was that of a sergeant in Tackett's platoon.

Hardly had the two parachutists hit the rock terrain than the enemy machine gun raked the precise area over which Tackett would have been dashing had not the unseen sergeant tackled him. The quick-witted sergeant, who had landed nearby, saw Tackett rushing toward the machine gun position, grasped the situation, and knew the youth would be riddled in seconds if he were not halted.

Minutes later there was a loud explosion and a flash of orange flame at the machine gun site. A parachutist had crawled near the weapon and tossed a grenade at its crew. The gun fell silent.

Some 14 miles inland, far from the DZ north and northeast of Gela, Pfc. Eugene G. Bennett, a scout with Company E of the 505s, landed in a field where the only sound that could be heard was the gentle tinkling of cowbells. The mission of Bennett and his squad was rapidly to grab prisoners in order to obtain information on enemy troop dispositions.

Back in North Africa, the specialized squad had practiced sand-table exercises for countless, tedious hours and knew precisely how many yards were to be covered on landing to capture the enemy soldiers. Bennett often had wondered how briefing officers knew that Axis soldiers would be there waiting to be taken prisoner once the precise yardage had been traveled.

During those sand-table exercises, Bennett had learned to identify landmarks until he felt he could do so in his sleep. Now, in the darkness of some unknown locale, he failed to recognize a single terrain feature.

Soon the 21-year-old trooper, who had joined the regular army before war broke out, made contact with five comrades. Not even certain if they were in the right country, the little group decided to hole up during the remaining hours of darkness in the farmhouse of a friendly native. Despite their dire situation, the men's spirits were lifted when the Sicilian farmer told them he had a teenage daughter living in the house. Thoughts of amorous adventure flashed through minds.

When the troopers saw the daughter, the fanciful contemplations vanished. The girl was skinny, gangly, homely and extremely filthy.

"The 'farmer's daughter' sure as hell don't look like that in Hollywood movies," a trooper opined to his comrades. All nodded their heads in agreement.

Shortly after daybreak, Bennett's tiny group began marching toward the south, hoping to reach the coast and locate other parachutists. They had yet to detect any sign of the enemy. Suddenly the tranquillity was broken. Bursts of machine gun fire sent bullets whistling past them. As hundreds of bullets hissed and sang past the heads of the prone Americans, Bennett and the others spotted their adversaries. Some 50 yards to the front were a German machine gun crew and several riflemen, all blazing away at the troopers.

"We've got to get the hell out of their line of fire!" Squad Sgt. Julius Axman shouted over the din of the machine gun's angry chatter. He hurriedly called out instructions for the little band of six troopers to skirt the enemy position and attack the Germans from their rear.

Axman shouted, "Let's go!" and leaped to his feet. Under a hail of fire, he raced to a nearby stone fence and jumped over it, then ran on for 10 yards and cleared another fence. His troopers were right on his heels. All six men flopped to the ground, breathless and contemplating their next move. Enemy machine gun bullets continued to hiss over their heads like angry swarms of bees.

One trooper, the smallest man in the company in physical stature, was furious at his tormentors. Without a word to his fellow troopers, the softspoken parachutist sprang to his feet and dashed toward the machine gun position, firing his rifle as he ran. He had gone only a few yards when a sudden burst from the enemy automatic weapon sent a slug through his head.

With the Germans' attention diverted toward the trooper charging them, other paratroopers maneuvered into positions that offered fields of fire. For 15 minutes a violent shoot-out echoed across the bleak, rocky terrain. Suddenly white pieces of cloth waved furiously from the enemy positions, and the Americans ceased firing.

Sergeant Axman, Bennett and the three other troopers cautiously advanced into the German line, weapons held at the ready. There they found 16 enemy soldiers, 7 of them wounded in the exchange of gunfire.

One of the Americans removed a small music box from a wounded German and began to examine it. "Careful," a comrade cautioned, "you know all we've heard about Kraut booby traps." Seconds later a component of the music box popped out. The parachutists flinched in momentary expectation of an explosion. The sudden movement in the box had caused the music to start playing, and the Americans grinned sheepishly at each other to the tune of "Lili Marlene," the Germans' favorite wartime ballad.

Hours earlier, when Col. James Gavin's flight of paratroopers was doglegging to the left near Malta for the final 70-mile run to the drop zone near Gela, Gen. Paul Conrath received word at his inland headquarters at

Caltagirone that an Allied landing in southeast Sicily was imminent. Only two weeks before, German battle commanders had been told by Field Marshal Kesselring, "If the Allies strike, don't wait for word from Sixth Army at Enna to attack. There may not be time."

At 10 P.M. General Conrath flashed word to his elite Hermann Goering Panzer Fallschirmjaeger (tank, paratrooper) Division to jump off southward for the beaches at Gela and Scoglitti.

Had Conrath known in detail the plan for the Allied invasion, he could not have selected a better locale in which to hold his division in readiness. Caltagirone was 22 miles from the beaches where the U.S. 45th Infantry Division would land at Scoglitti and the U.S. 1st Infantry Division would storm ashore at Gela.

Weeks before, General Conrath had drawn up a contingency plan for the prompt launching of the Hermann Goering Division in the event the Anglo-Americans were to land there. He had a good road network over which to move his columns from Caltagirone to the sea. Conrath was gambling that the Allies would land at Gela and Scoglitti, and he planned to have his tanks and grenadiers waiting for them to hurl the invaders back into the Mediterranean.

Chapter Six

THE ENEMY

Sgt. Frank Herkness and 17 comrades in the pitching, heaving C-47 were hooked up and standing in the aisle as the carrier plane approached the coast of Sicily. Herkness, tall and tough, was 27 years of age. Several years before, he had been a member of the University of Delaware football team when it played Army and was fond of reminding fellow paratroopers that "this time I'm on Army's side."

Herkness, waiting to bail out over Sicily, was inordinately proud to be flying in with Jim Gavin's 505th Parachute Infantry Regiment and elated to know that he and his comrades would be the first Americans to set foot on Adolph Hitler's Europe.

Now, only minutes away from combat, Herkness felt the surge of excitement that most of the other American troopers experienced that night of the initial parachute strike. For one year and three days Herkness and his comrades had been relentlessly engaged in the most rigorous training for this precise moment—their first battle action. Only three days ago the husky sergeant and his fellow troopers had celebrated the anniversary by killing three beef cattle for dinner back in the more tranquil surroundings of Tunisia.

Herkness was puzzled by the agonizing convulsions of his C-47 as he and others in his stick peered nervously at the red light near the open door, which would turn green at any moment—the signal to jump. The rolling and pitching of the transport plane was much more violent than anything he had encountered during 15 practice jumps.

The sergeant, in common with all in Colonel Gavin's flight, had been aware on boarding three hours previously that heavy winds had been gusting across their airfields near Kairouan. But now he had no way of knowing that these winds had become even more turbulent and had reached a gale-velocity force.

Above the roar of the motors and the torrents of wind howling through the open jump door, Herkness shouted to his comrades, "This crate is rocking so damned much that I now know how clothes feel going around in a washing machine."

The former football star would have been even more concerned had he been aware of another alarming factor: during the flight the carrier in which Herkness and his comrades were riding into battle, and a few other C-47s in his serial, had become totally disoriented and separated from the main aerial armada.

Still, Sergeant Herkness knew something had gone wrong. It had seemed like hours since the men in his C-47 had fastened their chutes to the jump cable as the red warning light had flashed on when the Sicilian coast was crossed. Yet the transport plane flew on and on into the night. All men aboard knew that the DZ north and northeast of the coastal town of Gela was only minutes inland and that the entire stick should have been on the ground and fighting long ago.

"If some goddamned thing can go wrong in this army, it sure as hell will," a voice called out in the gloaming of the cabin. "Amen," several responded.

Herkness glanced down the line of tense, yet curiously elated, paratroopers to where a rosy-cheeked young lieutenant was crouching in the open door. The lieutenant had been in this position since the red warning light had flashed on in what seemed to the troopers to have been ages ago, desperately seeking to locate a familiar landmark in the bleak terrain. No one on the plane had any way of knowing that this young jumpmaster would be dead in a few hours—murdered in cold blood.

Suddenly the long-awaited green light flashed on. This signal to leap out into the darkness over hostile territory sent brief electriclike tremors up the spines of the troopers who heard the young lieutenant shout "Let's go!" and saw him disappear into the night.

As best they could in the heaving and pitching C-47, the other men followed the jumpmaster through the yawning opening. So violently was the aircraft lurching that a trooper named Edmondson, third from the last, had to climb and be pushed out as the C-47 took a sudden surge upward. Herkness was the last to jump and, despite the extreme difficulties of the troopers farthest from the door in reaching the opening, the cabin was cleared in 15 seconds.

The sergeant's parachute snapped open with a terrific jolt, briefly stunning him. In the split second before the chute opened, Herkness reflected that the C-47 seemed to be moving far faster than the 100 miles per hour it was to have slowed down to in order for the troopers to be as close together as possible when they landed.

Glancing upward at the comforting sight of a magnificent blossoming parachute over his head, Herkness instinctively felt for his carbine. A sudden surge of alarm engulfed him—the carbine was not there. As was his practice, he had slung the strap of the weapon around his neck and even tucked the barrel under the emergency chute he wore on his chest. Yet, due to the terrific jolt of his parachute opening, his carbine had been torn loose and plunged into the inky blackness far below. Down there in the ominous night, the enemy, bent on killing or maiming him, were probably awaiting his imminent arrival, he thought, and all he would have to fight them with was his razor-sharp trench knife.

As he floated earthward in the moonlight, it flashed through Herkness's mind that it was a beautiful summer night in the Mediterranean. Such thoughts promptly vanished; there were too many other vital matters to occupy his time in the few seconds that remained before he touched the rocky soil of inhospitable Sicily—or whatever country he was descending upon. He tried to orient himself. For many weeks the paratroopers of the 82nd had studied their various drop zones on sand tables with such relentless intensity that they could see each boulder, tree and rock in their sleep. Now, in the reality of armed combat, so far he could spot nothing he recognized.

Had things gone according to plan, Sergeant Herkness should have been able to see scores of white parachutes floating to earth in the moonlight all around him. He nervously glanced in all directions and spotted one chute off in the distance.

Something—possibly everything—had gone wrong. Of that he was now positive.

Things indeed had gone wrong for Sergeant Herkness and his comrades n the lost C-47s.

The airborne operational plan had called for the paratroopers in Colonel Javin's assaulting force to be dropped from 600 feet with the C-47s slowed lown to almost stalling speed—100 miles per hour. This would maximize he grouping of the various parachute units on landing. Instead, the troop- rs in Herkness's plane had bailed out at 1,500 feet, and the C-47 had been acing along at nearly its top speed—200 miles per hour. As a result of this adical departure from the flight operational plan, troopers in Herkness's ircraft were floating to earth widely separated from each other. So Herk- ess could see only the one white parachute, which belonged to a trooper amed Machinski who had bailed out just in front of the sergeant.

Realizing he had jumped from a height nearly three times that called for y The Plan and at nearly twice the designated speed, Herkness found imself cursing violently as he descended to the ground far below. His nger was directed principally at the "fly boys," the C-47 crew that had lispersed his stick over a wide area by failure to follow the flight plan. He new that men and vital equipment bundles would be scattered for miles in he darkness and that it would require a minor miracle even for his stick to ssemble.

Sergeant Herkness kept his eyes riveted on his lone parachute compan- on. He tugged desperately at his shrouds in an effort to land closer to him. o add to his mushrooming concerns, Herkness was swinging like a pen- lulum, a condition referred to as oscillating. And we're using the new onoscillating chutes, Herkness reflected. An added thought flashed hrough his mind: I'd like to meet face-to-face with the son of a bitch back n the States who decided these chutes are nonoscillating!

Moments later, in the brilliance of the full moon, Sergeant Herkness ecame aware that the earth was rushing rapidly toward him, and he rashed into an orchard, a hard landing that left him dazed but otherwise nharmed. With the array of bulky equipment he was carrying, he wres- led for several minutes to shuck his chute, then took stock of his situation. Again he found himself cursing his luck. He had landed beside a dry canal 8 feet deep, with straight sides and a rock floor. Machinski, and hopefully ther comrades, had apparently landed on the other side of the formidable noat. A hurried inspection revealed there was no way for Herkness to ross—no bridges and no way to lower himself down into and climb out of the other side of the deep canal. Wherever he was, Herkness was alone and isolated.

The sergeant could see Machinski's billowing white chute across the dry canal and also the muted glow of little lights on equipment bundles, which burned for 10 minutes before flickering out. Herkness knew he had to get across that deep, forbidding rock moat, so he began cautiously walking along the side of the canal in an increasingly anxious search for a method of getting to the other side.

He had taken only a few steps when two shadowy figures suddenly loomed up in front of him in the darkness. Herkness's heart skipped a beat and he came to a complete halt. He reached down to his jump boot and whipped out his trench knife, his only means of protection. For what seemed like an eternity but was only several seconds, the tall sergeant froze in place. Only a few yards in front of him along the side of the dry canal, the two furtive figures did likewise.

There was not a sound to be heard, other than the incessant chirping of crickets elated to be apart from the madness of men all around them. Herkness squinted his eyes as he desperately sought to pierce the shadowy surroundings to determine if he was being faced by friend or foe. In what he hoped was a stage whisper, the parachute sergeant called out the password, "George!"

Unseen in the darkness across the canal, Machinski, who thought he was being challenged by a fellow parachutist, responded with the correct countersign, "Marshall!"

The pair of shadowy figures confronting Herkness alongside the dry canal remained silent. They stood motionless. Whoever they were, the sergeant realized, they now were aware that he was an American. Feeling his heart thumping furiously in his chest and cursing the loss of his carbine in the jump, Herkness began moving cautiously toward the two silhouetted men, gripping his long knife tightly. As the paratrooper neared the pair of men, he saw a metal object in the hand of one of the figures glisten briefly in the moonlight—the blade of a knife, unsheathed and ready for business. Now he knew that, for the first time, he was face-to-face with The Enemy. Outnumbered two to one, the sergeant was determined to take at least one of his opponents with him if he were to die in the confrontation.

In his anxiety to get in the first knife lunge, Herkness took a quick step toward his adversaries without realizing how close he was to the brink of the canal. The edge of loose dirt and sand began to give way under him as

This two-story concrete and steel structure was one of scores of pillboxes the Axis had built at strategic points behind the beaches where the Americans landed.

An improvised Axis pillbox which consisted of large boulders cemented together. Even one or two enemy soldiers with automatic weapons could cause heavy casualties for American parachutists before the pillbox could be neutralized.

Col. James Gavin (right), leader of American parachute elements in the initial strike on Sicily, confers with John H. "Beaver" Thompson.

Paratroopers of Maj. Mark Alexander's battalion of the 505th Regiment, with improvised transportation, move through Vittoria on D-Day plus two. Vittoria was the first large city in Europe to be captured by the Allies.

Maj. Gen. Matthew B. Ridgway (second from left) and aides during the 150-mile forced march by the 82nd Airborne to mop up the western portion of Sicily.

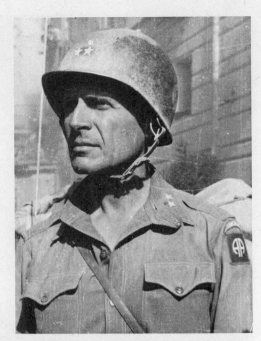

Matthew B. Ridgway.

The Liberty ship Robert Rowan *explodes off Gela, a victim of Luftwaffe bombers, the afternoon before Col. Reuben Tucker's flight. The* Rowan *smoked into the night, making nervous gunners still more jittery.*

Col. James Gavin's victorious troopers at Biazza Ridge with a knocked-out German Tiger.

The same Tiger after Lieutenant Swingler killed the crew.

A truck of the Hermann Goering Panzer Parachute Division captured by the 505th. Searching for booby traps.

Paratrooper tommy gunner wearing the complete equipment used when he jumped.

On Colonel Tucker's ill-fated flight the night of D-Day plus one when 23 C-47s were shot down by "friendly" fire.

Members of Colonel Gavin's parachute force make ready to board C-47s, on their way to Sicily.

Capt. John Norton (left) nearly had his head shot off minutes after landing when he mistook a heavily defended enemy pillbox for a farmhouse. Capt. Willard R. "Bill" Follmer (right) broke his ankle in the jump and led his company for three days on a mule.

Paratroopers of the 82nd Airborne gather around a Sicilian "recruit" during their six-day march to mop up western Sicily.

Facing east from the center of the Ponte Dirillo crossing over the Acate River. The road leads to Biazza Ridge and Vittoria.

Two seaborne Tommies and an American paratrooper after the small fortified town of Avola was captured.

The workhorse C-47. Carried a stick of 15 to 18 paratroopers, or towed Waco or Horsa gliders.

his Italian adversary, sensing an advantage in the American's being off balance, leaped at Herkness with a mighty swipe of his dagger, just as the paratrooper began plunging the 18 feet to the rock bottom of the canal. Herkness felt an excruciating pain in his leg as the needle-sharp point of the Italian's dagger caught him just below the knee and entered to the bone. He fell to the canal bottom and his body rendered a sickening thud as it hit. Dazed, the wind knocked out of him, and feeling sharp pains in his leg where he was stabbed and in his hand on which he had landed first, Sergeant Herkness, with his head spinning, became completely disoriented. Mercifully, he passed out.

Machinski, off in the darkness on the other side of the canal, was unaware what had happened. Herkness lay in the bottom of the canal, unconscious, for perhaps two hours. The two Italians had fled. When the parachutist slowly regained his wits, he became aware once again of the sharp pain in his leg and could see by the moon's shining light that his entire jump suit was saturated with blood. He was weak, woozy and ached from head to toe. Still he laboriously pulled himself to his feet and, to his surprise, discovered that he was able to walk.

At that moment a frightening sound rushed to his ears—the muted echo of footsteps in the canal bed moving toward him. He was convinced the Italians, probably with reinforcements, had returned to finish him off.

Herkness's mouth went dry and his heart began a hammering cadence. The footsteps in the darkness of the canal bed continued inexorably toward him—and this time he had not even a trench knife with which to defend himself, nor, wounded and aching as he was, could he flee those bent on killing him.

There was only one course of action open to him. In the unlikely possibility that the oncoming footsteps could be American, he called out the password, "George!" The footsteps halted. For several moments only silence hovered over the vicinity. Then Sergeant Herkness heard the word "Marshall!" drifting across the night air.

Herkness emitted a deep sigh of relief. The footsteps continued again, and moving out of the shadows toward him was a trooper he recognized as Sergeant Wood of his battalion's .81-millimeter mortar platoon. Wood also had been alone and lost. The two All-Americans clasped hands with a fervor reserved normally for those lost for years in an impenetrable jungle inhabited by countless man-eating tigers.

The pair began walking along the deep dry moat. Herkness, hobbling badly, was supported by Wood. On reaching a place where they could climb out, Wood helped his wounded comrade pull his way upward and followed him onto solid ground. There the two sergeants compared notes and concluded they had no idea where they were. Only later would they learn that they and a number of other lost planeloads of paratroopers had jumped a few miles inland from the coastal town of Avola, south of Syracuse in southeast Sicily and deep in the British zone. They were more than 50 miles from their drop zone on Piano Lupo, near Gela.

The two parachute sergeants moved on into the night and eventually came upon a mortar corporal named Fryer, who told them he thought that a bundle with a mortar and some shells had landed nearby. They easily located it by the luminous tape which kept glowing after the little light on the bundle flickered out.

In short order, Herkness, Wood and Fryer collected four other troopers and began a cautious overland march in search of a larger body of Americans. They still did not know if they were on Sicily or another island—Sardinia or Corsica, perhaps. They were moving across country dotted with orchards, and enemy troops seemed to be all about them. There were regular outbreaks of firing from the groves, but the Americans did not shoot back for fear of giving away their presence. They surmised, rightly, that the small arms and automatic weapons firing was being conducted by Italian troops highly alarmed over Allied paratroopers dropping about them and blazing away at shadows periodically to bolster their own morale.

Shortly the little band of All-Americans came across a main road and had cautiously moved along it for about 600 yards when from the shadows they heard: "Halt!" The seven troopers froze in their tracks as though made of concrete. Mouths went dry. Hearts beat furiously. Each felt naked standing in the road under the brilliant rays of the full July moon and expected to be cut down at any moment by enemy automatic weapons.

Each parachutist weighed the advisability of making a desperate bolt in an effort to escape the trap into which they had stumbled, but moments later came another shout from a thick clump of bushes a short distance from the rigid troopers: "George!" There were audible sighs of relief from Herkness, Wood, Fryer and the other four 82nd Airborne men as they responded, almost in chorus, "Marshall!"

"Come on in," a voice called from the bushes. "Who in the hell are you?"

The challenger had been posted along the road for the precise purpose in which he was now engaged—to halt any American parachutists who might wander by and lead them to a nearby farmhouse that was being used as an assembly point and first-aid station.

As the seven men moved up to the farmhouse, they saw a hodgepodge collection of human beings. There were 65 other paratroopers there plus 6 lieutenants. Charles E. "Pinkie" Sammon, intelligence officer of Mark Alexander's 2nd Battalion of the 505th Parachute Infantry Regiment, was in command. He was the senior officer present. Also crowded in the premises were 3 German prisoners and 12 Sicilian civilians.

"Where'd you get the Krauts?" Herkness asked a trooper out of mild curiosity. These were the first German soldiers he had ever seen. "Hell," he added, "they don't look like supermen to me."

"Lieutenant Brassell there brought the Krauts in, but he claims no great credit for it" was the reply.

The trooper went on to explain that after Brassell had bailed out and was about to land in an orchard, he spotted a cluster of armed enemy soldiers nearby who he thought would kill him as he floated helplessly in his parachute. Three Germans walked over to where Brassell lay stunned from the impact with the ground, and the young lieutenant expected a bullet through the head. Instead the Germans helped the American to his feet, removed his parachute harness, and handed him their weapons.

"We surrender," a German officer told the startled Brassell in perfect English. Later in conversation the enemy officer explained to the American parachutist, "For three years and eight months we've been fighting all over Europe, Russia and North Africa. That's long enough in any army. We're sick of it all."

The Germans' "illness" came at a most fortunate time for Lieutenant Brassell. Instead of being gunned down in his parachute, he became the captor of three enemy soldiers who had had enough of war.

The 12 Sicilian civilians had been in the house when the Americans had first taken it over. They were sullen at first over the arrival of the new tenants, and to be on the side of prudence the paratroopers confiscated several shotguns.

One of the troopers had landed a few hours previously; his chute had caught on the top of a tree and a house, leaving him dangling and helpless in his bulky equipment only a few feet off the ground. Wrestling mightily to free himself, the trooper looked up in alarm to see a Sicilian hurriedly emerge from the house and rush toward him, brandishing a long knife and shouting unintelligible words. This is the end, the dangling airborne man thought to himself. And not even a chance to fight back.

Still waving his knife, the Sicilian dashed up to the dangling trooper. He raised the dagger upward—and proceeded to cut the parachute straps from which the 82nd man was suspended. The native man then gently helped the paratrooper to the ground and assisted him in removing the balance of his harness.

Most of the older Sicilians gathered around the house were pleasant and helpful, assisting the wounded, bringing water and a few supplies. But soon the American troopers noticed that the older folk were being frightened by the sullen stares and mutterings of the younger Sicilians, so stopped aiding the Americans.

"You know, those younger Eyties are some really nasty sons of bitches," one trooper said to another. "If they don't cut out all that tough-acting crap, I'm going to lay down my tommy gun, take one or two of the bastards behind the barn, and beat holy hell out of them. They're starting to irritate me."

Lieutenant Sammon, as senior officer in charge of the collected American troopers, realized there was a serious need for transportation to round up several wounded, who had been left carefully concealed in various orchards in the vicinity, and to carry some of the heavier equipment that had been located after the drop.

Turning to an Italian-speaking American trooper, Sammon said, "Dicker with the guy who seems to own this layout and see if you can buy a horse and cart from him." The troopers had American invasion money which resembled the real thing but was good only in the country to be occupied—in this case, Sicily.

For several minutes there ensued an apparently heated discussion between the American who spoke Italian and the Sicilian who owned the property. There was much arm waving and shouting by each man.

Finally the American turned to Lieutenant Sammon and said in a disgusted tone, "The bastard wants too damn much for a horse and cart—200 bucks American."

"Go to work on him some more," Sammon directed.

Soon the Italian-speaking American and the Sicilian were engaged in another argument which grew increasingly more intense.

"All right," the American negotiator shouted, throwing his hands up in the air for emphasis. "If you don't want to sell the stuff at a fair price, we'll take it anyhow—for nothing."

The Sicilian then pleaded that the horse was old, skinny and ailing, and a quick examination of the animal confirmed that fact. "Then why in the hell didn't you say so in the first place instead of trying to screw us out of 200 bucks?" the American interpreter exploded. The Sicilian merely shrugged his shoulders. In order to survive in poverty-stricken Sicily, the native had spent a lifetime haggling for economic advantage.

Inside the old Sicilian farmhouse that was serving as a collection point for lost and strayed paratroopers, a combat medic, Pvt. Harlan Adams, had set up an aid station and was doing a brisk business. Many of the troopers had received relatively minor wounds in brief firefights in the darkness, and others were injured in heavy impacts with the ground after bailing out. The more seriously wounded parachutists were carefully concealed in assorted orchards, waiting for some mode of transportation to move them. Among those treated by the efficient aid man was Sergeant Herkness who had walked many miles during the night despite having received a painful stab wound and a mangled hand from his 18-foot fall into the dry canal.

As the first timid expressions of dawn began to illuminate the bleak Sicilian countryside, the troopers gathered around the farmhouse looked up to see two newly arrived 82nd Airborne men approaching. One of the parachutists was supporting a badly wounded man, the latter staggering with his arm around his comrade's shoulder. At first the watching troopers thought that the seriously injured man, his face a mask and his jump suit saturated with blood, must have been involved in a firefight. When they heard his story, it filled them with fury.

The wounded trooper's name was Mike Scambelluri. He was from Albany, New York, and of Italian descent. Scambelluri had parachuted into the center of a fortified Italian position, where he lay helpless as several sullen Italian soldiers, including a captain, stood over him pointing their weapons at his head. Hauling the American roughly to his feet, the Italian soldiers proceeded to rob him of his watch, wallet and all his belongings, including his last cigarettes.

When the enemy soldiers learned that Scambelluri spoke fluent Italian, they became furious. "You're a traitor, you bastard!" the Italian captain shouted in the captive's face. "We know how to handle bastards like you!"

The captain ordered, "Tie his hands behind him and stand him over against that wall."

As the enemy soldiers hurried to comply with the order, the Italian captain took out his revolver and, less than 15 feet away, aimed it at the helpless American. He did not intend to kill his captive—not right away, anyhow. At point-blank range, the captain's aim was true. There was a loud crack and a bullet tore through Scambelluri's thigh, causing blood to gush out of the wound. The captain grinned, pleased with his marksmanship.

The gun wielder then shifted his aim slightly and sent another bullet into the American paratrooper's other thigh. Scambelluri's face was contorted in extreme pain, but he refused to utter a cry or plea for leniency. This failure to beg for mercy further incensed the enemy officer who leisurely sent five more bullets ripping into the flesh of the parachutist—into both arms, the calf, and the final two into the body.

Mike Scambelluri, proud of his Italian ancestry but even more proud of being an American, finally fell to the ground. His tormentors, tiring of their savage game and believing the paratrooper was dead, began leaving. Only half-conscious and his mind confused, in a final gesture of defiance Scambelluri painfully pulled himself to his feet. As he did so, the Italians saw him and tossed two grenades—his own grenades—at him. The missiles exploded on the ground in front of him, sending white-hot pieces of shrapnel plunging into his abdomen.

Again Scambelluri collapsed and the enemy soldiers, this time convinced that they had finished the job, departed. Regaining consciousness some time later, the paratrooper, bleeding profusely from multiple wounds, regained his feet and staggered into a nearby orchard. There he ran onto several comrades who brought him to the farmhouse.

It was a group of grim-faced American paratroopers, shocked and angered, who gathered about young Scambelluri in the farmhouse aid station and heard from his own lips his frightening experience.

As Private Adams, the dedicated combat medic, bandaged the trooper's wounds, he moved to one side and whispered to a small knot of comrades, "He has no business even being alive. But there he is. And talking about his adventures." The troopers, tough fighting men in their own right, stared at Mike Scambelluri in amazement and admiration. They had no way of knowing that the All-American would die of his wounds several days later after being evacuated through a series of field hospitals back to Tripoli, North Africa.

Stunned on hearing Scambelluri's story, there was a brief moment of silence among the several troopers who had gathered inside the house. Finally one exclaimed in a matter-of-fact tone, "What happened to Mike has changed my whole outlook on this goddamned war. Hell, I wasn't really mad at the Eyties or Krauts. When we came over, I had a sort of Sunday school notion about how soldiers treat prisoners, lots of good fellowship and all that sort of stuff. Now I know what it's all about—the kind of bastards we're up against. I'll always remember what they did to Mike." He patted his tommy gun several times.

Mike Scambelluri's story within seconds had swept through the ranks of the other Americans outside the farmhouse aid station and quickly reached the ears of the Sicilian civilians. The young natives, so sullen and belligerent only a few hours before, sensed the white-hot anger of the paratroopers, and the scowls on their faces now turned to wide smiles when their furtive glances happened to make contact with the cold stares of the Americans.

"If one of those goddamned young Sicilian punks as much as lets out a peep, my tommy is going to suddenly accidentally discharge right at him," an angry trooper mused to a companion.

Shortly after dawn two paratroopers came up to the farmhouse with five Italian prisoners in tow. The enemy soldiers were led inside the building and were seen by the grievously wounded Mike Scambelluri through the doorway of the room in which he was lying in pain on a cot. The young parachutist raised up slightly, pointed a trembling finger at one of the Italian prisoners, and called out, "That's one of them! He's one of the bastards!"

The accused enemy soldier's face turned white with fear, and he vehemently denied any knowledge of participating in the savagery involving Scambelluri. But the American victim was positive of his identification. "He's one of the bastards!" Scambelluri repeated over and over. "There's no doubt about it. I'll never forget how those sons of bitches looked."

Minutes later the accused Italian was taken outside the farmhouse by three paratroopers, and the group moved out of sight over a low hill. There was the sound of rifle and tommy gun fire and then silence.

The three parachutists came back to the farmhouse without the prisoner. "The son of a bitch tried to escape," one observed.

Lt. Pinkie Sammon, the senior officer in charge of the hodgepodge collection of 75 paratroopers, had sent out patrols to determine the locale. On the return of these patrols, Sammon and the other troopers learned that seaborne forces of General Montgomery's British Eighth Army even then were attacking the nearby coastal town of Avola, a city of 22,000 population.

Two hundred yards from the Sicilian farmhouse stood a barren hill. Shortly after dawn, Lieutenant Sammon and several other troopers climbed the elevation and were fascinated with the panorama that unfolded before them. The hill offered an unobstructed view of the sea a couple of miles away, and as far as the eye could view, the coastal waters were dotted with British ships, hundreds of them. Sammon and the others could see little assault boats, skittering through the gentle swells of the Mediterranean like so many water bugs, bringing ashore British fighting men.

As the Americans watched, mesmerized by the scene, overhead flew black-bodied Junker bombers of the Luftwaffe which dropped angry loads of bombs on the ships, sending huge fountains of water gushing into the air as they exploded on impact. Here and there the aim was true; the paratroopers winced as bombs erupted in fury on the deck of a British vessel.

Suddenly, behind them, Sammon and his parachutists on the hill heard loud explosive noises. Unseen Italian artillery, concealed somewhere nearby, had opened up on the tempting targets anchored about the coastal waters, and the Americans could hear the whining and swishing of the enemy shells as they passed far overhead on their lethal journeys.

Transfixed as they were with the panoramic extravaganza of men at war, the troopers knew that they had urgent business of their own to attend to. Lieutenant Sammon called a council of war among the officers. "We're more than 50 miles east of where we're supposed to be on Piano Lupo," Sammon told the other officers. "But we're behind enemy lines and in a damned good position to help the British coming in by sea. We've only got 75 men, but we're a fighting force, and that's precisely what we're going to do—fight!"

A quick inventory of weapons disclosed that the little band of All-Americans had eight machine guns, two mortars, two light antitank guns, and each man was armed with a rifle, carbine, or tommy gun. "We've got enough firepower to provide a pretty good kick," Sammon observed to an officer.

A discussion was held as to how the group of parachutists could create the most havoc among the enemy. A decision was reached to aid the British coming in by sea by assaulting the coastal town of Avola from the rear.

Capturing a fortified town the size of Avola, with hundreds of houses and buildings to conceal enemy troops, would be a monumental task. In normal circumstances, at least a battalion of infantry, supported by artillery and armor, would be assigned the mission. Now Lieutenant Sammon intended to do the job with a force of only 75 paratroopers.

Hurried preparations were made to move out. The several German and Italian prisoners were left under the guard of two troopers, while the medic, Private Adams, remained behind with the seriously wounded Americans, including Mike Scambelluri. All the paratroopers, including several who were limping and wearing blood-stained bandages, set out down the road for Avola. The walking wounded refused to remain behind in the relative safety of the aid station farmhouse.

Avola was two miles from the farmhouse, and Lieutenant Sammon and his men arrived at the outskirts at 8 A.M. During the approach march they had not sighted a single Axis soldier. Suddenly the quiet was ruptured as an enemy machine gun to the front opened fire on the advancing troopers. Bullets hissed and sang past their heads as they dived for the nearest cover.

Several troopers worked their way behind a stone wall bounding a cemetery until they reached a point that brought the enemy machine gun crew into view. The Americans opened fire and in a few minutes had killed the three Italian gunners.

Lieutenant Sammon held a conference with his officers. From the cemetery the Americans could see the long streets of Avola leading in a gentle downward grade to the Mediterranean Sea, about a mile away. Sammon assigned each street to an officer who would take a group of troopers and clear out any enemy along his zone of advance. The several groups would then rendezvous at the shoreline.

Among the 82nd Airborne men getting ready to assault Avola was Sgt. Frank Herkness, limping from the stab wound in his knee and assorted other injuries. He had a fleeting thought: What had happened to the young lieutenant who had been the jumpmaster of his C-47? He had not been seen since bailing out. Herkness concluded that the jumpmaster was probably somewhere nearby fighting Axis soldiers.

The jumpmaster was not fighting, nor was he in a position to fight. At that very moment he was being held under guard by a detachment of Italian soldiers in a house along the coast. The lieutenant and a private had landed in the center of an enemy position and were taken prisoner while still struggling to get out of their parachutes.

Taken to the coastal house for safekeeping, the American officer and private soon became aware that British soldiers were attacking the position and that the alarmed Italian soldiers were hurriedly preparing to pull out. Before leaving the house, an enemy officer put a revolver to the head of each captive American and pulled the trigger. Entering the house minutes later, British Tommies found the two parachutists lying in pools of blood in the middle of the floor, still bound hand and foot with ropes.

On the outskirts of Avola, Lieutenant Sammon's little band of 75 paratroopers began edging into the built-up portions of the city. Within minutes they realized that they had entered a maze of stone and stucco houses, sturdy structures jammed up against each other, as well as a rambling assortment of narrow alleys and serpentine streets. It was a position ideal for the defenders.

Resistance was spasmodic. Troopers, drenched with perspiration from the Mediterranean sun, would clear out houses for a block without a shot being fired. Then suddenly an Italian machine gun up the street would launch an angry chatter, and bullets would ricochet off the stone houses and cobbled streets, sending the parachutists scrambling for cover.

Tired and hungry, the All-Americans fought all morning. The sun and the relentless tension of house-to-house combat were beginning to leave a brutal imprint on even the toughest of troopers.

Lt. Pinkie Sammon paused during a lull in the fighting and glanced at his watch. It was 2:30 P.M.—six hours after the band of paratroopers had entered Avola. The troopers had advanced only a mile through the maze of buildings and narrow, twisting streets, and Sammon was near despair over the enormity of the task he and his men had taken on.

Now the several bands of airborne men who had been mopping up the city reached the square, where they halted after coming under intense automatic weapons fire. There were at least a score of enemy machine guns in and around the square, and each effort by the paratroopers to advance was met by heavy bursts of fire. It was a situation that called for mortars, but no one knew where the mortarmen were in the maze of Avola buildings.

As Lieutenant Sammon pondered his next move, there was a sudden crescendo of firing in the square. From the other side of town a British Bren gun carrier had roared into the square with all guns blazing. Watching the unexpected action by their Allies, the pinned-down Americans sent cheers soaring into the torrid summer sky.

The Italian machine gunners in the square, their weapons aimed toward the advancing paratroopers, were taken by surprise by the charge of the British weapons carrier from behind them. Abandoning their guns, the Italians fled the scene.

Cheering in the ranks of the paratroopers was short-lived. A block away a company of British Tommies began advancing toward the Americans, not knowing allies were closer than 50 miles to Avola. The Tommies opened fire on the Americans and edged along the street until they were close enough to toss grenades, which fell short of the paratroopers' position. Knowing that the British had mistaken them for the enemy, the Americans did not shoot back; they concealed themselves and hoped the mistake would be recognized before major bloodshed occurred.

With the advancing Tommies only 40 yards away, two enterprising Americans placed their steel helmets on the tips of their rifles and held the weapons out from a doorway. A collective sigh of relief came from the paratroopers when they heard cries of "Cease fire! Cease fire!" ringing out from the British ranks.

Realizing that a mistake had been made, the English officer leading the attack cautiously advanced toward the paratroopers, and when he became certain that the begrimed airborne soldiers were indeed Americans, his eyes protruded with astonishment and he blurted out, "I say, what the bloody 'ell are you Yanks doing 'ere?"

His facial expression was much as though he had just spotted a ghost—or several ghosts.

The British officer was deeply apologetic over attacking the Americans. "Your bloody 'elmets look almost like the gawddamned Jerries from a distance, and when we spotted your 'elmets we opened fire. We didn't know there were any bloody Yanks in 50 miles of 'ere."

Despite the linkup of Americans and British in the town square, the enemy was not yet ready to abandon Avola. A British medical officer, wearing a Red Cross arm band, wandered into the center of the open space. There was a sharp rifle crack and the combat doctor fell to the cobbled surface, a bullet through his head.

A young British aid man, his Red Cross arm band glistening in the sunlight, dashed to the assistance of the mortally wounded doctor. Another rifle report rang out, and the first-aid man slumped to the street, dead before he could reach the medical officer.

Seeing the two comrades shot down by one or more snipers, a Tommie armed with an automatic weapon worked his way alongside the building where he suspected the enemy riflemen were concealed. He edged cautiously to the door, paused briefly, then kicked open the door, sprayed the room with a long burst and bolted inside.

For several minutes there was silence in the square. Then shots rang out from inside the structure. Moments later an Italian soldier emerged, arms held high and fear etched in his face. Another Italian followed with arms upraised. Then another. And still one more. Finally the Tommie came out with his weapon trained on the last Italian. Three enemy soldiers remained inside—dead as a result of the indoor shoot-out with a lone British soldier.

The fight for Avola was over.

Sgt. Frank Herkness was one of the several American wounded who were directed to a British mobile hospital just set up in a schoolhouse in Avola. Herkness had been marching and fighting for 24 hours after receiving the leg stab wound and other injuries in his 18-foot plunge into a dry canal. After his soiled and tattered bandages had been replaced, a wounded British colonel lying on a nearby cot said to the sergeant, "You American paratroopers being here by mistake saved us at least one hard day of fighting. And only God knows how many lives."

As orderlies began moving the English officer to another room, he called out to Sergeant Herkness, "And you Yanks pouncing on them unexpectedly from the rear scared the bloody 'ell out of those Eyties!"

CHAPTER SEVEN

ASSAULT BY SEA

I t was shortly after midnight. Capt. Willard R. "Bill" Follmer was
crawling along a rocky hillside on his hands and knees. It was a
painful trek. The 25-year-old leader of I Company of the 505th Parachute Infantry had crashed to earth with terrific impact only minutes
before. He heard a loud snapping sound and felt a pain like a white-hot
poker shoot up his leg.

Follmer's head was still spinning from the jolting landing against the
concrete-hard side of a hill. As he inched along, he peered intently into the
darkness for some sign of a comrade—or a foe. After negotiating 50 yards,
the parachute captain halted abruptly. Just ahead he heard a faint rustling
noise in the dark shadows.

Follmer quickly whipped out his .45 Colt automatic and, in a low voice,
called out, "George." He felt a relief to hear the response, "Marshall." Not
only did he know that it was a friend instead of an enemy, but he recognized the man's voice—his longtime batman, a young soldier who, in addition to being a fighting man, served as an aide to the company commander.

"Goddamn, I'm glad to see you!" Follmer whispered. Stealth was vital
because the enemy might have been lurking in the darkness. "I've got a
little trouble. I think I broke my ankle when I hit."

Unable to walk, Captain Follmer, at the suggestion of his aide, climbed
onto the rear of his husky batman, and in piggyback fashion the two men
set out through the ominous night in search of more I Company troopers.

As they moved along, other men of Follmer's unit silently emerged from the shadows and joined the growing column. Within an hour nearly all of the company had assembled. Only much later would the captain learn that his company was one of the few components of the 505th Regimental Combat Team to land on its designated DZ that night, northeast of Gela.

Follmer and his I Company had the mission of knocking out an Italian strongpoint near the lake, which served as a landmark near the drop zone, and of lighting huge bonfires to serve as beacons to guide in the seaborne U.S. 1st Infantry Division. I Company had also been assigned to block roads near its DZ to deny their use to the enemy seeking to reach the site of amphibious landings.

Captain Follmer had one immediate concern. The C-47 in which Lt. Walter B. Kroener was jumpmaster had apparently strayed from the flight or been shot down. None of Kroener's men had joined the I Company column.

As the file of paratroopers marched onward in the darkness, a small stone farmhouse, desolate and eerielike in the rays of the moon, loomed up to the front. The column halted and took cover in the shadows. Captain Follmer, still astride his wheezing, huffing batman, and several troopers approached the structure. One of the men knocked boldly on the ancient wood door with the butt of his rifle.

The sharp sound of the blows on the door echoed through the night, causing the parachutists to wish they had found another method for arousing the Sicilian occupants—or whoever might be inside. Presently, a dim light flickered inside the house, and the front door was thrown open, revealing a leathery-faced farmer in his long flannel nightshirt. Fear was evident in the old man's face as he found himself confronted with several armed soldiers, obviously not the German or Italian fighting men he had grown accustomed to seeing on the island in recent weeks.

Follmer tried to orient himself by questioning the native through an Italian-speaking trooper, and from what he could make out, the captain concluded that he and his men had landed almost directly onto the DZ.

On leaving the farmer's house, a trooper spotted a mule in a rickety old stable. "Just what we need for Captain Follmer," the man told his comrades. Several of the airborne men moved to the stable and started to lead the mule away. The farmer rushed up, protesting strongly and gesturing with his hands. He said he relied on the animal to till the soil and do other chores around the rock-strewn, barren little farm.

"We're not going to steal the damned mule," a parachutist told the pleading Sicilian. "We're just going to borrow it for awhile so's the captain can get around and help kick the Krauts and Eyties off this goddamned island."

Despite the vigorous protest by the owner, Captain Follmer was hoisted astride the old mule, and the group moved off into the night. The farmer had hurriedly thrown on clothes over his nightshirt, and he started trotting behind his prized animal.

"Well, let him come along," the parachute captain told his men, feeling pangs of guilt over taking the farmer's means of scratching out an existence. It will be only for a day or two and then the Sicilian can have his mule back, Follmer rationalized to himself.

The captain and his men were trudging along toward a high hill where Follmer planned to establish his command post. Far off in the distance, toward the beaches where American seaborne forces would soon storm ashore, the I Company men could see the occasional flash of guns and the faint pyrotechnics of streams of tracer bullets lacing the dark sky. Follmer peeked at his luminous watch. It was 2:05 A.M.

Suddenly the column halted abruptly. The quiet summer night around the troopers was broken by the pronounced rustling of reeds which grew in abundance at the bottom of a deep gully just to the right of the marching troopers. Follmer felt his heart skip a beat.

The captain sent two troopers into the deep, dark ravine to scout the cause of the rattling noises most of the men had heard. It was not an enviable task, but as comrades waited with weapons at the ready, the pair of All-Americans descended into the gully. Minutes after reaching the bottom, the scouts heard a much louder rustling of the weeds and caught a glimpse of shadowy figures scrambling up the far side of the ravine and disappearing into the darkness.

The mysterious figures could have been wild boars. Or an enemy force. Or even other American paratroopers who were not certain as to the identity of Captain Follmer's men along the edge of the ravine. The moon had gone down and the landscape had been plunged into blackness.

Resuming its trek, the column reached the top of the commanding hill where Follmer located his CP (command post). The mule stood contentedly by, and the Sicilian farmer kept a close eye on his four-legged property. Patrols were formed and sent out to determine if I Company men were among friends or foes.

As the patrols scattered on assigned missions, Captain Follmer peered intently into the distance toward the unseen beaches where the 1st Infantry Division was to storm ashore soon. Follmer was anxious to learn if his platoon under Lt. George Clark would be able to carry out its mission—lighting huge bonfires to guide in assault boats of the seaborne force.

Follmer had great faith in his men but knew the bonfire mission was facing huge odds. If Clark and his troopers were able to reach a point near the shoreline, they would have the task of locating large combustible objects to ignite. There was the distinct possibility that Clark's men would encounter enemy troops and get pinned down in a firefight.

At 2:45 A.M., the stipulated time for the seaborne landings, the parachute captain felt a surge of elation. Out in the darkness, between the lofty hill and the gray sandy beaches near Gela, the night sky glowed from the flames of several briskly burning haystacks. Clark, who had received a broken ankle in the jump, and his men had accomplished their mission.

A short distance from the hilltop, the angry rattle of small arms fire erupted near Biviere Pond which served as a landmark for C-47 pilots near the DZ. A platoon from I Company had assaulted an enemy strongpoint there and after a shoot-out of a half-hour's duration killed, wounded or captured the defenders.

Now two of I Company's three initial missions had been achieved. Captain Follmer had earlier sent out squads to block roads in the vicinity, and now he mounted the old mule, with the aid of two troopers, and set out to visit his men at the roadblocks. The animal's Sicilian owner marched along behind.

Meanwhile, I Company's missing stick of troopers under command of Lieutenant Kroener had jumped far inland and were lost. As Kroener's plane had reached the coastline, it came under intense antiaircraft fire, and minutes later the copilot came back into the cabin.

"We've lost the rest of the squadron," the Air Corps officer stated in a calm manner.

"When did we lose them?" Lieutenant Kroener demanded.

"Some time back."

"In other words, we're lost?"

"We're lost."

"Then pick out some sort of a goddamned field and give us the green light. Our orders are to jump, come hell or high water!"

The copilot returned to the cabin to locate a likely drop zone.

Within seconds the crisis in Kroener's C-47 compounded. The parachute of Kroener's .60-millimeter mortar gunner accidentally opened in the cabin, spewing great folds of white silk about the craft. It appeared that the mortar gunner had been issued an unexpected reprieve from having to bail out into the hostile landscape below. No one could foresee that this freak mishap with his parachute had been his death warrant.

Soon the red light flashed on. The pilots had located a likely DZ. Kroener took his place in the door of the lost C-47. Above the angry roar of wind rushing through the open door, the jumpmaster heard the shout of the I Company armorer, Henry Chappel: "Hey, lieutenant, thought you'd like to know that the port engine is on fire!"

Before he could respond, Kroener felt a tap on his leg by his "pusher," Chappel, the signal that the green light in the cabin had flashed on. Out the door the lieutenant leaped with Chappel, Platoon Sgt. James Robinson and several other troopers bailing out in quick succession.

Not all of the stick could clear the door of the burning C-47. The aircraft tilted crazily, went out of control, and began a wobbly glide to the ground. It skidded over the rough landscape for over 100 yards before smashing into a large tree. Killed instantly were the pilot, copilot and crew chief, as well as the mortar gunner whose chute had opened in the cabin. Four other troopers, whose static lines had been hooked up but who did not have time to jump, were seriously injured and taken prisoner by nearby Italian troops.

Lieutenant Kroener had landed heavily on one side of a deep ravine, and his platoon sergeant, Jim Robinson, slammed into the ground on the other side of the gully. The two men promptly got together but could find none of their C-47 comrades. While stealthily prowling about the vicinity, they came under fire periodically from enemy machine guns concealed in the dark. An hour later they decided to head in a southerly direction for the landing beaches, but as dawn approached they were near exhaustion, uncertain of their locale and fearful that in daylight they would be captured or killed. So they holed up in a dry riverbed.

As the first glimmer of light heralded another day, Lieutenant Kroener pulled out a small pocket diary and with a pencil stub scribbled:

This is the morning of D-Day. We are lost. We have maps but can't locate our position. Our pilot did say we are east of Gela. Very indefinite. Saw Italian tank and two trucks filled with Italians.

Elsewhere along the widely dispersed American paratroop landings, a small knot of parachutists led by 26-year-old Lt. Richard Janney and Sgt. Carl Hearn had landed amidst half a dozen enemy pillboxes guarding a key crossroads. There were only six of the All-Americans at first, but they took the ominous, thick-walled concrete fortifications under attack and a fierce firefight broke out. Attracted by the sound of the guns, eight other paratroopers arrived on the scene and promptly joined in the battle.

It should have been a one-sided affair. Only a handful of Americans were firing away at the narrow slits in the heavily manned pillboxes while others covered comrades attempting to sneak up on the concrete structures to throw hand grenades inside. These parachutists had only the minimum protection of trees and large boulders. But before daylight burst over the purple hills of Sicily, Lieutenant Janney's men had knocked out all six pillboxes and had captured in excess of 250 Italians who had fought desperately before surrendering.

War is never a one-sided affair. Of the 14 paratroopers engaged in the savage struggle of men against concrete and spitting machine guns, five Americans lay dead and three others were wounded.

In the same general vicinity, Pvt. Robert Games and a few comrades were also engaged in a savage struggle with the Italian-manned pillboxes. In a conventional infantry outfit, Games would not be involved in this perilous fight because he was a clerk in headquarters company. But in the paratroopers, each man was a combat soldier first and whatever was his military specialty second.

With the other handful of troopers covering him with small arms fire, Games began creeping through the darkness toward the pillbox, when he was spotted in the moonlight by the enemy inside. They loosened a withering blast of fire at the All-American, at the same time tossing several grenades at him. Peering intently through the darkness, Games's fellow paratroopers saw the explosions and were convinced their comrade had been killed. Actually, Games had been knocked unconscious by the concussion of the grenade blasts.

In a temporary lull in the fighting, several Italians left the pillbox, crept out to the unconscious American, and dragged him back inside the concrete structure. There they stripped Games of his clothes and left him lying naked on the hard floor.

Less than a half hour later, not knowing Games was unconscious inside the pillbox, the tiny knot of parachutists stormed the structure, burst inside, and sprayed the confines with automatic weapons fire. Those Italians not killed threw up their arms and cried out in surrender. Young Games was spotted lying naked on the floor. This lack of decency infuriated the Americans, and they proceeded to pump bullets into the cringing Italians inside the pillbox.

At another nearby concrete pillbox, Pvt. Leonard Rosenthal, who only months before had been a clerk in a Chicago drugstore, edged up close to the structure and blew its roof off with a bazooka rocket. Several Italians inside were wounded by the explosion. Moments later Rosenthal and the little band of troopers with him saw the shadowy forms of three enemy soldiers emerge from the battered pillbox, frantically waving a white flag. The Americans lowered their weapons, and as they did so, the trio of surrendering Italians opened fire on the paratroopers. Rosenthal whipped his Garand rifle to his shoulder, squeezed the trigger, and the enemy soldier who had been carrying the surrender flag fell dead, a red-stained bullet hole through his forehead. The other two Italians threw down their weapons and called out that they were surrendering.

No one involved in the parachute assault on Sicily had any way of knowing it at the time, but the mass drop by Colonel Gavin's 505th Regimental Combat Team had gone totally awry. Due primarily to the heavy gale which had blown the C-47s far off course, as well as the inability of inexperienced Troop Carrier Command air crews to navigate accurately a complicated flight course, the 3,405 American paratroopers were scattered over a width of 60 miles in southeast Sicily.

The tediously developed airborne plan called for the reinforced regiment to drop in neat patterns on the high ground of Piano Lupo, north and northeast of the coastal town of Gela, in front of the seaborne 1st Infantry Division, to block enemy reinforcements from rushing to the landing beaches. A handful of troopers was dropped on Piano Lupo, but the others were strung out all the way to Syracuse in the British sector, 60 miles to the east.

Finding themselves alone or in tiny packets on parachuting into Sicily, the All-Americans promptly realized the corporation had dissolved, so they went into business for themselves. Spontaneously, small raiding parties led by junior officers and noncoms stalked through the dark countryside, creating fear and confusion among German and Italian soldiers and commanders. In a manner reminiscent of Indian warfare tactics of America's Old West, these stealthy raiders, many wearing war paint and with heads shaved, lay in wait in the darkness along roads, then ambushed Axis couriers and officers taking urgent orders to German and Italian command posts.

Detachments of enemy troops moving toward the landing beaches were suddenly raked with tommy gun and rifle fire from the shadows, after which the paratrooper band would melt into the night to strike again later. Axis patrols were shot up without warning, and those not killed or wounded fled in panic to their bases where they told wild tales of being pounced on by "hundreds" of black-faced Americans in baggy pants. Actually, the ambushing raiding party on most occasions consisted of four or five paratroopers.

As the scattered 82nd Airborne men made their way through the night toward the drop zone near Gela, they blew up bridges the enemy had been using to move troops toward the landing beaches, planted mines in roads, and shinnied up poles to cut telephone wire used by the Axis to coordinate military operations.

Not knowing when the American paratroopers would strike, where they would be and in what numbers demoralized German and Italian soldiers along a wide sweep of southeast Sicily.

While hundreds of Colonel Gavin's troopers were marauding about in the darkness, at the ancient walled city of Enna, in the center of the island, Generale d'Armata Alfredo Guzzoni was calmly studying reports being flashed to Sixth Army headquarters from commanders in the field. Guzzoni was one of the few in the command center accepting the Allied airborne assault with a degree of equanimity.

But the able General Guzzoni was gripped with indecisiveness. Part of his confusion was caused by the vast number of conflicting and often panicky reports from field commanders that were pouring into Enna. As a result of this deluge of messages from scores of locales along the 60 miles of southeastern Sicily, aides to General Guzzoni estimated the Allies had landed three or four airborne divisions, numbering some 50,000 men.

Guzzoni, who held the ultimate responsibility for ejecting Allied invaders from Sicily, had had ample warning that the invasion was about to be launched. At 4:30 P.M. the day before, an Italian reconnaissance plane spotted five large Allied convoys sailing northward from Malta. At 6:40 P.M., some two hours after that flotilla had been sighted, all German and Italian troops and installations on Sicily were put on full alert. But due to the heavy swells in the Mediterranean Sea generated by gale velocity winds, Guzzoni and other Axis commanders did not expect a seaborne assault until the raging waves had subsided.

But now, at 1 A.M. on Allied D-Day, with reports of American and British Airborne men on the island arriving steadily at his headquarters, the Sixth Army commander knew the seaborne assault could not be long in coming. Guzzoni, only an hour after American paratroopers had bailed out of the first C-47s and before any landing craft had left their transports at sea, declared a state of emergency on Sicily.

With great perspicacity, the Axis commander only two hours later concluded that Allied seaborne forces would not land west of the coastal town of Licata. He ordered harbor facilities blown at Licata and Porto Empedocle, along the southern beaches, to deny them to the invaders. The German 15th Panzer Division and Italian mobile formations stationed west of Licata were ordered to proceed to the east as rapidly as possible.

Guzzoni, however, was not aware that by midnight hundreds of Allied vessels had stealthily closed in on Sicily and were lying silently a few miles off the southern coast. This powerful armada was coiled and waiting to strike.

On the bridge of one of these ghostly crafts, the USS *Ancon,* stood a tall, professorial-appearing officer wearing the three stars of a lieutenant general on his helmet. His looks belied the fighting heart of Omar N. Bradley, commander of the U.S. II Corps, whose troops would make the amphibious assault.

Earlier that evening General Bradley had gone to his cabin for a nap. He was seasick and hoped a short rest would remedy that discomforting illness. At precisely midnight he had returned to the bridge. The *Ancon,* along with several hundred other ships, had been maneuvered into the Gulf of Gela under the direction of U.S. Rear Adm. Alan G. Kirk, and from these ships shortly would emerge thousands of assault troops, their weapons and equipment.

A regiment from both the veteran 1st Infantry Division and the untested 45th Infantry Division would simultaneously storm ashore abreast in the American sector. Bradley concealed his deep concerns, but as he awaited H-hour, his thoughts returned repeatedly to the practice landing of these two divisions, conducted three weeks previously in North Africa. There the navy deposited one assault regiment one mile from its intended beach, and the other regiment was put ashore five miles from its targeted landing.

Bradley looked at his watch. It was 1 A.M. H-hour was less than two hours away.

Suddenly the general's heart skipped a beat. In the darkness ashore, an enemy searchlight flashed on and began sweeping the waters of the Gulf of Gela, crammed with Allied ships. The powerful beam came to a halt with its focus directly on the *Ancon*. There it stayed for what seemed to General Bradley and to others aboard like hours but was of some 15 minutes' duration.

Then, as quickly as the beacon had been turned on, it dimmed, flickered and was extinguished. Had the massive invasion fleet been detected and would Axis bombers soon be overhead?

General Bradley and other commanders on the *Ancon* had little time to ponder this question at length. Muffled sounds were heard on scores of ships in the Gulf of Gela as combat-loaded transports began hoisting landing craft down to the dark water. Grim-faced American infantrymen, burdened with heavy combat gear, struggled up steel steps from the cramped and stifling holds, climbed over railings and down slippery rope ladders into little assault boats.

Minutes after scores of the tiny landing craft began the nine-mile run to Axis-defended beaches of southern Sicily, many of the assault troops became violently ill, hanging their heads over the sides of the pitching, bucking boats and vomiting into the angry sea. The fighting men were soaked to the skin and shivered from a combination of the water spray, seasickness and their entry into combat.

As the assault waves neared a line of silhouetted warships, a tremendous roar rolled over the seascape and shafts of brightness illuminated the sky. Powerful guns on the vessels had started pounding the beaches in front of the assaulting troops. Coxswains on landing craft carrying the regiment of the 1st Infantry Division steered for the man-made homing beacons behind their targeted beaches—the glow from several haystacks set ablaze by paratroopers of Captain Follmer's I Company.

At precisely H-hour (2:45 A.M.) fighting men of the Big Red One, as the 1st Division was called, stormed ashore and hurriedly organized for the push inland. On the right flank the untested Thunderbirds of the 45th Infantry Division waded onto the sandy beaches.

Resistance had been unexpectedly light, and along most of the beaches not a single shot had been fired for the first 30 minutes. Only at Gela, in the 1st Infantry Division sector, did the defenders offer moderate resistance. Lt. Col. William O. Darby's force of Rangers, attached to the Big Red One, had stumbled onto an Italian light-tank unit in Gela, which was disposed of in short order.

Surprise on the American beaches had been so complete that the Italian occupants at one major command post near the shore had fled without firing a shot. One of the first to enter this just-abandoned enemy CP was Michael Chinigo, a war correspondent who had landed with the assault waves. Moments later the telephone rang and Chinigo, who spoke fluent Italian, picked up the instrument and said, *"Che e?"* ("Who's there?")

The caller identified himself as an Italian general.

"I've been awakened and told the Americans have just landed in my sector," the sleepy Italian commander stated. "I don't see how that could happen; they couldn't possibly land in that sea."

In an authoritative voice, Chinigo assured the caller that the report was untrue, that all was quiet in the vicinity of Licata. Satisfied and relieved, the Italian general rang off and went back to sleep.

As a grinning Chinigo replaced the receiver, American reinforcements were pouring ashore outside and moving inland.

Meanwhile, some 50 miles to the east, a similar scenario to the one unfolding in the Gulf of Gela was developing in the British sector in the vicinity of the large city of Syracuse, at the southeastern tip of Sicily. Under Vice Adm. Bertram Ramsay, Royal Navy, ships began landing Empire troops in much larger numbers than those available to General Patton in the American sector. The British seaborne forces were landed, against negligible opposition, on four groups of beaches that swept around the Pachino peninsula.

At the time the first seaborne troops of the British Eighth Army splashed onto the beaches, two airborne Red Devils were being held prisoner in a house near Syracuse. Father Frank Hourigan and a corporal, both members of Brig. Pip Hicks's 1st Air Landing Brigade, had been captured a few hours previously when their glider crash-landed near an Italian searchlight battery in the British glider assault to seize Ponte Grande bridge, just south of Syracuse.

The pair of Red Devils had heard the roar of naval gunfire and knew what it meant—Tommies were assaulting the beaches nearby and rescue seemed imminent. Suddenly the door to their room was thrown open, and an Italian soldier, acting either out of rage that the Allies were invading Italian soil or due to hysteria, tossed a hand grenade inside. There was a loud explosion, but the Red Devil corporal escaped with only a minor wound when he ducked under a bed which served as a shield from the blast and fragments. Lying in the center of the room in a bloody pulp was the British airborne chaplain, Father Hourigan—dead.

Elsewhere in the British sector as General Montgomery's assault troops were landing, a German medical major entered the room in a stone farmhouse where Pvt. Lawrence O'Mara of the U.S. 82nd Airborne Division was stretched out in pain on a wooden table. Only two hours before, he had been bayoneted in the leg by a German soldier as he dangled helplessly from his parachute harness caught in a tall tree. The nasty-looking wound was still bleeding.

The German doctor hurriedly examined the incision in O'Mara's leg, then told him in flawless English, "That wound must be cleaned inside and sewn up. It will be painful, so I will give you an anesthetic to knock you out."

O'Mara promptly thought that the injection was a quick and neat method for disposing of a wounded American. But he had no choice and merely replied, "Okay."

As the German officer shoved a syringe needle into the young paratrooper's arm, O'Mara had a frightening thought: It will be dawn soon. Wonder if I'll be alive to see daylight? Two hours later he awoke and gave a sigh of relief. It was daytime.

Also in the British sector, some 50 miles east of the American drop zone near Gela, another 82nd Airborne Division trooper was wandering about aimlessly through the night. The husky red-haired corporal was lost and confused—and angry. For the past two hours he had located none of his comrades but had periodically sighted British soldiers. He could tell that they were British by their distinctive pie-plate helmets. Yet what were all those English Tommies doing in the American sector? he thought to himself.

Periodically the American airborne corporal would steal up near a knot of Britons and call out the password, "George!" The reply would be a fusillade of small arms fire whistling past the trooper. He became more angry after repeating this process several times, and on each occasion the response was bullets sent in his direction from out of the darkness.

Determined to learn why his allies continually fired at him, the corporal concealed himself behind some vegetation, and when a lone British Tommie happened to walk by, the airborne man pounced on him and threw

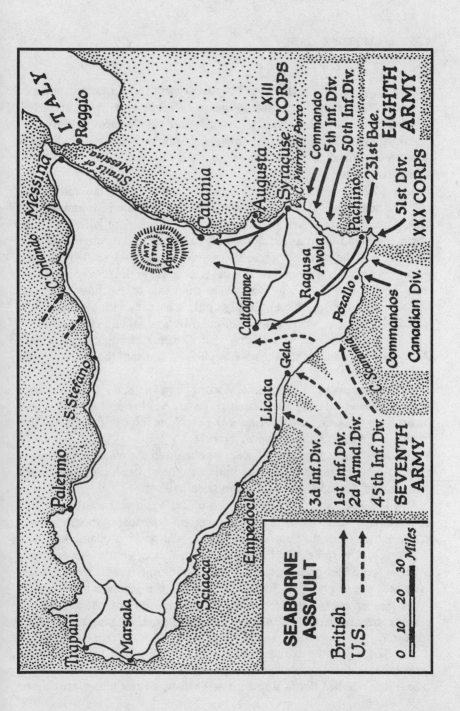

SEABORNE ASSAULT

British ━━━▶

U.S. ━━ ▶

0 10 20 30 Miles

ITALY

Reggio

Messina

C.'Orlando

Straits of Messina

S. Stefano

Palermo

Trapani

Marsala

Sciacca

Empedocle

Licata

Gela

Caltagirone

MT. ETNA

Adrano

Catania

Augusta

Ragusa

Avola

Pozzallo

C. Scaramia

C. Murro di Porco

Syracuse

Pachino

XIII CORPS

EIGHTH ARMY

Commando

5th Inf. Div.

50th Inf. Div.

231st Bde.

51st Div.

XXX CORPS

Commandos

Canadian Div.

3d Inf. Div.

1st Inf. Div.

2d Armd. Div.

45th Inf. Div.

SEVENTH ARMY

him to the ground in a firm hug. "Now tell me," the American sputtered as he held the struggling English soldier in a viselike grip, "what in the hell is going on? Every time I shout 'George' your people shoot at me!"

Aware by his accent that the antagonist was an American soldier, the Tommie explained to the airborne man, "We have a different password in the British sector."

At 4:30 A.M., some four and a half hours after American and British airborne men had landed, there was a light tap on the bedroom door of Gen. Dwight Eisenhower at his quarters on Malta. The Allied supreme commander had spent a fretful few hours twisting and turning in his bed, consumed by the knowledge that thousands of young Allied fighting men, under his orders, were engaged in a death struggle with the enemy only 70 miles to the north. And he was aware that, due to the heavy gale, his airborne and seaborne forces already could have met with disaster.

A British signals officer entered Eisenhower's room and reported that a message had been received stating that General Montgomery's Eighth Army assault elements were ashore as planned and that the operation was unfolding smoothly.

The supreme commander asked of word from General Patton's Seventh Army and was told none had been received. Neither had anything been heard from Col. Jim Gavin's American parachute force or from Maj. Gen. Hoppy Hopkinson's British glider brigade.

His deep concerns hardly relieved, he dismissed the officer with instructions to keep him advised on even minute reports from Sicily. Eisenhower switched off the light and once again tried to sleep.

It was 6 A.M. when the same British officer again entered the supreme commander's bedroom. In a cheery voice he reported, "Good news, sir! All of Patton's assault elements are ashore and pushing inland."

A trace of a smile of relief crossed Eisenhower's face. He promptly asked if word had been received from his airborne forces. "Sorry, none, General" was the reply. A furrow returned to the general's brow.

As the signals officer left the room, Eisenhower got out of bed and started dressing. What was the use of going through the pretense of trying to sleep?

The dark sky in the east began to dissolve into dawn of Allied D-Day in Sicily as Col. Jim Gavin and a small column of paratroopers were edging into a dry riverbed flourishing with tall weeds, to rest before moving on westward again. Most of the troopers were limping from jolting parachute landings; all were near exhaustion.

Colonel Gavin was disconsolate. During 20 years of military service he had prepared for the physical and moral challenge of leading fighting men against the enemy in desperate battle. It had been nearly five hours since he had leaped from a C-47, and he was not yet certain what country he was in. His only confrontation with the enemy was the episode with the drunken Italian soldier—and even that was botched.

Jim Gavin, who had taken off from North Africa in command of 3,405 paratroopers, counted the force with him. It totaled five individuals—two officers and three enlisted men.

As a disspirited Colonel Gavin was taking stock of his situation, across the Mediterranean in Algiers a telephone jangled impatiently in the room of civilian newspaper correspondent Richard Tregaskis at the Hotel Aletti. The journalist flipped on the light and looked at his watch. It was 4 A.M. The caller identified himself as an officer at Allied Force Headquarters and said, "You might want to get right over here. We've got an announcement of major significance."

Tregaskis slipped on his clothing and rushed to the nearby headquarters building where a number of sleepy-eyed reporters had gathered. The door of the conference room flew open, and a British colonel, Cedric McCormick, entered and started reading from a prepared text: "British, Canadian and American troops began landing operations in Sicily early this morning . . ."

The announcement came as no surprise to the reporters. General Eisenhower had briefed them on the operation a month before.

At the conclusion of the press conference, the sky was beginning to lighten. Tregaskis spotted a solitary figure standing solemnly on a balcony, staring down at the empty rue Michelet. It was Hugh Baillie, president of United Press.

As Tregaskis joined his friend on the balcony, Baillie said in a low voice, "Well, Dick, I guess plenty of our boys have gone to their glory by this time."

CHAPTER EIGHT

HEROES OF PIANO LUPO

D awn on D-Day burst forth over a bustling sea off the coast at Gela. At 6 A.M. minesweepers began energetically combing the waters offshore, even though a large convoy had already charged into the vicinity during the darkness and was now anchored just outside the beaches. No mines were detected, so the troop transports and cargo ships moved even closer to land.

Landing craft scurried between the beaches and the ships offshore, and LSTs (landing ship, tanks) lumbered steadily through the water. Far off in the distance subchasers patrolled back and forth, protecting the scores of ships lying at anchor from possible sudden disaster from underwater torpedoes.

With the arrival of daylight, loud swishing sounds echoed across the waters off Gela as four light spotter planes were catapulted from the cruisers *Savannah* and *Boise* whose job it was to detect the approach of enemy forces and radio firing information back to the gun batteries aboard ship. Without fighter-plane cover, the pilots of the light aircraft had a perilous mission. And the closest Allied fighter bases were nearly 200 miles away, in North Africa.

The appearance overhead of the naval spotter planes triggered a quick response from the German Luftwaffe. Within minutes five ME-109s based at Gerbini airport, only minutes away by air, swept in over the beaches near Gela and promptly attacked the unarmed, fragile, slow-moving

American spotters. It was an unequal contest. Within seconds Navy Lt. C. A. Anderson, senior pilot on the *Savannah*, was machine-gunned in his seat, dying almost instantly. His radioman, Edward J. True, took over the controls of the spotter plane from the dead pilot and, although not a qualified flier, skillfully landed the bullet-riddled craft on the sea as the ME-109s continued to blaze away at him. True's plane sank almost immediately on hitting the water, but the young radioman crawled out of the twisted wreckage and was rescued by a nearby vessel. He sustained only minor injuries in his close brush with death.

The veteran Luftwaffe pilots, with the scent of blood in their nostrils, then shot down the second spotter plane from the *Savannah*, which crashed into the Mediterranean just offshore and disappeared from sight.

Capt. R. W. Cary, the *Savannah*'s commanding officer, knowing the great value of furnishing aerial "eyes" to the paratroop and seaborne forces on shore, sent his two remaining spotters into the air. Another flight of Messerschmitts arrived overhead, shot one spotter out of the sky, and forced the other to fly far out to sea.

The German fighter pilots then turned their attention to Lt. C. G. Lewis, piloting one of the spotters from the *Boise*. At 8:27 A.M. shipboard monitors heard the calm voice of Lewis report: "Two Messerschmitts are on my ass. Stand by to pick me up out of the water!"

Moments later Lieutenant Lewis's voice was heard again: "Delay that. The Krauts know it's me up here and they've gone back for reinforcements."

Undaunted by the knowledge that German fighter planes would soon return, the navy pilot continued to hover over the bustling beaches and reported to the *Boise* over his radio: "Enemy tanks and vehicles moving south down Niscemi road toward the beaches at Gela."

The enemy column, trailing thick clouds of dust in its wake, belonged to the Hermann Goering Panzer Fallschirmjaeger Division. Shortly after 10 P.M. the previous night, the column had been sent rolling toward the landing beaches from its assembly area near Caltagirone by its commander, Gen. Paul Conrath. The pugnacious German general a few weeks before had been told by his superior, Field Marshal Kesselring, to "smash 'em on the beaches!" That is what Conrath intended to do.

It was a situation fraught with peril for the 1st Infantry Division which was still coming ashore and at its most vulnerable point to determined armor attack.

Standing between the oncoming Hermann Goering column and the landing beaches of the Big Red One was a small band of paratroopers belonging to Lt. Col. Arthur "Hard Nose" Gorham's 1st Battalion of the 505th Parachute Infantry Regiment. Gorham's men, numbering less than 100, were on the high ground known as Piano Lupo, which was to have been the drop zone for Col. James Gavin's 3,405 paratroopers.

Piano Lupo was a bleak hill mass that dominated a key road intersection seven miles northeast of Gela. The junction had been code-named Objective Y by airborne planners and marked for early seizure.

Objective Y, guarded by a complex of large, thick pillboxes bristling with machine guns, was the point where roads from Vittoria and Caltagirone (by way of Niscemi) met. The Hermann Goering Division tank column would have to sweep past this intersection in its most direct route to the landing beaches near Gela.

Most of the American parachutists on Piano Lupo were members of A Company, commanded by Capt. Edwin M. Sayre, a 27-year-old farmer from Texas, who had risen through the ranks from a private in the 36th Infantry Division. During the night the nine-plane formation carrying Colonel Gorham's staff and two platoons and headquarters of Sayre's company kept in formation. Although coming under heavy fire on crossing the coast, all nine C-47s dropped their paratroopers on the DZ.

Captain Sayre was the first man out when the green light in the C-47 flashed on, and he landed with terrific impact in a vineyard on the side of a steep hill, a collision with the ground that caused his head to spin and his eyes to lose their focus. Because much time had been lost while the nine-plane flight flew around off the southeastern tip of Sicily trying to locate familiar landmarks, the moon was now descending, and Sayre could see only a few feet around him.

As he momentarily contemplated his next move, he became aware that enemy machine guns, which had been firing at his overhead flight and then at the paratroopers as they floated to earth, had lowered their trajectory and were now raking the terrain on which the paratroopers had landed with heavy bursts of tracer bullets. Despite the darkness, normal confusion of an air drop at night, and the relentless firing of the six enemy machine guns, in about an hour Sayre had assembled 15 of his men and their equipment. By 5 A.M., with daylight at hand, 30 more of his parachutists had joined him. Sayre was encouraged to learn that, in the darkness, his

ightly armed men had managed to recover two .60-millimeter mortars
with 50 shells and three machine guns with 2,000 rounds for each weapon.
Colonel Gorham by now had determined that he and his headquarters
group and most of Captain Sayre's A Company had landed four miles
south of Niscemi, about two and a half miles from their true DZ. They
were just east of a sturdy, thick-walled, two-story farmhouse that had been
urned into a fortress. It was surrounded by pillboxes. The farmhouse was
oristling with enemy machine guns, and thick strands of nasty-looking
oarbed wire and deep trenches protected approaches to the strongpoint.
Sayre decided to attack this heavily defended position with the men at
his disposal before enemy reinforcements arrived. At 5:30 A.M. the two
60-millimeter mortars of the little band of paratroopers began dropping
rounds on the fortress as the Americans peppered the sturdy structure
with rifles, tommy guns, rocket launchers and grenades as they moved
steadily forward. Inside the thick-walled farmhouse the enemy spotted the
parachutists advancing toward them and sent long bursts of automatic
weapons fire hissing angrily past the Americans. Sickening thuds told that
enemy bullets had found their marks among the attackers, and several
paratroopers went down.

Firing bazooka rounds and bullets into the supporting pillboxes, Sayre's
men killed or drove out the defenders and took over the concrete structures. The pillbox machine guns were manned by the Americans who
began raking the fortress with heavy bursts of fire from the Italians' own
weapons.

Captain Sayre was lying on the ground with several men as bullets
ripped past just over their heads. "We're going to charge 'em!" Sayre
called out above the chatter of machine guns. Turning to a trooper lying
next to him, who the captain thought was armed with a tommy gun, Sayre
said, "You come along and cover me."

The company commander shouted, "Let's go!" and with a forward wave
of his hand, leaped to his feet and charged the fortress. Sayre had a grenade in his teeth, another grenade in one hand, and a carbine in the other
hand. His men dashed forward with him.

Under cover of heavy fire by the Americans from the just-captured
machine guns in the pillboxes, Sayre and several troopers reached the side
of the thick-walled farmhouse and tossed several grenades through open-
ngs. A trooper fired a rifle grenade at the front door from 10 feet, blowing

it open. But the door swung shut. Creeping up to the door, Captain Sayre kicked it open and tossed in a grenade.

As the paratroopers got ready to rush in through the opening, shouts of surrender were heard from inside the building. "Come on out with your hands in the air, you bastards!" a trooper shouted. As the wary Americans leveled their weapons at the opening, a German soldier emerged carrying a piece of white cloth. The defenders continued to parade out of the stone farmhouse until 40 Italians and 10 Germans had emerged. Inside, Sayre and his men found 15 dead enemy soldiers. Four Americans had been wounded in the charge, one of whom later died.

Inside the thick-walled, two-story fortress, Sayre and his men took control of a wealth of enemy booty: 20 machine guns and nearly 500,000 rounds of ammunition for the weapons. The captain was elated. These would come in handy.

Contemplating his next move, Captain Sayre casually remarked to the paratrooper he had designated to cover him in the final charge to the bristling fortress, "Where's your tommy gun?"

"What tommy gun?" the trooper replied.

"Well, the one you had when you covered me."

"I lost my tommy in the jump. All I had was a trench knife."

Meanwhile, from prisoners captured in the pillbox complex, Sayre learned that the Germans were an outpost from a kampfgruppe (battle group) of the elite Hermann Goering Panzer Division which was only two miles to the north. The company commander was startled by this revelation. The parachute combat team had been told by U.S. intelligence officers before takeoff from Tunisia that "only a few German technicians" were in Sicily.

Armed with this new information, Captain Sayre immediately organized his small group of paratroopers into a defensive position, utilizing the 20 enemy machine guns in his line. Now the training back in Africa designed to make men of the 82nd Airborne capable of firing enemy weapons was about to pay off.

Sayre for the first time glanced at his watch. It seemed as though he and his men had been on Sicily for a lifetime. It was 6:25 A.M.—barely six hours since the captain and his troopers had jumped.

A short time later a lookout spotted a small column of men approaching the farmhouse strongpoint. It was Lieutenant Colonel Gorham, the 1st Battalion commander, at the head of 29 men, including the two battalion surgeons. Assisted by other troopers, the medical men were carrying several All-Americans who had been wounded in fighting during the night.

The 28-year-old Gorham, a 1938 graduate of West Point, had the nickname "Hard Nose" due to his toughness and insistence on strict discipline in his battalion. On Piano Lupo he and his men would need all the toughness they could muster.

At 7 A.M., only a half hour since preparations began to organize the strongpoint for defense, a trooper rushed up to Gorham. "Colonel, there's some vehicles coming down the road toward us from Niscemi," the lookout stated. "They look like they're about a mile away."

Gorham, Sayre and a few others scrambled to a nearby high point and with the aid of binoculars saw that the approaching "vehicles" were armored cars and tanks preceded by two motorcycles and a Volkswagen.

"All right, men, get ready," Colonel Gorham called out. "A column of Kraut armored stuff is heading toward us." He told his parachutists to "wait until the 'point' gets right up to us, then open up on them with everything we've got." Gorham added that he would give the word when to commence firing.

Nervously fingering the triggers of their rifles, tommy guns and machine guns, the tense and perspiring troopers lay in wait. They felt a peculiar mixture of elation that a German force was unknowingly falling into their ambush and a gnawing anxiety as to whether less than 100 lightly armed parachutists, without antitank guns, artillery or tanks, could ward off an armored column backed by grenadiers (infantrymen).

Rolling along totally unaware of lurking danger, the Germans in the Volkswagen and two motorcycles, acting as the point for the main body, neared the line of concealed Americans. The only sound to be heard was the steady purring of the vehicle motors. Suddenly a loud shout "Fire!" rang out. A crescendo of noise echoed across the bleak landscape as the paratroopers poured bursts of machine gun and rifle fire into the approaching Germans.

It was over in seconds. Both motorcyclists were killed, as were two Germans in the Volkswagen. Two other enemy soldiers in the camouflaged automobile, trembling uncontrollably and ashen-faced from the sudden confrontation with death, scrambled out of the vehicle with cries of *"Kamerad! Kamerad!"* ("I surrender!").

Hearing the bursts of gunfire half a mile to their front, the main body of the armored column ground to a halt. The American paratroopers, grim-faced and tense, waited for the next enemy move. It would not be long in coming.

From a vantage point on a low knoll, Gorham and his troopers looked on as two companies of German grenadiers, numbering about 300 men, fanned out into a skirmish line and headed across the barren, open ground toward the Americans' position. The German commander, either due to a faint heart or because he feared rushing into a tank ambush, held back his armor.

Onward came the line of enemy grenadiers. The boiling Sicilian sun beat down on the attackers as they advanced steadily to a point some 200 yards in front of the Americans. Not a single shot had been fired by either side. The Germans trudged ahead, out in the open and devoid of cover or concealment. Now they were 100 yards away. Then 80. On they came toward the concealed Americans.

Again the shout "Fire!" rang out over the paratrooper positions, and ear-piercing fusillades of machine gun and rifle fire riddled the ranks of the exposed German infantrymen. Scores of enemy soldiers were cut down in the initial bursts. The others, caught in the open, milled about in fear and confusion. Most of the attackers flopped to the ground and lay there as the Americans continued to rake them with fire. So intense was the paratrooper firing that few Germans could raise up to shoot back.

Those toward the rear of the attacking force began to crawl away from the hailstorm of fire. About half of the Germans managed to pull back. Soon shouts of "Cease firing! Cease firing!" echoed over the American positions. There were no targets remaining at which to shoot.

An eerie silence fell over the Piano Lupo terrain. Out in front of the Americans, scores of German bodies lay grotesquely sprawled in death, scorched by the brutal rays of the Mediterranean sun. Other forms interspersed among the dead could be seen writhing in agony. Low moans and cries from these mutilated enemy soldiers wafted over the landscape to the ears of the paratroopers.

There was nothing the Americans could do to relieve the suffering of the wounded and maimed Germans sprawled out before them on the rock-hard, flat terrain. The paratroopers had no medical facilities to care for their own wounded.

Now Colonel Gorham and his troopers awaited the next German move against their blocking position. The little band of paratroopers was keeping the enemy armored column from its urgent mission of reaching the landing beaches and shooting up the 1st Infantry Division before it got all of its firepower ashore. The minutes ticked by and there was no indication of another assault by the German force. Perhaps the ear-piercing chatter of the 20 captured Italian machine guns riddling the ranks of the attacking grenadiers resulted in the enemy commander believing that a much larger force was confronting him.

Less than a half hour after the two companies of German grenadiers were riddled at point-blank range, a high-velocity .88-millimeter gun began firing shells into the paratroopers' position. The field piece was located on a hill and was shooting in a flat trajectory. Cccrraacckkk! Sswiissh! The speed of the projectile was so fast that the troopers heard the explosion in their ranks before the swishing noise of the shell in flight.

Colonel Gorham had no method for combating the .88. If his troopers remained in place, they would be chewed up by the relentless shelling. He ordered his 90 men to pull back to a new blocking position several hundred yards to the rear.

A frontal assault by grenadiers against the paratroopers having met with disaster, the German commander now employed a new tack. He launched several of his tanks around the right flank of the American parachutists at the time they were moving to the new position.

Within minutes after Hard Nose Gorham and his men heard the ominous sound of enemy tanks clanking around toward their rear, the echo of a series of explosions reached their ears. The troopers could not see the enemy tanks on their flank and had no way of knowing that the iron-plated monsters had run up against a little knot of Captain Sayre's tank-destroyer troopers armed with bazookas.

The tank-destroyer squad had landed during the night about two miles from the main body of A Company and were marching toward the DZ, when they heard the roar of powerful diesel motors and saw the panzers flanking Colonel Gorham's position grinding toward them.

The bazooka squad hurriedly got into firing position as six German tanks bore down on them. Buttoned up inside, the enemy tankers could not see the bazooka men. Suddenly there were loud swooshing sounds— American rockets were launched toward the oncoming iron monsters. Although aimed by steady hands, the rockets found their marks mainly by luck. The missiles struck the tanks in vulnerable spots, and the two leading tracked vehicles swerved crazily and ground to a halt, their crews dead inside.

Unaware that they were opposed by only a handful of Americans and fearing that they had stumbled into an ambush, crews of the four remaining tanks backed out of bazooka range and began raking the tank-destroyer squad with machine gun bursts. Minutes later a contingent of German infantry moved up in support of the panzers and took the pinned-down Americans prisoners.

The 90 American paratroopers with Colonel Gorham and Captain Sayre had no way of knowing it at the time, but they had taken the steam out of the drive by the western column of the Hermann Goering Division to reach the landing beaches at Gela. At the same time, the eastern column of the elite German panzer and paratrooper division was heading hell-bent for the shoreline where the U.S. 45th Infantry Division was moving into Sicily.

Using German prisoners to carry American wounded, Gorham and his troopers arrived at the new blocking position on a commanding hill mass on the drop zone. Gorham promptly sent out patrols to locate other members of the 3,405-man parachute force that was to have dropped on Piano Lupo. Not a single other All-American could be located.

Lieutenant Colonel Gorham, taking stock of his situation, now knew that it was up to his band to try to accomplish the mission of the 505th Parachute Regimental Combat Team. "We're going to do our damnedest," he defiantly told Captain Sayre. That mission was to block Axis forces from rushing south to 1st Infantry Division landing beaches.

Gorham sent Captain Sayre and his A Company men to attack and seize the enemy strongpoint at Objective Y, the key road intersection a short distance to the south, which would have to be passed by Axis forces headed for the shoreline. As Sayre and his men reached a point about 1,000 yards from the pillbox complex at Objective Y, they heard the roar of airplane engines overhead and looked up in dismay as a Luftwaffe fighter plane shot down a slow-moving, unarmed spotter aircraft, probably one from the USS *Savannah* lying offshore.

The spotter plane apparently had been directing naval gunfire on Objective Y, as heavy salvos were crashing to earth about 100 yards in front of the pillboxes. Although Sayre and his troopers were 1,000 yards away from the impact area, they could feel the ground trembling from the force of the explosions.

Before assaulting the thick-walled pillboxes bristling with automatic weapons, Captain Sayre decided to attempt a *ruse de guerre*. He ordered a

German prisoner brought to him and through an interpreter told him, "Go to those pillboxes at that road junction out there and tell those bastards inside that if they do not surrender immediately, I am going to call that naval gunfire right down on top of them and blow them all to hell. Do you understand?"

The prisoner nodded his head that he did comprehend his role. He set out at almost a trot for the pillboxes at the road intersection.

Actually, Captain Sayre had no communication with the warships offshore and therefore no means for influencing their firing. He was banking that the enemy manning the pillboxes had no way of knowing that crucial point.

A combination of the apparent eloquence of the German prisoner and the looming destruction by naval gunfire of those inside the pillboxes had the desired effect. Only three minutes after the POW entered the first concrete structure, enemy soldiers bearing white flags and hands held high in surrender emerged from the three pillboxes.

Captain Sayre and his troopers took over the pillboxes from the evicted tenants—and not a minute too soon. The sound of clanking treads and powerful diesel motors echoed across the landscape and told the new proprietors of the pillboxes that enemy tanks were approaching. Four German panzers were grinding down the Niscemi road toward the intersection. The paratroopers opened up a blistering round of machine gun and rifle fire at the enemy tanks which promptly spun around and rumbled back in the direction from which they had come.

A half hour later, at 11:30 A.M., a parachutist lookout called out, "Foot soldiers closing in from the rear. They look like straight-legs." Minutes later several scouts from the Big Red One reached the intersection. Their regiment had landed by sea near Gela during the night.

Captain Sayre located a 1st Division radioman and sent a signal to General Ridgway, commander of the 82nd Airborne Division: "Mission of combat team accomplished."

Lieutenant Colonel Gorham's paratroopers, somewhat reduced in number due to casualties from the fierce clashes that morning, were attached to the 2nd Battalion, 16th Infantry Regiment, of the 1st Division, commanded by Lt. Col. Joseph Crawford. The infantry battalion and its attached parachutists were ordered to push inland at once, and by dusk the combined force had advanced a mile against light opposition. There the Americans dug in for the night.

Despite nearly 30 hours of flying, marching and fighting, and on the brink of exhaustion, Captain Sayre was worried that American paratroopers might be lying wounded to his front. Just after dark, Sayre led a patrol of eight parachutists from the positions of the main body out toward German lines. Stealthily edging along in the darkness, ears and eyes alert for any sign of a lurking enemy or wounded American paratroopers, Sayre and his men advanced for nearly half a mile in the eerie hush of night without hearing a sound.

"I don't like it," a trooper whispered at a comrade. "It's too goddamned quiet."

Hardly had the words left his mouth than the tranquillity was pierced by the savage chatter of enemy machine guns which opened up on them from the darkness to the front. Caught in the heavy fusillade at almost point-blank range, the troopers flopped to the ground as white tracers crisscrossed the air just over their heads, much like a swarm of angry bees in search of a hated victim.

Seeking to escape the withering bursts of fire, Captain Sayre and his eight men began arduously to crawl away from the line of fire. After edging along for more than 200 yards, they reached a dry stream bed about five feet deep and scrambled into its protective confines. Enemy machine gun bursts were still sweeping the area.

Sprawled about in the pitch-black darkness of the defile to rest and regain their breaths, the troopers were silent. Minutes later they heard a shuffling of feet nearby, and the shadowy silhouettes of perhaps 10 armed men suddenly leaped down into the dry river bottom almost directly on top of the reclining paratroopers.

In the blackness Sayre's men were unable to identify shoulder patches of the new arrivals but presumed them to be a patrol of the 1st Infantry Division seeking cover from the enemy machine gun fire searching the terrain periodically.

The newcomers appeared as startled to detect the dim outlines of the soldiers occupying the riverbed as the paratroopers were to suddenly have the newcomers leap nearly on top of them. But none in either group showed any outward concern over finding themselves side by side in the pitch-black defile.

Moments later a curious newcomer called out in a hushed voice to the men who had occupied the dry riverbed first, *"Kompanie zu welcher Einheit gehosen Sie?"* ("What company do you belong to?")

"They're Krauts!" an American shouted as he whipped out his trench knife and tackled the nearest enemy figure, plunging the sharp point of the weapon into the German.

As if the shout had been a starter's gun at a track meet, the American paratroopers leaped to their feet and charged into the nearest Germans. In seconds the dry riverbed was a whirling mass of thrashing bodies as opposing patrols fought each other in the blackness with daggers, rifle butts and swinging fists. Loud curses in two languages punctured the night air amid the rustle of entangled bodies rolling in the dust. An occasional grunt could be heard when a trench knife had found its mark.

Captain Sayre, who had picked up a pistol from a dead parachute officer earlier, had a weapon in each hand. When he could clearly identify a combatant as German, he fired at him with both pistols.

The hand-to-hand fight in the dark was savage—and brief. The German grenadiers were no match for the American paratroopers in close-quarter combat. Those enemy soldiers who could do so tore themselves from the grasp of adversaries and fled into the night toward German lines. Left behind in the defile were one dead and three wounded comrades.

Sayre and his patrol returned to the main body of the 1st Infantry Division battalion, bringing their three wounded prisoners with them. It was now midnight of D-Day. Ed Sayre and his men had engaged in continuous activities for 48 hours. As they fell to the ground in exhaustion, Colonel Gorham edged up to Sayre and said, "Better get some sleep, Ed. We've received orders to attack Hill 41 half a mile to our front at dawn."

Dawn was only a little more than four hours away.

Unknown to Colonel Gorham, Captain Sayre and their handful of troopers, other 82nd Airborne men had landed during the night along the northern portions of Piano Lupo. They were members of Lt. Col. Charles W. Kouns's 3rd Battalion, 504th Parachute Infantry Regiment. Most of Kouns's battalion was scattered over a wide expanse southeast of Niscemi. Only one of Kouns's companies was able to reorganize, and this unit promptly moved into an ancient castle which they prepared for defense.

Shortly after daylight, the troopers in the medieval castle heard the noise of vehicle motors approaching and, while remaining carefully concealed, peeked out to see a company-sized convoy of Germans grind to a halt along the road at the bottom of a hill just to their front. The enemy formation was part of a .120-millimeter mortar unit on its way to shell the American landing beaches.

There were shouts along the convoy for the Germans to dismount and take a 10-minute break before moving on toward Gela. Unaware that the prying, hostile eyes of a band of determined American paratroopers were focused on their every move from less than 50 yards away, the enemy troops, numbering around 200, began to relieve themselves along the sides of the narrow road. Suddenly and without warning, their relief activities were interrupted as the concealed paratroopers opened up a withering fusillade of fire.

Panicked by the abrupt and totally unexpected raking by small arms fire, those who were able attempted to flee the scene. Others were cut down by the parachutists' salvos.

Soon there were shouts of "Cease firing!" in the ancient, thick-walled castle, and the American weapons fell silent. The lieutenant in charge looked around. With the thick walls of the castle offering protection from enemy small arms fire, not an American paratrooper had been hit. Down at the bottom of the hill many German bodies lay grotesquely sprawled in death. Here and there, dispersed among the lifeless forms of comrades, wounded enemy soldiers writhed and moaned in agony. Those remaining in the enemy force had fled the scene and abandoned their heavy mortars, large stores of shells, and all of their vehicles.

Learning of the ambush of the vitally needed .120-millimeter mortar unit, German commanders were furious. They were particularly irate over the survivors fleeing the scene. A German force, supported by several tanks, was hurriedly launched toward the old castle with orders to seize it, wipe out the American occupants, and regain the mortars, ammunition, vehicles and equipment sitting at the bottom of the hill.

The assault force of the Hermann Goering Division hit the paratroopers in their stronghold with fury but were unable to budge the stubborn defenders. Efforts by the Germans, under cover of darkness, to sneak patrols into the abandoned mortars and vehicles and drive them away were detected by the parachutists, who drove off the enemy grenadiers with withering small arms fire.

During the next two days and nights, German formations made periodic attacks against this thorn in their sides, but the band of American paratroopers refused to budge. Low on food and out of water, ammunition nearly exhausted, the troopers in the castle were relieved by elements of the advancing 1st Infantry Division on D-Day plus three.

Other paratroopers of Colonel Kouns's battalion, early on the morning of D-Day, were marauding the countryside in small batches led by lieutenants and noncoms. Lt. Peter J. Eaton had landed at midnight two miles northeast of Biscari and rounded up 36 troopers who had landed in the vicinity. Eaton's column headed for the DZ of his battalion near Niscemi, and by dawn another 14 parachutists had joined the little band.

Marching under the scorching Sicilian sun, Eaton and his men about noon spotted two Italian trucks towing .57-millimeter antitank guns moving along the road toward the paratroopers. The column scrambled into concealment alongside the road. The unknowing Italians drove their vehicles into the ambush and were cut down in a blistering fusillade of fire, mostly before they could get out of their seats.

Lieutenant Eaton's men mined the road and covered it with the newly captured Italian .57-millimeter guns. At 12:35 P.M. a long column of German infantry, supported by a tank, was spotted marching along the road toward the concealed Americans. Eaton estimated the force as a battalion.

The paratroopers nervously fingered the triggers on their weapons as the Germans marched closer. When the enemy column reached Eaton's position, the officer shouted "Fire!" and an ear-shattering noise echoed through the surrounding hills as rifles and tommy guns poured bullets into the startled German ranks. A trooper armed with a bazooka crept near to the tank and fired a rocket into its side, knocking out the tracked vehicle and killing its crew.

Surprised and caught in the open without cover or concealment, the German column was able to mount only feeble efforts to fight back. The ambushed enemy force milled about in confusion, then rapidly withdrew toward the rear. Outnumbered and the advantage of surprise lost, Lieutenant Eaton and his troopers withdrew, leaving many enemy dead and wounded behind them.

Elsewhere on Piano Lupo shortly after dawn on D-Day, Lt. F. E. Thomas of Colonel Kouns's battalion and several of his men were eating a meal served them by friendly Sicilians. They were seated under a shade tree outside an old farmhouse. Suddenly Thomas and his men glanced up from their food and into the muzzles of a mass of Schmeisser machine pistols leveled at them.

After the Americans were disarmed, Lieutenant Thomas engaged the German officer in earnest conversation. The parachute officer first explained that the Axis had already lost the war, then shifted to a more

personal tack: the German patrol could never get back to its own line with
the American prisoners because it would be killed or captured by the
"thousands" of paratroopers swarming over Piano Lupo. Thomas's persuasive powers were not inhibited in the least by the fact that he was not
aware of the presence of a single other airborne man outside of his own
little group.

Thomas was a gifted salesman. When he concluded, the German officer
sat silent for several minutes in contemplation. Suddenly he cleared his
throat and said, "I have one seriously wounded man with me. I would very
much like for him to receive medical attention. I can never get him back to
our lines alive, and even if I did, there is very little medical help for him
there."

He paused briefly and fondled the Schmeisser automatic pistol he was
holding across his lap. "I'll strike a bargain with you," the young German
officer said in fluent English. "We'll give you back your weapons if you
give me your personal word that you will take charge of my wounded man
and see that he receives the excellent medical attention you Americans can
give him." Again pausing briefly, the German added, "And as part of our
agreement, once we give your weapons back to you, we promise not to fire
on you in return for your word not to fire on us."

"Agreed on both points," the paratroop lieutenant replied, knowing that
he and his men had gotten the best of this impromptu agreement.

Weapons were returned to the paratroopers who took custody of the
seriously wounded German. Several hours later he was turned over to
medics of the 1st Infantry Division and evacuated to a hospital ship offshore.

Along the road leading from Niscemi to the intersection at Objective Y
and then on to the American landing beaches, 21-year-old Lt. James C.
Ott and 12 men stumbled onto an enemy force of 350 men marching
southward. Ott and his troopers scrambled into bushes beside the road to
allow the enemy column to pass; opening fire on such a large body of the
enemy would be disastrous for only 13 paratroopers.

As the marching formation reached the hiding place of Ott and his men,
a lone German fell out of line and moved to the side of the road to relieve
himself. He picked the same large bush the young parachute lieutenant
was concealed behind to perform his urgent task. The German's face
turned white as he saw himself staring into the muzzle of the American's

rifle at five-foot range. Ott squeezed the trigger and the enemy grenadier toppled over backward, a large red hole in his forehead.

Hearing the rifle shot, a German command car filled with officers halted directly opposite Ott to investigate. The parachute leader grabbed a bazooka and fired a rocket which caught the command vehicle in its center and sent bodies hurtling into the air. Lieutenant Ott pitched down the bazooka and with a yell of "Let's go!" he and his concealed troopers leaped to their feet and raced off through vegetation and disappeared over a low hill. German bullets nipped at their heels every step of the way.

At headquarters of the Hermann Goering Division at the end of Allied D-Day, Gen. Paul Conrath was furious. His anger was directed at the failure of his western column to reach the beaches at Gela. One of his colonels was relieved for cowardice; several others received severe reprimands.

But tomorrow would be another day. Conrath's division, named for Adolph Hitler's exalted right-hand man, would jump off again at dawn.

CHAPTER NINE

PILLBOX RESISTANCE

Dawn of D-Day broke over the Via del Fori Imperiali and the ruins of the ancient Colosseum in Rome as an excited announcer took to the airwaves to inform an alarmed homefront that Allied forces were ashore in Europe. Reflecting the confusion within Axis ranks due to the wide dispersal of Col. James Gavin's paratroopers in adjoining Sicily, the voice on Radio Rome told millions of listeners: "Five and perhaps 10 American parachute divisions landed in Sicily ahead of troops landing by sea."

Instead of the 60,000 to 120,000 paratroopers that Radio Rome estimated had jumped, less than 3,400 American parachutists were creating havoc among Axis forces.

Back at the bivouac areas of the remaining 82nd Airborne elements around Kairouan, Tunisia, daylight brought a deluge of rumors which spread like a raging brush fire on a dry prairie. The basis for the "reports" among the paratroopers and glidermen still in North Africa was obscured behind a veil of optimistic wishful thinking by those who soon would join Colonel Gavin's men on the embattled island.

A young corporal of Col. Reuben Tucker's 504th Parachute Infantry Regiment burst into a tent filled with comrades and blurted out, "Our guys landed right on the target and had only minor losses!" A chorus of cheers greeted the report.

"Where the hell did you hear that?" a skeptical trooper inquired.

"A cook said one of his helpers overheard two lieutenants talking in the chow line," the bearer of the report explained.

Two hours after this initial rumor sped through the GI grapevine, a sobering item of gossip was introduced among the anxious airborne men in North Africa. Dashing into a small, ramshackle building which served as a supply room for his company, a grim-faced trooper called out, "Bad news, fellows! Really bad news! Our guys have been wiped out in Sicily! A total disaster!"

This latest version of results of the American parachute strike saturated the tent camps, casting a thick cloud of gloom over the paratroopers and glidermen.

Within an hour the weighty cloak of despair was partially lifted around the tent camps outside Kairouan as a modified report made the rounds.

"It's not as big a disaster in Sicily as we thought," Lt. Kenneth R. Shaker, a 27-year-old platoon leader in the 509th Parachute Infantry Battalion, told a tentmate, Lt. Ernest "Bud" Siegel, "but it's still bad. I just heard a reliable report that the entire force had not been wiped out, but at least half of the 505s were killed in their C-47s or shot while parachuting down."

"Where did you get that info?" Siegel asked.

"Sol Weber told me just a minute ago," explained Shaker, a professional soldier who had fought as a private in the Spanish Civil War. This report could have had credence, Siegel thought. Sgt. Solomon Weber was communications noncom for the battalion and as such had electronic equipment available.

"Did he get the info on his radio?" Lieutenant Siegel pursued.

"No, he overheard it in the latrine."

In Berlin, on the morning of D-Day in Sicily, General of the Fighters Adolph Galland was conferring with Reichsmarschall Hermann Goering, the bombastic chief of the Luftwaffe. Galland, in his late thirties but already a general, was one of the Luftwaffe's outstanding aces, having shot down scores of enemy aircraft in nearly four years of war.

General Galland, a Hitler favorite and something of a folklore hero among the *herrenvolk* of the Third Reich, was greeted by his chief with little enthusiasm. "You must return immediately to Sicily," Goering declared. "The Allies landed there earlier today."

Galland had spent several days in Sicily less than two weeks before, trying to breathe life into his exhausted airmen. For weeks Luftwaffe fighter pilots based on the island had been relentlessly battling Anglo-American bombers pounding Sicily, Sardinia, Corsica and southern Italy.

In the face of overpowering Anglo-American air superiority, General Galland knew that there was nothing to be achieved by his going to Sicily. Leaving Goering's ornate office suite, Galland resignedly remarked to an aide, "As soon as our new fighter planes arrive in Sicily, they are blown to hell by enemy planes. And our replacement pilots are killed before they even have a chance to open fire."

Despite his pessimistic outlook, General Galland knew that there were still several hundred Axis fighter planes and bombers in Sicily, nearby Sardinia and mainland Italy. He would do the best he could to inspire the pilots. Three hours later, at the controls of a Messerschmitt, the general was winging toward the embattled island the Allies had invaded earlier that morning.

Meanwhile, about noon on D-Day, 82nd Airborne Capt. Bill Follmer, who had broken three bones in his ankle slamming into a rocky hillside while parachuting into Sicily 12 hours previously, was seated on the hard ground at his I Company CP on a hill, poring over maps. Standing nearby was the skinny, ancient mule the injured captain had been riding to his company outposts.

Follmer sensed the presence of someone looking over his shoulder and turned to gaze into the stern face of Gen. Matthew Ridgway, commander of the 82nd Airborne, who had landed by boat after daylight. Ridgway was disturbed. He could locate only a handful of his paratroopers who were supposed to be swarming over this region.

Unaware that Follmer was injured and noting that the company commander remained on the ground, Ridgway snapped, "What are you doing there sitting on your ass, Captain? Where are your men?"

"Sir, I think I broke my ankle and I'm having a hard time getting around," Follmer replied. "But most of my men are accounted for and they've carried out all of our missions. I've been going to see them at roadblocks on this old mule."

Ridgway's features softened as he realized Follmer had been injured but appeared to have a firm grasp on his company's situation. "Well, keep at it, Captain," the general remarked as he and his two aides marched off in search of more paratroopers.

At 10 A.M. that morning, Maj. Mark Alexander, commander of the 2nd Battalion of the 505th Parachute Infantry, sent for his adjutant, Lt. Clyde

R. Russell. Alexander had no way of knowing it at the time, but his battalion was the only one to drop in a cluster and rapidly assemble. But Major Alexander was worried. He and his troopers had been dropped 25 miles southeast of the drop zone on Piano Lupo.

"What's our strength?" the battalion commander asked Lieutenant Russell.

"About 475 men, sir," was the reply. Alexander was pleased. This was the bulk of his battalion.

It had been an exceedingly difficult 10 hours for Major Alexander and his troopers. First his excited men had tried to shove him out of his C-47 door when they thought it was time to jump. Instead of the 600- to 700-foot bail-out height called for in the operational plan, the men of the 2nd Battalion leaped out at only 350 to 400 feet. This resulted in a tight landing pattern—but broken legs and ankles for 24 parachutists.

Many of Major Alexander's force had crashed down onto a complex of Italian pillboxes, and a confused and intense firefight broke out in the darkness. These pillboxes were huge, some three stories high, and were bristling with machine guns. Thick walls protected the occupants who raked the descending paratroopers with small arms fire through the apertures that dotted the concrete structures. The pillboxes were situated so as to provide interlocking fire.

Lt. Robert Clee, a young battalion surgeon, dropped heavily just in front of one of the pillboxes. Stunned by the violence of the impact, Clee tried desperately to free himself from the wire entanglements into which he had fallen. Moments later enemy soldiers in the pillboxes spotted Clee as he struggled to break loose and poured a stream of automatic weapons fire into the surgeon, killing him instantly.

Nearby, Sgt. Harold Freeland was in the same predicament as Lieutenant Clee—entangled in barbed wire in front of a menacing pillbox. Unlike the battalion surgeon, Sergeant Freeland did not attempt to free himself. He feigned being dead for several hours and lay motionless under the eyes and guns of the enemy in the pillboxes as the savage firefight continued around him. When the concrete structure he was laying in front of was captured by his comrades after dawn, Freeland pulled himself loose from the tight grasp of the barbed wire and joined in the fight.

Capt. John Norton, Alexander's second in command, had landed alone and began to wander through the darkness in search of comrades. Norton came upon the silhouette of a building and could hear the faint sound of voices inside. Thinking that fellow parachutists had taken cover inside the structure, the captain called out the password, "George!"

A booming voice with a heavy accent shouted back out of the dark, "George, hell!" after which streams of tracer bullets whizzed past Norton's head. He flopped to the ground and crawled away into the shadows. The building Captain Norton had approached in the dark was in reality a large pillbox, manned by enemy troops.

As daylight erupted over Sicily, Major Alexander could see for the first time the entire complex of pillboxes he and his men had dropped onto. The battalion commander promptly launched an attack to wipe out the concrete structures. Having no high-velocity guns, the job would have to be done with rifles, tommy guns and grenades.

Lt. Norman Sprinkle and five men charged across open ground toward a massive pillbox, 3 stories in height and 40 feet in diameter. All six troopers were killed by withering machine gun fire, but their actions distracted the enemy long enough to allow other All-Americans to slip up to the pillbox and toss grenades through the fire ports and a ground-level door.

Minutes later a white flag waved from the pillbox. The parachutists held their fire and shouted for the occupants to emerge. Out trooped 36 Italians with hands held high in the air. Inside, many of their comrades remained, some dead and others seriously wounded. By 10 A.M. Major Alexander and his men had captured all four of the massive concrete pillboxes.

On receiving the report from his adjutant, Lieutenant Russell, that 475 of his men had assembled, Major Alexander prepared to move the battalion southward to the coast, two miles away. The gnawing problem of what to do with his 37 wounded men who could not navigate was solved when Lt. Lester Stein, the other battalion surgeon, volunteered to remain behind with the injured troopers, hoping that American seaborne forces would reach them before the enemy did.

A short time after the last of Alexander's marching column disappeared toward the south, Lieutenant Stein looked up to see a body of armed men approaching his position. He was elated, as it appeared a rescue was on the way much sooner than expected. But his elation was short-lived—these were Germans approaching.

Holding their weapons at the ready, the grenadiers marched up to Stein and gazed around at the bloody and bandaged Americans sprawled about. Recognizing Stein as a doctor tending to a group of wounded men, the

German leader barked out orders, and his group retraced their steps and disappeared behind some low hills.

Reaching the southern shoreline near the village of Marina di Ragusa, Major Alexander and his battalion halted on detecting a complex of concrete fortifications containing several large-caliber guns which were fixed in place to fire at invaders from the sea. Alexander ordered an immediate assault on the menacing fortification.

As the paratroopers moved into position to attack, members of the 456th Parachute Field Artillery rolled their lone gun, a .75-millimeter howitzer, into place. Lt. Col. Harrison Harden, Jr., commander of the parachute artillery battalion, and 21 of his men had joined Major Alexander's column and dragged the heavy field piece by hand the two miles from the pillbox complex.

The small howitzer opened the attack by sending several rounds into the concrete coastal fortification. There were only 30 shells available, which had been lugged by hand on the two-mile trek. Before the Americans could jump off toward the defensive position, Major Alexander saw a white flag raised over the concrete structure. Soon other white pieces of cloth were fluttering in the hot breeze. The battalion commander breathed a sigh of relief that the Italian navy officer commanding the installation had no desire to fight. The troopers took over 100 prisoners.

Darkness by now was approaching, so Alexander moved his battalion to high ground just northwest of Marina di Ragusa and prepared defensive positions for the night. As soon as night fell, machine gun and sniper fire from the north began pouring into paratrooper positions. As his men were exhausted from continuous fighting and marching for many hours, the major thought it impractical to send out patrols to attack the enemy weapons in the darkness.

Earlier in the day, Alexander had noticed a British cruiser standing offshore and now from the high ground could discern the vessel's silhouette in the darkness. The major sent for a young officer, Lt. Arthur Miller.

"Art," Alexander inquired, "do you know Morse code?" The lieutenant replied that he did. "Well, do you see the outline of that British cruiser out there just offshore?" Alexander asked, pointing a finger in the direction of the vessel. "Affirmative," Miller responded.

"Then get a flashlight and signal that cruiser in Morse code that there's a bunch of Krauts or Eyties out to our front and ask if they can plaster them with some big stuff."

A flashlight was located and Lieutenant Miller went into action. Numerous skeptics among the troopers looked on, but all hoped the scheme would work. The blinking flashlight, even if picked up by someone on the British warship, could be construed as an Axis trick to bring down heavy salvos upon an American position.

His task concluded, Miller and the others waited for some reaction from the cruiser. Minutes ticked by, and the only sound was the occasional chatter of the enemy machine gun sending bursts into paratrooper positions. "Well, it was a good idea, even if it didn't work," a parachutist observed.

A short time later, loud barks were heard from the direction of the offshore British cruiser, and shimmering flashes of whiteness lit up the sky. In moments Major Alexander and his men instinctively ducked on hearing an eerie swishing noise as several large projectiles raced by them through the night air and exploded precisely on target. The entire slope where the enemy machine guns and snipers were in position seemed to erupt in a flash of fire.

Minutes afterward another salvo from the cruiser smashed into the slope.

"Flash our British friends a message that they were right on target," Major Alexander told Lieutenant Miller. He added, "And be damned sure to thank them."

During the remainder of the night, not a single round of enemy fire came from the slope plastered by the cruiser's big guns.

It had been the longest day of Jim Gavin's 36 years on earth. He was convinced that he had been a total failure. But the fierce determination that had been a hallmark of the young colonel all of his life came to the forefront—he was obsessed with finding his regiment and engaging the enemy wherever they might be found.

With the setting of the sun, the parachutists collected their gear, climbed out of the muddy ditch that had been their home for nearly nine hours, and set a course which they hoped would take them to Gela. At this point Gavin cared little if he ran onto a large opposing force; anything would be better than what he had been doing.

Marching through the dark and silent night, Gavin and his men had been moving for about an hour when they heard the shout "Halt! Password!" ring out from the shadows to their front. It was an American voice.

Gavin felt a surge of elation that he had finally located a substantial force of his paratroopers. But his hopes were promptly dashed. There was only a small group of 505s, all wounded or injured, under Lt. Al Kronheim. After learning that Kronheim and his men did not know where they were either, Gavin prepared to move on toward the drop zone. Before departing, a mutually beneficial exchange was conducted. The colonel and his men traded their morphine syrettes for the Garand rifles and ammunition of the wounded and injured paratroopers.

As Colonel Gavin and his troopers melted into the darkness on a course for the drop zone near Gela, some 20 miles to the northwest on Piano Lupo, Col. Art Gorham, Capt. Ed Sayre and the remaining paratroopers were deep in exhausted sleep. Sayre and the eight parachutists who had just returned from a hand-to-hand fight with a German patrol in the inky blackness of a dry riverbed were particularly drained, physically and emotionally.

Soon dawn of D plus one arrived, and the 2nd Battalion of the 16th Infantry Regiment of the Big Red One and the attached paratroopers jumped off to assault Hill 41, half a mile to the front. With Colonel Gorham's 505s leading the attack, the American force was on the barren hill in an hour, encountering only light opposition. There the troopers and the straight-legs were ordered to dig in—and not a minute too soon.

Peering out of their shallow slit trenches, the paratroopers saw six German tanks headed directly toward their position. These were Mark VI and Mark IV panzers. From their positions Colonel Gorham's men could see 400 yards to their left where 21 German tanks, trailing plumes of dust clouds and motors roaring, were bearing down on the defensive line of the 16th Infantry Regiment of the Big Red One.

As the swarms of German tanks rolled ever closer to American lines on Hill 41, their long, menacing .88-millimeter gun barrels glistening in the sun, heavy bursts of machine gun fire were poured into the ranks of the parachutists and the 1st Division infantrymen. Periodically the advancing iron monsters halted briefly to fire flat-trajectory shells into American positions.

Now German artillery opened up and a thunderous barrage pounded the Americans clinging to the bottom of their holes. As if on cue, infantrymen of the 2nd Battalion of the 16th Regiment, to which Colonel Gorham's troopers were attached, scrambled out of their holes and began rushing pell-mell to the rear. At first it was only a handful, then more and more joined in, until within minutes two-thirds of the Big Red One battalion had urgently departed.

Most of those fleeing were recent replacements, in battle for the first time. However, the other one-third of the battalion remained in their holes and blazed away at the onrushing German tanks with rifles, Browning automatic rifles and machine guns. Not a single paratrooper budged from his hole.

Now the enemy tanks reached Hill 41 and began running over American foxholes. Some of the defenders were in holes deep enough so that they could crouch and fearfully gaze up at the underside of a German tank as it passed over. Other Americans were crushed to death in shallow slit trenches.

Some tanks halted along the line of foxholes and began firing machine guns up and down the American line with lethal effect. But the parachutists and the remaining men of the Big Red One battalion fought back with bazookas and grenades and by firing weapons into the vision slits of the iron monsters swarming over them. A few American paratroopers leaped up onto the enemy tanks and tried to jerk open the turret doors to get at the German crews inside.

Col. Art Gorham, the paratroop commander who had been totally frustrated because he could assemble only a handful of his battalion, scrambled from his hole, picked up a bazooka, and dashed toward an onrushing tank. Crouching on one knee, Gorham aimed the bazooka and, when the tracked vehicle was only a few yards from him, squeezed the trigger. The rocket struck a vulnerable spot, causing the tank to spin around crazily and grind to a halt. Inside were three dead German crew members.

As the German tanks were rolling toward the American positions, two officers of the Big Red One battalion managed to move a .57-millimeter antitank gun forward. The gun's crew had abandoned the weapon and fled, and now Big Red One infantrymen, who had no training in firing the gun, took over. The riflemen fired several rounds before a shell struck a tank at close range, knocking it out and killing the crew.

Now, with two tanks destroyed, the four remaining German panzers assaulting the 1st Division battalion and attached paratroopers on Hill 41 had had enough. They spun about and clanked off to their rear.

On the left of the Americans on Hill 41, other elements of the Big Red One had been engaged in a savage fight against the 21 German tanks that had assaulted that sector. Unable to break through the determined Ameri-

can resistance on hilly Piano Lupo, the enemy panzers skirted the un-
manned left flank of the Big Red One and onto the flat ground, ideal
terrain for a mass armored attack against Gela.

In view of heavy casualties suffered in the German tank assault and a
line weakened by the flight of two-thirds of his battalion, Lieutenant Colonel Crawford of the Big Red One ordered the remaining American force
on Hill 41 to pull back to a hill 500 yards to the rear. The new elevation
was steep and crisscrossed with ravines, making it virtually inaccessible to
enemy tanks.

Moving back to the new positions, the paratroopers picked up six Browning automatic rifles and thousands of rounds of ammunition for the
weapons, where they had been tossed by the 1st Division Infantry replacements who had bolted before the onrushing German tanks. To the lightly
armed parachutists, these automatic weapons were welcome additions to
their limited arsenal.

At 3 A.M. the following morning, orders arrived for Colonel Crawford.
His force was to immediately assault and seize back Hill 41. Capt. Ed
Sayre's parachute company was designated to lead the attack, with the Big
Red One battalion to follow in a column of companies. It was pitch-black
when the paratroopers jumped off.

In order to locate the objective, Captain Sayre, at the head of his company, held a German telephone wire in his hand, which he was confident
would lead up onto Hill 41. Inching along in the blackness, nervous and
tense, the paratroopers began to breathe sighs of relief as they neared the
top of Hill 41 without a shot being fired at them.

Suddenly the silence was shattered. Enemy machine guns dug in on the
crest of the hill opened up a withering fusillade of fire, and white patterns
of tracer bullets crisscrossed the black sky. Hill 41 was steep, so most of
the enemy bullets were hissing past over the heads of Ed Sayre and his
parachutists. But the plunging machine gun fire was raking the Big Red
One companies following along behind.

Lieutenant Colonel Crawford, commanding the combined group as-
saulting the hill, was hit and seriously wounded by a machine gun bullet.
He was carried to safety from an exposed position by his executive officer,
Capt. Bryce F. Denno. The youthful Denno then took command of the 1st
Division battalion and its attached paratroopers.

Ed Sayre's parachutists began crawling forward in the darkness until
several reached a point almost at the mouths of the spitting enemy ma-

chine guns. Detaching grenades from belts while prone in front of the weapons, the troopers pulled the safety pins and tossed the missiles forward. There were bright orange flashes and loud explosions on the peak, together with screams which pierced the night air above the din of battle. The enemy machine guns fell silent.

German riflemen, left without automatic weapons and with American infantrymen closing in on them, fled down the back side of the hill and melted into the darkness.

On top of Hill 41, the paratroopers found deep trenches and many foxholes, indications that the enemy had planned to hold the elevation. Captain Sayre and his men took over the German holes and signaled for the remainder of the attacking battalion to join them atop the objective.

Dawn would arrive in about an hour, and the Americans on the hill fell into an exhausted sleep. They were unaware that when they awakened they would find themselves caught in a German iron trap.

CHAPTER TEN

BIAZZA RIDGE

L ate in the afternoon of D-Day, Gen. Fridolin von Senger und Et-terlin was standing on a high hill south of Biscari, surveying the battlefield. Out in the distance was the demoralizing sight of hundreds of Allied vessels riding at anchor in the Gulf of Gela. Von Senger knew the Anglo-Americans were pouring troops and equipment ashore, but he did not despair.

Sent to Sicily by Adolph Hitler several weeks previously as an "advisor" to Sixth Army commander, Gen. Alfredo Guzzoni, an Italian, von Senger and other Wehrmacht generals gave lip service to serving under Sixth Army control. Actually, German generals in Sicily called the shots for their own units and tried to coordinate efforts with the Italians. Now, on the sunbaked hill a few miles inland, General von Senger sensed the opportunity for a great victory—perhaps a decisive one.

Some five miles southeast of where von Senger was observing the panorama, leading elements of Maj. Gen. Troy Middleton's green U.S. 45th Infantry Division had rapidly pushed inland to the vicinity of Vittoria. A National Guard outfit whose members were mostly from Oklahoma and New Mexico, the Thunderbirds had had their advance smoothed by the work of American paratroopers, who had destroyed pillboxes along the beach near the little town of Santa Croce Camerina and had seized the key Ponte Dirillo bridge after driving off its Axis defenders. But in moving inland, the 45th Division had left its flanks wide open.

General von Senger was aware that the Hermann Goering Division had sent a *kampfgruppe* rolling southward through Niscemi and onto the high ground at Piano Lupo to smash into the seaborne U.S. 1st Infantry Division coming ashore around Gela. This was the western column of the elite Wehrmacht armored division. At the same time, another *kampfgruppe* of the Hermann Goering Division, the eastern column, was attacking southward through Biscari on a roughly parallel course to the western column. The distance between the two German armored columns varied between 12 and 15 miles.

Now, realizing that the U.S. 45th Division had a long, unprotected flank, von Senger directed that the eastern Hermann Goering column pivot to the southeast four miles south of Biscari and strike a devastating blow unto the vulnerable flank of the American division.

Von Senger, a battle-wise former corps commander on the Russian front, knew the 45th Infantry Division had not yet been tested in combat. Finding themselves hit unexpectedly and with fury by veteran German panzer units on the unprotected flank might well cause the Americans to flee in chaos and panic, von Senger believed. The Hermann Goering Division then could cut up the disintegrating 45th Division and drive it into the sea.

A short distance from where the German eastern column had halted for the night, Col. Jim Gavin, the commanding officer of the entire American parachute element in Sicily, was trudging along in the darkness at the head of the combat force he had collected along the way. It had grown from five troopers to eight.

Suddenly from out of the shadows came a sharp command: "Halt!" Gavin identified himself and found that he and his men had stumbled onto an outpost of the 45th Infantry Division. It was 2:30 A.M. on July 11— D-Day plus one. For the first time since he set foot on Sicily, he learned precisely where he was—five miles southwest of Vittoria.

Gavin and his men set out again, heading toward Vittoria. A short time later the little band heard the rumbling of a tank off in the distance and a few minutes later discerned its shadowy silhouette moving down the road toward them. The troopers scrambled for cover along each side of the road as Colonel Gavin called out a warning, "Be sure to hold your fire until you're certain it's an enemy tank. It might be one of ours."

Moments later, as the tank came closer, the excited troopers opened fire. Bullets ricocheted off the steel skin of the monster, casting sparks like hundreds of fireflies flittering into the air. "Cease firing! Cease firing!" Colonel Gavin shouted above the din of the small arms fire. He had detected that it was an American Sherman tank.

The tankers were buttoned up, so the rifle and tommy gun fire caused no casualties or damage to the tracked vehicle. A group of sheepish paratroopers, new to warfare, got to their feet and set off down the road once more, leaving behind a cursing and ranting American tank crew.

Reaching Vittoria, Colonel Gavin secured a jeep and driver and took off down the road at a fast clip for Gela, 20 miles to the northwest. He still was intent on gathering together his scattered parachute combat team and assaulting the enemy in force wherever it might be found. Dawn had now broken out across Sicily.

Along the way Gavin spotted about 250 paratroopers slowly and sleepily climbing out of foxholes. Approaching their commander, Lt. Col. Cannonball Krause, the regimental combat team leader ordered him to move his 3rd Battalion at once toward the high ground at Piano Lupo which was the objective of the parachute elements. Krause's men would follow the same road Gavin was taking to reach Gela.

Taking a platoon of engineers commanded by Lt. Ben L. Weschler, Gavin again struck out on foot along the road to Gela. At about 9 A.M. he and his troopers arrived at a point where a railroad crossed over. Next to the crossing was a house where the railroad gatekeeper and his family lived. Preparing to march on past, Gavin and his men heard heavy small arms fire erupt from a ridge about half a mile to their front. So intense was the firing that the colonel knew that a large enemy force was on the ridge.

Colonel Gavin did not know at the time that the elevation with the gentle slope leading to its crown on which the enemy force was located was named Biazza Ridge, nor did he have any way of knowing that on that ridge he and his small number of 82nd Airborne troopers would fight one of the most critical actions of the invasion.

Through an incredible roll of the dice by Dame Fortune, Colonel Gavin, who had been inadvertently dropped some 25 miles southeast of the DZ, happened upon the precise point where the powerful eastern column of the Hermann Goering Division was advancing to smash into the open flank of the U.S. 45th Infantry Division. Had Gavin and other paratroopers been dropped north and northeast of Gela as planned, there would have been little in front of the German *kampfgruppe* to halt its rush to the shoreline.

Coming over the ridge toward Colonel Gavin and his men was a German force of 750 grenadiers, backed by a company of 60-ton Tiger tanks and an armored artillery battalion. The American parachutists, a hodge-podge collection of engineers, cooks, orderlies, riggers, clerks and riflemen, had no field guns, antitank guns or tanks and would be vastly outnum-bered in the looming confrontation.

A short time before Colonel Gavin and his little band of paratroopers reached the scene, a few All-Americans in the vicinity on the way to the drop zone had bumped onto the German battle group on the ridge. The little knot of paratroopers opened fire on the leading elements of the German armored column. Pvt. Philip Foley, a young trooper from Boston, was flat on the hard ground, squeezing off shots from his Garand rifle, when he heard a sickening thud next to him and a comrade gasp. Foley glanced toward his fellow trooper. The man was dead, a neat, blood-stained hole through the center of his forehead. He was the first 82nd Airborne trooper to die in the struggle for Biazza Ridge.

German grenadiers reacted swiftly to the parachutists and were soon raking them with small arms fire. Now .60-millimeter mortar rounds ex-ploded around Foley and his handful of comrades. A shriek echoed above the din of the firefight, and Foley turned around to see a comrade writhing in agony, his arm ripped off at the shoulder by an exploding shell. Blood was gushing out of the ugly, jagged hole.

Private Foley began crawling toward the man with the severed arm as enemy automatic weapons raked his position. As he neared the wounded soldier, he felt a sharp blow on his heel, much as though someone had taken a sledgehammer and struck the bottom of his foot with tremendous impact. Foley was convinced that a large chunk of shrapnel had sliced off his foot. Fearfully glancing downward along his body, he expected to see his bloody foot lying nearby. Instead he breathed a sigh of relief; both of his jump boots still encased his feet which were attached to his legs. A bullet had neatly chopped off the heel of one boot without touching him.

Reaching the trooper with the severed arm, Foley knew there was noth-ing he could do for him. The youth, his face an ashen mask from loss of blood, had lapsed into unconsciousness. In minutes he would be dead. Foley went back to firing his rifle at the enemy.

Back near the railroad gatekeeper's house, half a mile from Biazza Ridge, Colonel Gavin made a decision. Although he had only some 40 troopers with him, he would launch an attack against the large enemy force. Gavin promptly began issuing orders for the assault to his collection of assorted troopers from many units and military occupational specialties. It was not the type of cohesive formation a commander would want to lead into battle. But Gavin had great confidence in the individual bravery and resourcefulness of his troopers.

Preparing to launch the initial attack against Biazza Ridge, the small band of All-Americans would be top-heavy with brass. In addition to Colonel Gavin, taking their places as assault infantrymen in command of no one but themselves were the two official airborne observers, Lt. Col. Chuck Billingslea and Lt. Col. Bill Ryder; the executive officer of the 505th Regiment, Lt. Col. Herb Batcheller; plus several captains and lieutenants.

Colonel Gavin deployed Lieutenant Weschler's engineer platoon on the right of his skirmish line and his assorted riflemen, artillerymen, clerks, lieutenant colonels, cooks and riggers elsewhere along the line. Before jumping off for Biazza Ridge, Gavin sent a runner back to locate Lieutenant Colonel Krause with orders to hurry forward with the 250 troopers of his 3rd Battalion.

As soon as all of the parachutists were in place, Colonel Gavin, from the center of the skirmish line, gave the signal for the jump-off. The All-Americans moved forward.

Seeing the Americans advancing toward them, the Germans along Biazza Ridge opened up a withering burst of automatic weapons and rifle fire, cutting down the three 505 scouts leading the assault. A heavy fusillade of bullets hissed and whined past and into the ranks of the parachutists. Here and there other troopers went down, but Gavin and his men pressed forward. One of those who fell to enemy fire was Lieutenant Weschler, commander of the engineer platoon.

As the shoot-out raged on the forward slopes of Biazza Ridge, Gavin's small force, despite numerous casualties, steadily expanded. Maj. Walter Hagen, executive officer of Cannonball Krause's 3rd Battalion, appeared with leading elements of his unit. Gavin ordered Hagen and his men to drop their packs and immediately join in the attack.

Also hustled into Colonel Gavin's assault force was a lost platoon of the 45th Infantry Division and part of a company of the 180th Infantry Regiment. Individually, in pairs and in tiny knots, paratroopers who had been wandering about the vicinity heard the guns and rushed to embattled Biazza Ridge.

It was no longer solely an army operation. Two young U.S. Navy ensigns, who had parachuted into Sicily with the 505th Regimental Combat Team to coordinate fire support from warships offshore, were handed rifles and told to join the attack as infantrymen.

Trapped alongside the road leading to the crown of Biazza Ridge in the midst of the fighting was an elderly Sicilian peasant. Clad in a dirty black suit coat and tie on a shirt that had once been white, the old man, his jackass and cart huddled beneath a tree throughout the battle as streams of bullets from both adversaries whizzed past.

During the height of the battle, Luftwaffe fighter-bombers, black and menacing, appeared overhead in the cloudless blue sky. But instead of attacking the Americans on the slope of the ridge, the enemy aircraft dove on the gatekeeper's house half a mile to the rear and bombed and strafed the structure. Apparently the German pilots believed the house was a command post for the assault on Biazza Ridge.

Inside the gatekeeper's home, combat surgeons were operating on wounded paratroopers, but after being attacked twice by Luftwaffe aircraft, the medical men moved to a farmhouse a quarter of a mile away to perform emergency operations.

One of the contingents rushing toward the sound of the guns on Biazza Ridge was a 50-man force led by Lt. Harvey J. Ziegler, a member of Service Company of the 505s. It was a mixed bag of troopers; Ziegler knew none of them.

When the young lieutenant had parachuted into Sicily, he was alone and lost. He eventually rounded up 12 troopers that night, one a corporal named Murone who spoke fluent Italian. As a few of the men were wounded or injured, transportation was vital, so Corporal Murone disappeared for a time and when he returned, he was driving an ancient, wheezing, coughing Italian flatbed truck. "A Sicilian 'agreed' to let me borrow it," Murone explained.

As Lieutenant Ziegler and his troopers wandered about after dawn, seeking to gain their bearings and a larger force of comrades, they continued to pick up stray parachutists. The old truck now proved to be of even greater value, as other newcomers were wounded or injured.

Late on the morning of July 11, Ziegler and his band and wheezing truck were some two miles southeast of Biazza Ridge. The intense firing in the distance provided a homing beacon, and an hour later Lieutenant Ziegler and his men were fighting Wehrmacht grenadiers. Several of the wounded climbed off the old Italian truck and joined the fray.

That afternoon Colonel Gavin's hodgepodge group of fighting men had clawed and fought their way to the top of Biazza Ridge and, with ear-piercing whoops, charged the enemy foxholes. Those among the enemy force who were not killed or wounded rapidly pulled back down the reverse slope of the ridge. The Americans took over occupancy of German foxholes to rest from the rigors and emotional drain of the daylong assault.

Now, with Biazza Ridge's former tenants evicted by the new landlords, the Germans began to pound American positions on the elevation with mortar and artillery fire. Explosions rocked the ridge as paratroopers labored feverishly to deepen German foxholes or dig new ones into the hard shale which served as earth in this part of Sicily. Entrenching tools were too frail to make headway against the concrete-hard surface, so shallow foxholes were scraped out with the use of sturdy steel helmets as cutting edges.

Colonel Gavin, who was occupying a shallow trench on the ridge which served as the CP, had learned a military axiom in his first week at West Point: when the enemy is on the run, keep him on the run. That was precisely what the colonel intended to do.

Gavin ordered his men to pursue the Germans over the ridge. Hardly had the paratroopers charged off than a chilling sound struck their ears—the roaring of powerful diesel motors and clanking of steel treads to their front. The Germans had thrown their 60-ton Tiger tanks against the All-Americans who had only ineffective 2.36-inch bazookas with which to fight back. In any confrontation between human flesh on one side and iron monsters armed with .88-millimeter cannon and machine guns on the other side, the odds are obvious.

A young paratrooper out in front of the attack was confronted by an enemy panzer clanking directly toward him. Kneeling in the open with a bazooka over his shoulder, he fired a rocket at point-blank range, only to watch in rage and fear as the missile bounced harmlessly off the front of the huge iron monster. The tank rumbled on, crushing the trooper and his comrade who had loaded the bazooka.

As the lightly armed paratroopers battled German infantry and tanks on Biazza Ridge, a concerned Colonel Gavin began to see his wounded men coming back past his CP foxhole in increasing numbers. Major Hagen, the executive officer of the 3rd Battalion of the 505s, limped past the colonel on his way to the rear. Hagen was holding his leg which was bleeding profusely from a gaping hole torn out of flesh and bone by an .88-millimeter shell fired by a Tiger tank.

Also filing back over the ridge toward the American rear, hands clasped behind their necks, bareheaded, and some wearing bloody bandages, were the first prisoners taken by the paratroopers in the Biazza Ridge fighting. Colonel Gavin halted the first batch of prisoners and was astonished—and alarmed—to learn that the Germans were members of the elite Hermann Goering Panzer Fallschirmjaeger Division.

"My God," Gavin said to his personnel officer, Capt. Al Ireland, "we were told that there were only a few German technicians on Sicily. Now we're confronted with one of Germany's best armored divisions—and we've got nothing to fight them with but these damned peashooters [bazookas]."

It would be long after the war before Gavin learned of the decision that had been reached by the Allied high command not to inform the American paratroopers of the nearby presence of the Hermann Goering Division in order to protect the secret of ULTRA—even if it meant destruction of the 505th Parachute Regimental Combat Team.

As the fight on Biazza Ridge raged, Colonel Gavin's firepower was increased—but barely. Under Lt. Robert May, several troopers manning two .81-millimeter mortars began lobbing an occasional shell onto German positions. The mortar ammunition was limited and had to be hoarded for even more serious crises. May and his men were promptly taken under fire by enemy artillery, and the young lieutenant was hit and seriously wounded by shell fragments.

During a brief lull in the fight, Colonel Gavin hurried back to his sole artillery support—two .75-millimeter pack howitzers a few hundred yards to the rear on the lower slope of the ridge. "You remain concealed here for the time being," the colonel instructed the crews. "If enemy tanks come over the ridge, you can hit them in their underbellies as they reach the rise."

"Yes, sir," replied a sergeant, not overly enthused over the prospect of tangling in a cannon duel at point-blank range with his relatively low-velocity .75 howitzer against the high-velocity .88 gun on the German Tiger tanks.

As Gavin started to leave to return to the front lines on the ridge, he assured the howitzer crews, "We're staying on this goddamned ridge—no matter what happens!" If the tanks overran his troopers, the colonel in-ended to remain in place and fight the German infantry advancing behind them.

Back on top of the ridge a few minutes later, Gavin and his troopers spotted a chilling sight. Less than 400 yards to their front, a 60-ton Tiger tank poked its menacing .88-millimeter gun out from behind a small stone building. The German crew edged the tank forward until it was totally in view, then slowly traversed its high-velocity gun until it was pointing toward the Americans on top of the ridge.

Learning of the sudden appearance of the Tiger, a paratrooper gun crew at the bottom of the slope decided on its own to move a howitzer to the top of the elevation and try to knock out the enemy tank. Undaunted by the fact that the howitzer was a light weapon for use against other ground troops and not as an antitank weapon, the artillery parachutists muscled the howitzer up the slope. One trooper was riding on its barrel.

Reaching the top of the ridge, the gun crew lined up the howitzer and lay down beside it to wait for the marauding huge Tiger to show itself again. The German tank crew had already spotted the American howitzer men, and moments later there was a loud explosion just in front of the .75-millimeter gun. Crew and gun were blanketed with a thick cloud of dust and smoke from the explosive. Other troopers on the ridge heard and saw the detonation next to the howitzer and thought the artillery parachutists had been wiped out.

A split second later, the four-man gun crew leaped to their feet, bolted out of the cloud that had enveloped them, and instinctively raced for the relative safety of the rear. Not one of the crew had been killed or wounded, although shrapnel from the .88 shell had hissed past their prone bodies.

After racing only about 15 yards, the four troopers realized that they had abandoned their weapon, and with sheepish expressions they turned and headed back to their howitzer. There the crew rapidly loaded a shell into the breech, took aim and fired at the Tiger tank. The missile exploded on or near the huge Tiger, and in the ensuing cloud of dust kicked up around it, the enemy tank withdrew behind the stone building where it had been concealed. It was not seen again.

On the reverse slope of Biazza Ridge, Jim Gavin's paratroopers were battling the smaller German tanks they confronted in the orchards and vineyards. Edging up to the sides of Mark IV 30-ton tanks, troopers sent bazooka rockets into gas tanks and ammunition racks, the vulnerable spots on the tracked vehicles. Three of the Mark IVs were knocked out and their crews killed.

At the 18-inch-deep foxhole on the ridge that served as his command post, Colonel Gavin heard the clanking of a tracked vehicle to his rear. He glanced around to see two troopers riding forward in a small Italian armored weapons carrier they had confiscated the previous day after killing its crew.

As the tracked vehicle reached the top of the ridge, it was halted by Gavin who inquired of the two parachutists, "And where in the hell do you think you're going?"

"We want to scare the shit out of those goddamned Krauts, Colonel," a young trooper replied. "When they see us coming, they'll think that we've got armor, too."

While appreciating their courage and initiative, Gavin tried to dissuade the pair from the venture.

"Oh, we'll be okay, Colonel," one responded breezily. "We can take care of ourselves."

With many pressing matters on his mind, Gavin shrugged his shoulders in resignation. The small Italian armored vehicle and its two-man American crew clanked onward. Moments later there was a terrific explosion and the track-laying vehicle burst into flames. It had received a direct hit from a German .88. Still clutching rifles, two grisly, charred bodies sat upright as flames consumed the vehicle.

The struggle to drive the Hermann Goering battle group from Biazza Ridge was growing more intense for the outnumbered Americans. Enemy tanks were destroyed, but others were sent into the fracas. Now, several hundred yards to the front of the ridge, German grenadiers were massing for a major assault to seize back the ridge.

Colonel Gavin was prone on the ground, firing away at the enemy with his Garand rifle. He sensed a form approaching from behind and turned his head to see a large, bushy-bearded man crawling toward him as enemy bullets whistled just overhead.

"Beaver, what in the hell are you doing up here?" Gavin scolded the reporter. "We're about to get overrun."

"I heard all the shooting and came up here to see what's going on," Thompson replied.

"Well, what we don't need is a dead or captured civilian reporter," the colonel said. "Now get your ass back to the rear where it belongs!"

Maj. Gen. Matthew B. Ridgway (far side) and Colonel Gavin address the 82nd Airborne troopers in North Africa just prior to the mass jump.

Trooper setting up mortar moments after landing in a practice jump in North Africa.

Three troopers of the 505th Parachute Infantry at Alcamo, Sicily, after airborne phase of Operation Husky. (Left to right) William Eppler, William Embury, Irvin Seelye.

Many Red Devils of the British 1st Airborne Division were killed or seriously injured when their gliders (such as the one above) were smashed on the night crash landings near Syracuse.

Captured German weapons carrier (foreground) and Italian ambulance (rear) being brought into Gela by troopers of the 82nd Airborne.

Capt. Edwin Sayre (right) receives the Distinguished Service Cross from General Ridgway for his action on Piano Lupo. Maj. Herbert Batcheller (center), executive officer of the 505th.

Going into battle for the first time, Col. Reuben Tucker boards a C-47 to lead the 504th on the night of D-Day plus one. (Photo courtesy Phillips Publications)

Lt. Ivan Woods being decorated with the Silver Star by General Ridgway for leading 28 troopers in the capture of Egadi Islands off Sicily.

British Foreign Minister Anthony Eden inspects the 505th Parachute Infantry Regiment at Fort Bragg, North Carolina, just before 82nd Airborne left for North Africa. Trailing Eden is Colonel Gavin.

Maj. Mark J. Alexander

Commander of American forces in Sicily, Lt. Gen. George S. Patton (left) and Brig. Gen. Theodore "Teddy" Roosevelt, confer in Gela.

Lt. Col. William Yarborough

Brig. H. W. Hackett, CO,
British 4th Parachute Brigade
(left) with Gen. Maitland
"Jumbo" Wilson.

Field Marshal Kesselring

Gen. Fridolin von Senger und Etterlin

Brig. P. H. W. "Pip" Hicks, CO, British 1st Air Landing Brigade (Imperial War Museum, London)

Maj. Gen. G. W. "Hoppy" Hopkinson, commander, British 1st Airborne Division, briefs officers on impending airborne strike.

Brig. Gerald Lathbury, British 1st Airborne Division (Imperial War Museum, London)

Maj. R. T. H. Lonsdale (Imperial War Museum, London)

Brig. Eric Down (center), leader of the British 2nd Parachute Brigade, discusses a battlefield problem with two of his officers.

Properly chastised, Thompson crawled back off the ridge and returned to the gatekeeper's house where the railroad crossed the road. Aware that a strong enemy force was about to overrun the lightly armed paratroopers on Biazza Ridge, his thoughts turned to the notes he had been carrying, fearful that the penciled notations might be of value to the enemy if he were captured—or the notes taken off his dead body.

Yet these notes were invaluable to him and would be useful eventually as a basis for writing stories to be dispatched back to the States. Spotting a culvert, the heavyset Thompson squeezed into the tight enclosure, secreted his notes and emerged. Seeking something constructive to do to occupy his time, the reporter trekked to a nearby aid station and helped out with the wounded.

Colonel Gavin, in the meantime, returned to firing his rifle. A crouching figure dashed up to him. Capt. Al Ireland, personnel officer of the regimental combat team who had been fighting on Biazza Ridge as a rifleman, flopped to the ground beside his commanding officer.

"Colonel . . ." he began. Both men held onto their helmets and hugged the ground even closer as a cluster of mortar shells exploded around them. There was an eerie whirring sound after the detonations as white-hot, jagged shrapnel skimmed over their heads.

When the smoke, dust and acrid fumes from the explosives started to dissipate, Captain Ireland, known to fellow officers as "Irish," resumed talking in a calm voice, yet one tinged with urgency. "Colonel, it might be a good idea if I went back to the beach and got some help up here for us," he stated.

"Irish, that's the best idea I've heard today," Gavin promptly responded.

The regimental commander, in his initial major combat action, had been so deeply involved in the battlefield crisis he was facing that the thought of securing reinforcements and firepower from the beaches had not entered his mind.

There was a pause as two mortar shells plunged to earth nearby, scattering clouds of dust about the pair of parachute officers.

"Tell them," Gavin said as he raised up to fire at a bobbing target, "tell them that if they want this ridge held, we're going to have to have more firepower." A defiant look crept over the colonel's face as he added firmly, "And tell them even if we're overrun, we aren't moving off this place."

Knowing it was several miles to the beaches and having no transportation, Captain Ireland set out at a trot. Having gone about a mile, the parachute captain came to an old stone farmhouse along the narrow gravel road and spotted a bicycle parked nearby. I certainly wouldn't steal anyone's bicycle, Ireland thought to himself. I'll just borrow it.

He went over to the two-wheeled vehicle, a rather battered one, and threw a leg over the saddle just as an irate Sicilian came charging out the door. Speaking rapidly and gesturing wildly with his hands, the native was vigorously protesting his bicycle being stolen. Ireland merely shrugged his shoulders and pedaled off on his urgent mission.

Luck was with him. Some three miles farther along he came onto the CP of Maj. Gen. Troy Middleton, commander of the 45th Infantry Division. Middleton was in his command tent when Captain Ireland rushed inside. There he came face-to-face with not only the divisional commanding general but also with Lt. Gen. Omar Bradley, the soft-spoken leader of II Corps.

Ireland hurriedly explained the dire situation at Biazza Ridge in which the American paratrooper force was in imminent danger of being wiped out. Maps were promptly brought out, and the paratroop officer explained the situation in rapid yet thorough fashion.

"We need help up there—and in a hurry," Ireland stressed.

Bradley, always imperturbable, asked in his high-pitched voice, "What do you need up there, Captain?"

"Mainly artillery, but we can use some tanks also. There are Kraut tanks all over the place."

General Bradley said to Middleton, "Give him what he wants."

"Well, we've just had some .155s come ashore and they're into position," the bespectacled Middleton replied. Like Bradley, the 45th Division leader was inevitably calm in stressful situations.

"Good," Bradley responded. Turning again to Captain Ireland, the II Corps commander asked, "What else do you need?"

"Well, as I said, we could sure as hell use some tanks, sir."

"Can you hustle him up some tanks, Troy?" Bradley asked his fellow general.

"I'll send up what I can spare," Middleton stated.

Only minutes later a heavyset artillery observer, the "eyes" of the .155-millimeter guns, appeared at the command tent with a jeep and driver. "Hop in," called out the artillery officer to Ireland. The three men roared off in a cloud of dust, bound for the ridge.

Arriving at the scene of the battle, Ireland and the two artillerymen parked the jeep a few hundred yards to the rear of the ridge and hurried on foot to the top of the elevation. The jeep driver had now placed a radio on his back and was prepared to send firing information back to the battery of .155s. On reaching the crown of the ridge, the three men were greeted with several salvos of enemy artillery shells which sent them sprawling into the dust.

Although the rotund artillery observer had not been under fire before, the enemy shelling did not faze him. He leaped to his feet and grabbed the radio transmitter from the operator. Captain Ireland heard the observer give map coordinates to his battery back near the beach. Then the artillery officer shouted into the mouthpiece, "To hell with zeroing in. There's so goddamned many targets out there, you can't miss. Fire for effect!"

Minutes later troopers on the ridge heard a loud swishing noise over-head as a cluster of American .155 shells rushed through the air on the way to the target area. With terrific impact that shook the ground on the ridge, huge shells began exploding among the German infantry and tanks. Salvo after salvo was poured into enemy ranks. The enemy force, which had been advancing toward Biazza Ridge, wavered, then halted and finally pulled back. The shelling by the .155s ceased, and an eerie silence fell over the battleground.

At 7 P.M. the paratroopers on the ridge were preparing to jump off once more in pursuit of the disorganized Wehrmacht battle group. Then a chilling sound was heard to the rear of the Americans—the faint hum of tank motors. The noise became louder, and soon the clanking of tank treads could be heard. Had the enemy skirted the open flanks of the paratroopers on Biazza Ridge to move in behind them with panzers?

The tanks approaching from the rear were not yet in sight, as they were cloaked by vegetation and low hills. But the roar of powerful engines became more pronounced. Then a curious sound was heard on the ridge: several troopers were cheering. Then more joined in, and finally Americans all along the embattled ridge let loose with a full-throated chorus of gleeful shouts.

The approaching tanks were not German but six American Sherman tanks and several half-tracks pulling antitank guns. Like the cavalry in the Old West riding to the rescue at the final minute, the armored column roared up the slope of Biazza Ridge, trailing tall plumes of dust, as cheers continued to rock American positions. This was the tank assistance Captain Ireland had been promised by General Bradley a few hours previously. Now Colonel Gavin's paratroopers, although still far outnumbered, could battle the enemy force on something like even terms.

The six Shermans and several antitank guns lined up along the ridge and opened fire on German positions, and the paratroopers moved forward again to close with the enemy. Despite the added firepower, the All-Americans soon ran into the customary tenacious resistance of the Wehrmacht. The Germans raked the advancing parachutists with machine gun bursts and pounded them with artillery and mortars. Many Americans went down, but their comrades pressed forward.

Lt. Harold H. Swingler, a 25-year-old officer from St. Louis who was a collegiate boxing champion, worked his way some 200 yards in front of the ridge. Two troopers were with Swingler as he started crawling along the edge of a cut through which ran the road that bisected Biazza Ridge. The three Americans were taken under fire by an enemy machine gun, and the pair of men with Swingler were killed instantly.

Still under heavy fire, the former boxer continued to edge forward along the lip of the cut. He cast a glance down into the cut and there, several feet directly below him, a 60-ton Tiger tank had halted and its crew was standing outside next to it. Swingler fished out a grenade, pulled the safety pin, reached an arm over the side of the rim, and dropped the missile. The explosion killed the three tankers. Minutes later other All-Americans moved up the road, and the 82nd Airborne Division captured its first Tiger tank.

Elsewhere along the line paratroopers moved forward as the 45th Infantry Division's .155-millimeter guns continued to pound the enemy. The Germans began to pull back and eventually abandoned the battlefield, leaving behind their dead and wounded. In their haste to retreat, the Hermann Goering Division battle group left several tons of supplies and equipment, and the paratroopers, in addition to the Tiger tank, captured several field guns, two trucks, numerous machine guns, and twelve large mortars together with stacks of shells.

Green American paratroopers had driven a *kampfgruppe* of the battle-tested Hermann Goering Division from the battlefield. Colonel Gavin's parachutists had blocked the German effort to smash into the unprotected flank of the 45th Infantry Division and push on to the American landing beaches. But the 82nd Airborne men had paid a price for the victory.

Surviving paratroopers tenderly carried the bodies of dead comrades to a collecting point near the top of Biazza Ridge. Graves were dug, the regimental chaplain fashioned crude wooden crosses out of K-ration boxes, brief but appropriate services were held, and the excavations filled in. The troopers noticed that several of their comrades were buried with twisted pieces of bazookas ground into their bodies.

Head bowed in prayer, Capt. Al Ireland peeked at the resolute regimental commander who stood looking down at the graves. There were tears in Colonel Gavin's eyes.

CHAPTER ELEVEN

THE "FRIENDLY FIRE" DISASTER

At 8:45 A.M. on July 11—D-Day plus one—Lt. Gen. Omar Bradley, leader of the assaulting II Corps, threw a long leg over the railing of the *Ancon* and climbed down the rope ladder for the choppy ride into the beach on an LCVP. Bradley was anxious to get ashore to establish communications with his units before the inevitable Axis counterattack.

The corps commander headed immediately for the coastal town of Scoglitti where his first CP had been established in the confining *carabinieri* (Italian police) headquarters. Bradley had been ashore only minutes and already was deeply worried. He could hear the constant roar of heavy guns in the direction of Gela, to the west, and knew that Gen. Terry Allen and his 1st Infantry Division were engaged in heavy fighting there.

Field Marshal Kesselring, from his headquarters south of Rome, the previous night had ordered the tank column that had been butting its head against Colonel Gorham's paratroopers and elements of the Big Red One on Piano Lupo to skirt the Americans' left flank there and onto the plain of Gela. Over flat terrain ideal for maneuvering, the panzers would charge south to the port of Gela. Standing in the way of the German armored column reaching the sea were other elements of the 1st Infantry Division and attached Rangers under Lt. Col. William O. Darby.

With scores of German tanks bearing down on Gela, the plain erupted in a montage of exploding shells, fires, smoke and thick clouds of dust. It was this savage encounter that General Bradley heard at Scoglitti. The lead panzers reached a point just west of Santa Spina, 2,000 yards from the shoreline. From there they pounded supply dumps, installations and landing craft and prepared to push on to the sea.

Bradley promptly departed Scoglitti and headed for Gela where he found a disheveled, exhausted, yet confident Terry Allen.

"Can you hold 'em?" Bradley asked.

"It's the Hermann Goering Division," the aggressive Allen responded. "They've goddamned near broken through to the beach. We're having a hell of a fight, but we can hold 'em!"

At his headquarters at Caltagirone, some 20 miles inland, Gen. Paul Conrath, commander of the Hermann Goering Division, flashed a signal to Kesselring: "Pressure by the Hermann Goering Division [has] forced the enemy to re-embark."

The U.S. Seventh Army did *not* intend to re-embark. A signal to that effect had been misinterpreted when the Axis Sixth Army headquarters at Enna intercepted it. Nor did the lead tanks of the German force get any closer to Gela.

A combined force of infantrymen from the Big Red One, Rangers, Sherman tanks, field artillery and later naval fire sent the assaulting German tanks reeling back. Sixteen panzers remained on the plain of Gela—burning, smoking, twisted hulks.

Now, with the situation around Gela stabilized—at least for the present —General Bradley headed back for his musty headquarters in Scoglitti. On the way the corps commander was nearly killed in action—by his aide. The young officer accidently discharged a carbine, and the bullet whizzed past the general's head.

Always imperturbable, Bradley said to his shaken aide, "Please be more careful with that thing."

Walking into his headquarters, Bradley was handed a message by his chief of staff, Brig. Gen. William B. Kean, Jr.

"It's from Patton," Kean said. "Matt Ridgway is going to bring in another regiment by air tonight."

Taking the penciled message, Bradley read: "Notify all units, especially AA, that parachutists 82nd Airborne will drop about 2330 [11:30 P.M.] tonight on Farello landing field."

"That's the airfield west of Gela?"

Kean nodded his head.

"Has everyone been notified?"

"We've got the antiaircraft people checking their units on the beach."

"Good, we don't want our guys being shot down by our own guns."

One general officer was not so sure that "everyone had been notified." At his makeshift headquarters on the beachhead, Gen. Matthew Ridgway was deeply worried. As commanding general of the crack 82nd Airborne, he recognized that the flight of Col. Reuben Tucker's 504th Regimental Combat Team was fraught with peril.

Ridgway promptly contacted British Gen. Frederick A. M. Browning, airborne advisor to General Eisenhower and an old antagonist of Ridgway's. The American commander sought an "assurance" that the C-47s lumbering along overhead at low altitude would not be fired on by the navy. In a condescending tone that so irritated Ridgway, Browning replied that the navy could "make no such promises."

Every precaution would be taken by the navy, but due to the fact that there were many merchant vessels and smaller ships in the convoys, it would be impossible to give a guarantee, Browning pointed out.

Ridgway considered this explanation vague and uncertain. In fact, it increased his alarm. He immediately went to General Patton's Seventh Army staff, and in a tone that left no doubt as to his deep concern for the safety of Colonel Tucker's impending flight of reinforcing paratroopers, Ridgway issued what amounted to an ultimatum.

"Unless you give some assurance that the navy won't open up on my men, I'm going to officially protest this follow-up drop," Ridgway stated.

Patton needed Colonel Tucker's tough paratroopers on shore. So the Seventh Army staff approached the navy once again and obtained assurances that "friendly" antiaircraft fire would be withheld over previously designated airborne routes.

Convinced that he had done all he could to maximize the safety of his 504th Regimental Combat Team, General Ridgway agreed to the plan for the reinforcing drop at Farello airfield.

Despite some relief from concern by the assurance of the navy that his 504th combat team would not be fired on, Ridgway was still worried. On the surface it appeared to be a routine operation with only the normal hazards of a mass drop, for Colonel Tucker's command was to land behind 1st Infantry Division lines. But Ridgway knew, as did other airborne leaders, that there were enormous potential dangers not always evident to nonairborne commanders.

The largely inexperienced troop carrier pilots would again have to fly the same dogleg route of two nights before when Colonel Gavin's combat team was scattered over 60 miles of Sicily. But there was an even greater danger looming in the 504th combat team's drop: the flight would pass over, at low altitude, 35 miles of "friendly" beach, packed with American guns manned by jittery troops, to reach the DZ west of Gela.

Later on the morning of July 11, with Reuben Tucker's drop only some 12 hours away, General Ridgway left his headquarters to pay a personal visit to antiaircraft units in the surrounding sector of the 45th and the 1st Infantry divisions. He wanted to assure himself that all batteries had been notified that the 504th combat team would be flying overhead that night.

Accompanied by an artillery officer, Ridgway called on six AA batteries. Five were aware of the impending paratrooper flight, but the sixth one knew nothing about it. The embarrassed artillery officer hurriedly told the airborne leader that a meeting was set for early that afternoon of all AA commanders and that he, personally, would see that each was notified.

Ridgway departed for his CP only partially relieved. The fact that even one antiaircraft unit would be uninformed was considered an ominous omen.

That afternoon had been a haunting one for American troops along the beachhead. In midafternoon 30 black JU-88 Junker bombers appeared over Gela and rained their explosives on the town and the docks. Some supply ships at anchor offshore were struck by bombs. Loaded with ammunition, the USS *Rowan* received a direct hit, blew apart and sank in shallow water. For hours it smoked and exploded, a constant eerie reminder to troops along the beaches that the German Luftwaffe could strike with devastating effect at any time.

Across the turquoise Mediterranean from Sicily, 2,304 of Col. Reuben Tucker's 504th Parachute Regimental Combat Team clustered about their bulky C-47s at several airfields around the holy city at Kairouan. Jumping that night at Farello airfield near Gela would be Tucker's own 504th regiment (minus the 3rd Battalion which had jumped with Colonel Gavin's strike force two nights previously), the 376th Parachute Field Artillery Battalion, Company C of the 307th Airborne Engineer Battalion, plus Medical and Signal units.

It was nearing time for takeoff, and the fiery Colonel Tucker jeeped from plane to plane, halting only long enough to stand up in the vehicle, shake his fist in the air and shout, "Let's give the bastards hell, men! You know what to do!"

The grim-faced parachutists checked their weapons, then checked them again. One of those making preparations to board a C-47 was Brig. Gen. Charles Keerans, the former motorcycle daredevil and assistant commander of the 82nd Airborne Division. Although a nonjumper, Keerans was going along on what promised to be a routine flight to observe men of the division in their first combat operation. Charlie Keerans expected to be back in Tunisia and in bed in his quarters by dawn.

Under one of the broad wings of a transport plane, Brig. Gen. Maxwell D. Taylor, the division's artillery commander, was involved in animated conversation with Colonel Tucker, the leader of the parachute force. Taylor's neat, trim khaki shirt and trousers were in contrast to Tucker's steel helmet, jump boots and assorted combat gear. Taylor would remain in Tunisia to expedite the movement of other airborne units and equipment to the battlefield on Sicily.

Busily inspecting his personal weapons and gear alongside another C-47 was Lt. Col. William P. Yarborough, commanding officer of the 2nd Battalion of the 504th Parachute Infantry. Yarborough, regarded as one of the up-and-coming young officers in the army, was a relative newcomer to the 82nd Airborne Division, having been "drafted" into the All-Americans only several weeks before by General Ridgway.

Although only 30 years of age, Yarborough was one of the true pioneers of the fledgling U.S. airborne service. He was one of the first army paratroopers, back in mid-1940, and had designed the American parachutist's two most coveted possessions—his jump boots and wings.

Despite his relative youth, Colonel Yarborough had been selected in July 1942 to be Maj. Gen. Mark W. Clark's chief airborne planner for Operation Torch, the massive Allied invasion of North Africa in November of that year.

Yarborough was also one of the handful of men in the 82nd Airborne who had been under fire prior to the Sicilian invasion. Not only did he plan the airborne spearhead assault in North Africa by the independent 509th Parachute Infantry Battalion, but at his own insistence he went along on the 1,600-mile flight to Algeria from England.

Once the Axis had been driven out of North Africa by the British and Americans, Yarborough hoped to gain a troop command with Brig. Gen. William H. Lee's new 101st Airborne Division, then still in training in the

United States. Lee, regarded as the "father" of the U.S. airborne movement, was a close friend of Yarborough.

But Matt Ridgway was about to take his 82nd Airborne into Sicily; he had an opening for a battalion commander and urgently requested the War Department to assign Yarborough to his command. The request was granted, and now the paratrooper pioneer was about to lead his battalion of All-Americans into battle.

Around the dusty, stiflingly hot airfield suddenly were heard the cries: "It's time to move out! Get aboard!"

This was it. There was no turning back. For the first time, each man, in his own way, would face the violence of combat against a strong and determined foe.

Across the wide expanse of the airfield could be heard the rattling of equipment as the men got to their feet and into their parachute harness. Seated in his C-47 and waiting for takeoff, S. Sgt. Sam DeCrenzo, the 31-year-old cartographer of the 1st Battalion, removed a small diary from his jump suit pocket and scribbled an entry: "Glad to be going. The tension of waiting is over."

The 504th Parachute Infantry had originally been scheduled to make the drop in Sicily 24 hours previously, but the mission had been postponed pending clarification of the fate of Colonel Gavin's paratroopers on the island.

Looking toward the door of his waiting C-47, DeCrenzo spotted Lt. Col. Warren R. Williams, 27-year-old commander of the 1st Battalion. The sergeant added in his diary: "The colonel, a human dynamo, is raring to go!"

Minutes later there were ear-splitting roars at several airfields scattered over the bleak Tunisian landscape as engines of the 144 C-47s were started. One by one, the transport planes carrying Col. Rube Tucker's 2,304 paratroopers to Sicily raced down runways and lifted off. Circling over the airfields, the C-47s maneuvered into flight formation and headed in an easterly direction for the initial checkpoint of Malta.

Soon it was dark. The summer night was cloudless and would have been beautiful on some other more tranquil occasion. The dancing waves only a few feet below the lumbering planes reflected the pale light of the moon hanging high in the heavens.

In two hours the checkpoint of Malta was reached, and the sky armada, as it had 48 hours before with Col. Jim Gavin's parachutists aboard, made a sharp dogleg to the left and began the final 70-mile run to the drop zone in Sicily.

As the sky armada neared the embattled island, American troops on land and scores of navy ships anchored off Gela had just received the fourth massive pounding of the day by swarms of Luftwaffe JU-88 bombers. It was dark over Sicily, but scores of American gunners on land and in the water down below blazed away at their winged tormentors high above. For nearly an hour the Luftwaffe bombers rained high explosives on the beaches and facilities along the Gulf of Gela.

Anchored near the still burning and exploding USS *Rowan*, sunk in shallow water just offshore earlier that afternoon, was the Liberty ship *Christopher S. Shales*, named after the inventor of the typewriter. That afternoon on the bridge of the *Shales*, 21-year-old Signalman Harry C. Taylor had engaged in a brief but heated dispute with the ship's gunnery officer. Both men had seen a flight of 12 airplanes heading in the direction of the *Shales*, and Taylor promptly called out, "They're German!" Taylor had been involved in combat in the Pacific theater earlier in the war and, while making the long trip by convoy from the United States to the Mediterranean, he had spent many hours studying the silhouettes of German bombers and fighters.

The gunnery officer, new to combat, glanced upward and replied, "No, they're not German. They're ours."

"But, Lieutenant," Taylor persisted, "I'm positive they're German bombers!"

In a matter of moments the argument on the bridge of the *Shales* came to a sudden halt. The eerie whistle of falling shells told the two navy men that these planes were indeed German and that they had loosened their bombs on the Allied ships off Gela. As the pair flopped to the deck, loud explosions were heard in the vicinity. Several bombs straddled the *Shales*, and others made direct hits on the nearby *Rowan*.

Shortly after 11 P.M., the hum of JU-88 motors faded in the distance. Jittery Americans relaxed fingers on machine gun triggers and nervous officers shouted, "Cease firing!" An eerie silence fell over the beaches along the Gulf of Gela where much of the day the ground had been quaking from exploding bombs and the air saturated with the sharp barks of antiaircraft guns and staccato of automatic weapons.

But soon the ears of the fidgety troops on land and navy men at sea again picked up the faint purr of airplane motors far off in the dark sky.

Again the Americans along the Gulf of Gela tensed and waited for the arrival of yet another Luftwaffe bomb force. This was no flight of JU-88s, however. It was the rapidly approaching flight of the 504th Parachute Regimental Combat Team on the way to a routine mass drop at the Farello airstrip just west of Gela.

Unaware that the beaches had been pounded several times that day and night by German bombers, the first serial of Colonel Tucker's parachute force flew over the shoreline precisely on course and, in accordance with the operational flight plan, turned northwest for the 35-mile dash over the bridgehead to the DZ.

Arriving over Farello airfield without incident, paratroopers in the first serial bailed out and landed right on target. It was an operation so uneventful and routine that it might have been one of those conducted back at Fort Bragg, North Carolina.

None of the 504s hauling in their parachutes after touching down had any way of knowing that the routine flight over the American beachhead and subsequent drop on the airfield by a few planeloads of troopers would be the final thing to go right that night for the 504th Parachute Regimental Combat Team.

As Col. Bill Yarborough's C-47, droning along in the wake of the first serial, neared the Sicilian coast, Lt. John O'Malley, a 25-year-old platoon leader seated next to his battalion commander, craned his neck to peer out the tiny window behind him. He was particularly anxious to see what was occurring over the sandy gray beaches up ahead. As with all paratroopers and air crews in the flight, O'Malley uttered a silent prayer of thanks that all was quiet along the shores of Sicily.

Suddenly, somewhere in the darkness far below, a lone machine gun sent a fountain of tracers into one of the low-flying, slow-moving transports packed with American paratroopers. Almost immediately another machine gun, either on a naval vessel or on shore, followed suit. Then another and another. Soon scores of antiaircraft guns joined in, and shells and bullets filled the sky around the C-47s.

Taking in the frightening scenario of gunfire and death that was unfolding to his front, Lieutenant O'Malley saw that a wide sweep of the coast was aglow with a kaleidoscope of color: yellow flares, grotesque patterns of streams of red tracers, black, acrid puffs of smoke from bursting antiaircraft shells, puffs so thick that it appeared a person could leap from one to the other.

Gunfire from scores of vessels in the Gulf of Gela, dim silhouettes in the darkness, and land-based weapons in the American bridgehead increased to such an intensity that a curtain of explosives had been draped across the sky as if to bar entrance to Sicily by outside intruders, be they friendly or enemy. Directly into this hailstorm of man-made fire the lumbering, troop-laden C-47s flew, only 700 feet or less above the gunners blazing away down below. The furiously blinking amber signal lights on each C-47, whose purpose was to identify the aircraft as friendly, failed to be recognized by, nor did it deter, the panicky gunners.

Streams of tracer bullets whizzed into and past the C-47 carrying Lieutenant Colonel Yarborough, Lieutenant O'Malley and others.

Something definitely had gone awry, each trooper in the C-47 knew. Stomachs, already churning, twisted into tight knots. Palms and foreheads broke out with heavy beads of perspiration. Knees quivered. Hands trembled. Throats went dry, and those who tried found it difficult to speak. Still, out of the eerie darkness of Yarborough's plane came a voice: "Someone try to say something funny."

Seated across from Lieutenant O'Malley, Sgt. John Magee, a tough trooper, held his rosary beads in his hands, and his lips were moving almost imperceptibly in prayer. Magee would do his duty if he reached ground alive, but right now it appeared he and his comrades would plunge to a flaming death.

Next to Magee another man was vomiting violently in his helmet. Despite the extreme peril of the situation, O'Malley somehow thought the sight of the trooper throwing up in his steel headgear was humorous, and he fought for a few seconds to restrain a smile. In other planes many parachutists did not have the same foresight of the man using his helmet for a practical purpose—they simply vomited on the floor of the cabins.

Just outside Yarborough's plane, shells exploded with ear-shattering noise, tossing clusters of shrapnel against the fragile aircraft. Ripping sounds were heard through the open cargo door—bullets tearing through the wings and fuselage.

Seated down the aisle from Yarborough and O'Malley, Lt. Louis Fern, like the others his nerves drawn and taut, had a vagrant thought: Now I know what the expression means to be a "sitting duck."

Colonel Yarborough, straining mightily to remain outwardly calm through the holocaust the air armada had suddenly been plunged into, could see out the open cargo door opposite his bucket seat. He was sickened by what he saw. All around him C-47s, paratroopers and air crews still inside, burst into flames and plummeted crazily to earth. Others, receiving direct hits, exploded in midair and simply disintegrated. The transport plane on Yarborough's left wing, in its frenzy to escape the lethal inferno, veered sharply to its right, almost struck its neighboring C-47, then tilted awkwardly and plunged to earth. Seconds later, the twisted wreckage of the plane exploded in a huge ball of fire—it had been carrying mortar ammunition.

Lieutenant O'Malley watched in horror as the plane fell to earth and crashed. "Oh, my God, no!" he called out in anguish. Blown into dust in the explosion of that crashed C-47 were half of O'Malley's platoon. Tears rolled down the cheeks of the lieutenant who might at any moment join his platoon comrades in a fiery death.

Much in the fashion of a covey of quail suddenly and without warning fired upon by concealed hunters in the bush, the flight formation quickly split up. Planes continued to receive direct hits, explode in flight or crash to the ground as fiery torches. Machine gun bullets ripped through the floors of the ambling C-47s, killing and wounding many troopers inside and causing the decks to be slippery with human blood and gore.

A few damaged planes, crammed with paratroopers, sideslipped into the sea among the Allied ships where frenzied naval gunners lowered their sights and blazed away with machine guns and .20-millimeter cannon at the helpless paratroopers and air crews desperately clinging to the twisted, floating wreckage of their aircraft. Already hooked up, many of Colonel Tucker's men bailed out pell-mell and landed in sectors occupied by American infantry divisions. Not having been informed of the reinforcing airborne flight, ground soldiers mistook the descending Americans for German paratroopers and shot them while they were still in their harnesses. Some parachutists, their C-47s aflame, leaped out without static lines hooked up, desperately seeking to escape a fiery death. In front of Col. James Gavin's positions on Biazza Ridge, sickening thuds were heard in the darkness as bodies of All-Americans, parachutes neatly packed on their chests, struck the hard earth.

A few oncoming C-47s, noting the cauldron of gunfire and death into which they were inexorably heading, veered to the right instead of to the left as called for in the flight plan and dropped their loads of paratroopers into the less violent British sector. At the tag end of the 144-plane armada, seven pilots, believing they would be sentencing their passengers and themselves to certain death if they continued onward, turned around before reaching the beaches and headed back for the airfields in Tunisia.

As the streams of tracer bullets continued to climb into the night, seeking out the bulky flying targets just overhead, several officers involved in the airborne operations looked on in horror as they watched plane after plane tumble out of the sky like flaming torches. General Patton, commander of Seventh Army, and General Ridgway, leader of the 82nd Airborne Division, had gone to Farello airfield to greet the parachuting 504th on their arrival in what was thought to be a routine nighttime mass jump. Now, consumed with excruciating inner torment, the two generals stood side by side and witnessed the unfolding disaster, powerless to intervene.

"My God!" Patton muttered over and over. Tears welled in the eyes of Ridgway. Two of the toughest fighting commanders in the U.S. Army were nearly overcome with grief and frustration.

Standing outside his moldy headquarters in Scoglitti, General Bradley was also gazing toward the dark heavens at the tragic aerial spectacular. So consuming was his deep compassion for the young American parachutists and air crews being disintegrated in the sky or plunging to mass deaths in flaming torches, Bradley failed to notice that he, too, was in mortal danger. Countless fragments from exploding antiaircraft shells were plunging to earth all around the II Corps commander as he stood in the open gazing skyward. Any one of the jagged pieces of metal could have killed him.

On Biazza Ridge, where earlier that day 82nd Airborne troopers had fought an epic action and routed a German force numerically far superior, Colonel Gavin watched the pyrotechnics over the beaches with deep anger, frustration and sorrow.

In the skies over Gela and Scoglitti, within minutes death had claimed 318 American paratroopers and scores of Troop Carrier Command crews. Twenty-three C-47s had been shot down by friendly gunfire. Scores of other aircraft had been damaged and many of those on board killed or wounded.

One of those who perished in the flaming wreckage of a C-47 was Brig. Gen. Charles Keerans, his plan to remain aboard for the flight back to Tunisia after the 504th Parachute Infantry Regimental Combat Team had made its routine mass drop west of Gela abruptly terminated.

Suddenly, as though some huge supernatural force had thrown a switch, a blanket of eerie silence fell over the Gulf of Gela and the beachhead. The flying targets were gone—shot down, scattered, or somehow managing to wing inland through the curtain of gunfire.

One of the C-47s that had flown through the lethal barrage was carrying the 2nd Battalion commander, Lieutenant Colonel Yarborough, and his stick. Seeking to inject a tone of calmness into his voice, Yarborough inquired of the trooper in an adjoining seat, Lieutenant O'Malley, "Well, what do you want to do now?"

"Well, sir, I sure hope to hell we don't have to fly through something like that again," the lieutenant replied.

"I won't argue that point with you," the battalion commander remarked. He quickly added, "We've got to get the hell out of this plane before we're hopelessly lost. Go tell the pilot to slow the plane down and we'll jump—wherever in the hell we are."

O'Malley struggled from his seat under the burden of his combat gear, waddled to the cockpit and gave the pilot the colonel's orders. The red light in the plane was promptly flashed, the men hurriedly prepared to jump, and Yarborough took his place in the cargo door, crouched and ready to leap. Moments later the green light glowed and Yarborough jumped, followed by Lieutenants Fern and O'Malley and the rest of the stick. I'm bailing out into the unknown, but at least I'm not being shot down in flames, each man thought as he went through the yawning door.

Meanwhile, another C-47, its amber recognition lights blinking with the utmost urgency, was rapidly closing in on the fireswept coast of Sicily. Pfc. Richard Wagner, a member of the reconnaissance platoon of the 504th Regiment, was for the first time becoming inwardly alarmed. This was to be a "milk run" repeatedly flashed through Wagner's mind. Then what's all that shooting going on up ahead, and whose planes are those being shot out of the sky?

Wagner's recon platoon had been splintered for the jump—two troopers to a plane—and Wagner and a private named Rozman were among the few enlisted men aboard. The majority in the C-47 were officers of various regimental components, including a lieutenant colonel, two majors, several captains and three lieutenants.

As the plane carrying Wagner began its flight into the hailstorm of fire from "friendly" navy and army gunners on the ground, an order was shouted: "Take off your Mae Wests!" The troopers hurried to comply, and the inflatable life preservers were tossed about the floor of the cabin.

"Stand up and hook up!" echoed through the airplane, and there was a rustle of equipment as the parachutists struggled laboriously to their feet. As the men tensely awaited the warning red light to change to the green one that signaled "go," they heard the chilling sound of machine gun bullets ripping through the skin of the fragile aircraft. Screams rang out from the front of the dim cabin, and Wagner could see a commotion taking place there. Troopers were milling about, and he could not detect precisely what had happened.

"What the hell's going on up there?" a voice shouted from the rear of the cabin.

Came back a yell: "The regimental sergeant-major was standing in the door and he's been shot!"

Angry streams of tracers continued to rip through the fabric of the C-47 as troopers dragged the badly bleeding sergeant from the door opening. There was no panic, even though the All-Americans were under fire for the first time and their chances for survival appeared marginal.

A shout rang out from the semidarkness of the C-47: "The sergeant-major's dead!"

The glowing red light, which was to signify four minutes until bail out, was still burning. Five minutes ticked by. Then ten minutes. Twenty minutes. The green light failed to flash on. The pilot of the C-47 was lost and had been flying up and down the shell-racked night skies of southeast Sicily, anxiously seeking some recognizable landmark. Periodically, American gunners down below in the darkness opened fire on the low-flying transport plane despite the winking amber lights.

Twenty-millimeter shells exploded near the plane, leaving holes 10 inches wide in the fuselage. Twice streams of tracers ripped through the floor of the plane, missing Private Wagner's feet by only inches. Several others on board were not so fortunate—the bullets found their mark and the troopers were wounded or slumped over in death.

Another command rang through the bullet- and shell-shattered cabin: "Unhook! Sit down! Hold on to your seats! We're out of control and are going to crash-land on the water!"

Wagner and the other parachutists felt their hearts skip a beat with this ominous revelation. What chance would they have to survive a crash landing in the darkness on the sea? Very little, each silently concluded to himself. Outwardly, the All-Americans in the doomed C-47 remained calm. This is it! Wagner thought to himself. And I didn't even get a crack at the Germans.

Moments later the bullet-pierced airplane's lower body struck the water with tremendous impact, spilling the combat-loaded paratroopers out of their bucket seats and into assorted piles of bodies with arms and legs entangled. Wagner could feel the C-47 skidding along the surface at a high rate of speed. The hopeful prayer passed through his being that the aircraft would come to a halt before it struck some object in the water and burst into flame, incinerating those inside. The young trooper's silent prayer and those of his comrades were answered: the C-47 slowed and then came to a stop.

The bodies on the cabin floor remained motionless for several moments as each trooper digested the fact that the airplane had skidded to a halt and was floating precariously in the gentle swells of the Mediterranean.

Wagner disentangled himself from the arms and legs of comrades, struggled to his feet in the several inches of water that now covered the cabin floor, and with his trench knife began hacking at his and other troopers' static lines which were still hooked up to the anchor cable.

Most of the 504s had pulled themselves to their feet when a machine gun and several rifles on shore began raking the half-submerged C-47. Strangely, this gunfire sent a renewed surge of hope through most of the beleaguered troopers; it proved that the plane had ground to a halt near land instead of far out to sea where it most likely would be swallowed up by the dark, murky waters of the Mediterranean.

As Wagner and the others were cutting away their heavy personal equipment, a trooper standing in the partly submerged door suddenly shouted, "You dirty sons of bitches!" His anger was directed at those unseen tormentors on the beach, fellow Americans, who were firing at the disabled aircraft floundering around in the sea. He whipped out his .45 Colt and fired several shots toward the gun flashes on the shoreline.

"Cut out that goddamned firing!" a shout rang out from the blackness of the cabin. "You'll just cause those crazy sons of bitches on shore to keep shooting at us!"

The chastised paratrooper, inwardly less frustrated because he had briefly fought back, replaced his .45. As predicted, in moments red machine gun tracers were zipping past and into the floating winged hulk.

"Fer Chrissake!" a trooper exploded. "Those aren't Krauts shooting at us. Those are our own goddamned dogfaces. Those tracers are red and the Krauts' are white!"

A loud chorus of curses echoed through the floating cabin.

Soon the shooting from the beach tapered off, and the troopers in the cabin conversed in normal tones as to their next course of action. "Well, we sure as hell can't spend the war in this floating coffin," one observed, summing up the feelings of all.

As the discussion was under way, a shout was heard from just outside the swaying aircraft: "Help me! Save me! I'm going under!" The plea was coming from a parachute captain who, without informing anyone of his intentions, had edged through the partly submerged door into the sea. He apparently had intended to swim to shore and had become entangled in the twisted wreckage of the C-47.

Troopers near the door tried to reach out helping hands but were unable to locate the officer. His frantic calls ceased as he slipped beneath the sea to a watery grave.

Now the water was up over the bucket seats. Wagner decided that if he stayed longer, he would be doomed in the bobbing C-47 when it would suddenly plunge to the bottom. He put on his Mae West and started wading through the partially flooded cabin and came upon a trooper whose body was blocking the door. He leaned over to determine if the man was alive and could see by the faint rays of the descending moon that it was his pal, Private Rozman—dead from bullet wounds.

Wagner had been inside the floating C-47 for about 20 minutes when he pushed Rozman's body aside. He heard two rifle shots ring out at the shoreline and felt a breeze on his neck as one bullet whizzed past within inches of him and the second pellet whipped through the fuselage near his legs.

Wagner slipped out of the plane on the far side to avoid drawing more gunfire from shore. As he dropped down into the water, he could discern the dim silhouettes of invasion vessels and worried whether nervous gunners aboard would also fire at him.

Wagner saw he was only about 100 yards from shore and debated with himself whether to swim for the beach or a ship. He heard a shout from land and recognized the voice as a comrade in the C-47 who had already made it ashore: "It's okay to come on in now. Whoever the bastards were that were here are gone!" Wagner swam to shore and waded up onto the sand, near exhaustion.

The young private huddled on the beach until daylight, then began walking along the coastline. Soon he came upon the pilot and copilot of his ill-fated C-47, lying on stretchers at an aid station. One had been hit by a

.20-millimeter shell and was in danger of losing his arm, and the other was also wounded.

"What happened up there?" Wagner asked softly.

"We couldn't find the DZ," the ashen-faced pilot, weak from loss of blood, stated. "I got hit. Then my copilot got badly hit. But we kept flying around trying to locate a place for you guys to jump before we crashed."

The young airman paused to gasp for breath, then added, "But before we could spot a DZ, one motor was knocked out by a shell, then the other motor was hit. We tried to crash-land on the beach but couldn't control the plane, so we guided it into the water the best we could." His voice drifted away and he lapsed into unconsciousness.

At a nearby aid station, Wagner saw a wounded soldier from the 45th Infantry Division being carried on a stretcher. A white bandage on the man's shoulder was stained with blood. "What happened to you, pal?" Wagner inquired gently.

"Well, I ran into one of your paratroopers in the dark last night," the ground soldier replied. "Your guy called out that he was an American paratrooper and not to shoot. I yelled back, 'You're a goddamned *German* paratrooper.' "

Painfully wounded but not in serious condition, the soldier paused briefly before continuing. "Well, I thought sure as hell he was a Kraut 'cause we'd been told earlier that the Krauts might drop paratroopers. So I raised my rifle to shoot him. But before I could squeeze off a shot, your guy whipped out his .45 and shot me instead."

Wagner trekked off inland in search of comrades.

Fifteen miles from the DZ at Farello airfield, Lt. Col. Warren Williams, commander of the 504th's 1st Battalion, had bailed out with his stick at only 400 feet and slammed into a hillside with great impact. Minutes later he spotted a shadowy form which turned out to be Staff Sergeant DeCrenzo, his battalion cartographer.

Williams gathered several other men and arrived at a firm conclusion— he was lost. Walking across the bleak landscape, Williams and his little band saw a farmhouse with a dim light inside.

"Sam," the colonel said to DeCrenzo, "we'll stay here and cover you. You go in the house and see if you can find out from the resident where in the hell we are and where the Krauts are."

DeCrenzo moved toward the house as Williams and the others watched from the shadows, aware that the enemy could be occupying the house.

They were relieved to see a Sicilian answer the door and admit Sergeant DeCrenzo.

The minutes ticked by and DeCrenzo still had not left the house. Williams was becoming worried about his man's safety. After 20 minutes had gone by, the colonel whispered to his men, "Something must have happened to Sam. We're going to crash the door down and see what's going on."

The battalion commander and his men stole silently up to the house, and one of the husky troopers crashed open the door, using his shoulder as a battering ram. They bolted into the front room, weapons at the ready. There, at a table, sat Sergeant DeCrenzo and his Sicilian host leisurely draining a bottle of wine.

"Oh, hello, Colonel," DeCrenzo called out breezily. "Sit down and have a drink."

Williams was furious, convinced that the sergeant had forgotten his mission, and the others had been waiting anxiously outside. "Let's get going!" the colonel growled at DeCrenzo. The little knot of troopers moved out into the darkness.

When Colonel Tucker's combat team approached the coast of Sicily, Capt. Mack C. Shelley, a former Regular Army sergeant who had been commissioned when war broke out, was standing in the door of his C-47. Shelley's plane was flying on the left wing of Lieutenant Colonel Yarborough's aircraft. Before anyone in Shelley's C-47 jumped, it was hit by a shell, caught fire, and spun crazily downward and crashed. Shelley was flung out of the door, where he had been standing, and into a heavy growth of brush which cushioned the impact.

The captain lost consciousness, but minutes later revived and became aware that his comrades were in the burning airplane. With great effort he freed himself from his harness and, although in great pain, crawled to the twisted wreckage. He edged inside and began tugging at the limp bodies of comrades, hoping that some were still alive.

Moments later an explosion sent an orange flame cascading into the air —a load of mortar shells had detonated. The force of the blast pitched Shelley like a rag doll from the wreckage. An undetermined amount of time later, the captain once more regained consciousness and was aware that two shadowy figures were hovering over him.

Despite his physical condition, the parachute officer realized the pair of dim silhouettes were armed Italian soldiers who apparently had been in the area and stopped to see if there had been any survivors in the crashed American aircraft.

Shelley had limited knowledge of the Italian language, but he was able to discern the thrust of what the two enemy soldiers were discussing. One Italian wanted to "finish off the bastard," while the other insisted that Shelley be carried to an aid station. A heated debate continued between the pair, after which the American became vaguely aware that he was being lifted off the ground. Again he lapsed into a coma.

Ten days later Captain Shelley, wounded, burned over the body, hazy of mind and bedridden, was in a German field hospital on the eastern coast of Sicily. He realized that an intense firefight had broken out in the town. His spirits rose as it appeared rescue was near. The American officer noticed that German army personnel had vanished from the hospital, and a short time later Canadian soldiers, wearing their distinctive pie-plate helmets, burst into the building. Shelley was again a free man.

Canadian medics removed the parachute captain, who was swathed in white bandages, to a nearby aid station. There he would await transportation to a field hospital in the rear for required treatment of his critical wounds. Shelley had other ideas. He was mad—mad at the Germans.

Presently a Bren-gun carrier arrived at the medical facility with a wounded British officer. While the medics had their backs turned, Shelley took the injured officer's gun, hobbled out to where the crew in the Bren carrier was starting back to the front, and called out, "Hold on, I'm going with you." He hopped aboard.

Rounding a curve in the road, the men in the gun carrier suddenly were confronted by the menacing muzzle of the main cannon of a Mark VI tank aimed directly at them. The three-member British crew leaped from the still-moving vehicle and attempted to flee for cover. A burst of machine gun fire erupted from the ponderous Mark VI, and the Tommies were cut down in flight.

Unable to run due to his wounds, Captain Shelley rolled out of the gun carrier before the tank opened fire on the three English soldiers and slid into a roadside ditch. The German tank crew apparently did not spot the American as they revved the iron monster's engine and rolled forward, close enough to Shelley that he could feel the heat from the motor.

Moments later Shelley peered over the rim of a grassy ditch and spotted a squad of Wehrmacht soldiers leap over a stone wall less than 50 yards away and, with Schmeisser machine pistols at the ready, move directly toward him. The German grenadiers apparently had viewed the episode with the Mark VI and now were coming after Shelley.

One of the parachute officer's arms was badly burned, had a broken bone in it and was useless. Shelley propped himself up and, holding his unfamiliar British automatic weapon in the left hand, opened fire on the German squad. He killed three of the enemy, but a fourth German, although wounded, continued to crawl closer to the American captain and hurled a potato-masher grenade. A fragment from the exploding missile tore into Shelley's badly burned shoulder, but he managed to fish out a grenade, pull the pin and heave it at the German, killing him instantly.

Again the American captain lost consciousness. Hours later he was discovered by Canadian medics who, for the second time, removed him to an aid station to await evacuation to a rear area hospital. Shelley revived sufficiently to understand a Canadian medical major who was berating him, without conviction in his voice, for slipping away from the aid station and getting himself involved in a fight with the enemy.

"You managed to break at least 10 army regulations," the Canadian doctor observed, "including stealing a British officer's gun and being absent without leave."

Medics treated Shelley's most recent wound, the grenade fragments lodged in his burned shoulder, and loaded him into an ambulance which started back for the beach in a convoy with other vehicles. Halfway to its destination, the convoy came under attack from the air. Shelley heard the roar of powerful engines overhead, followed by the whine of diving airplanes. Seconds later he heard a hissing sound as the chattering machine guns of the Luftwaffe fighter-bombers sent streams of .50-caliber bullets into convoy vehicles.

Now the American heard loud explosions as the German pilots released their bombs. One bomb scored a direct hit on a half-ton truck just in front of the ambulance. Concussion from the blast badly damaged the medical vehicle, and Shelley was thrown out of the ambulance and onto the road. He was alive but had sustained yet another wound—a broken left arm.

As the German planes banked and sped for home, another Canadian medical crew placed Shelley into a passing ambulance, and he continued the journey to the beach. There he was evacuated to North Africa. Capt. Mack Shelley simply refused to be killed.

Shortly after bailing out of their C-47 along the southeastern coast of Sicily on the night of D-Day plus two, Pfc. James M. McNamara of the reconnaissance unit of the 504th Parachute Infantry regimental headquarters and his close friend, Pfc. Joseph Hart, were huddled in scrub brush in the darkness, trying to gain their bearings. They had jumped from the same plane, along with the rest of the stick, without waiting for the green light after the C-47, flying at only 500 feet, was raked with machine gun and .20-millimeter gun fire.

McNamara and Hart conversed in hushed tones and agreed that they had no idea where they were. They did realize they had landed within 150 yards of the sea and would have drowned in their parachutes had they leaped out only three seconds earlier.

As the pair of troopers pondered their next move, above the roar of antiaircraft guns they heard a nearby loudspeaker blare out in English: "Be on the alert! German paratroopers have just landed all around us!" The panicky American voice continued to boom out: "Be on guard! German paratroopers are landing!"

Unsure whether the greatest danger lay with enemy troops or friendly ground forces, McNamara and Hart edged into a ditch and began crawling away from the panicky voice on the loudspeaker. Presently they heard American voices in the darkness and determined that these were members of a quartermaster company bivouacked along the beach.

Crawling closer and spotting several shadowy figures, the pair of troopers decided to take a risk and make their identity known. McNamara got out of the ditch, stood in the open-and shouted, "We're American paratroopers."

There were several moments of silence, and then bursts of automatic weapons fire from the bivouac area sent McNamara diving back into the ditch. As the two friends contemplated their next action, McNamara whispered to Hart, "You know, Joe, I think we should have stayed in the States as latrine orderlies."

The pair of parachutists crawled off into the night.

Meanwhile, Capt. Delbert A. Kuehl, a Protestant chaplain in the 504th Parachute Infantry regiment, and several troopers were facedown on the ground behind the 45th Infantry Division beaches, with American bullets whistling just over their heads. Chaplain Kuehl was suffering from blurred vision; only minutes before he had slammed into a stone wall after parachuting to earth.

Before Captain Kuehl and several of his comrades had shucked their chutes, they were taken under intense rifle and machine gun fire by a group of nervous 45th Division Thunderbirds who mistook them for German paratroopers. The parachutists flopped to the ground with angry bullets whistling past them.

When the intense firing tapered off, Kuehl shouted that his group was American. The call was greeted by a withering burst of gunfire. When the Thunderbirds relaxed their trigger fingers, the chaplain yelled, "We're Americans!" Each effort to identify themselves brought a renewed fusillade of fire into the band of paratroopers.

Knowing the paratroopers could not remain in this predicament, Chaplain Kuehl hatched a plan of action. With the handful of parachutists firing their weapons into the air, Kuehl arduously began crawling through the vineyards and the tall grass to skirt around the flank of the skirmish line of 45th Division troops. After what seemed to him an endless period of time, the chaplain arrived at a point behind the Thunderbirds who were still firing furiously toward the "German paratroopers" to their front.

Kuehl stealthily crept up to the nearest infantryman and tapped him on the shoulder. As the startled soldier glanced around from his prone position, Chaplain Kuehl asked in a matter-of-fact tone, "Just what do you people think you're doing? Those are Americans you're shooting at."

Elsewhere in the ill-fated flight of Col. Rube Tucker's regimental combat team, Flight Officer J. G. Paccassi's C-47 was taken under intense antiaircraft fire as it crossed the coast and was struck by a shell just as the final pair of 504s bailed out. Paccassi banked the craft and headed out to sea. Just offshore the C-47 was hit again, the rudder was shot away and both engines failed.

Paccassi began a glide to crash-land into the Gulf of Gela as guns on navy ships continued to blast away at the disabled aircraft. Hitting the water and skidding to a halt, the twisted wreckage remained afloat as the U.S. destroyer *Beatty* raked it with .20-millimeter shells. Minutes later the *Beatty* lifted its fire and lowered a small boat to pick up the dazed Flight Officer Paccassi and two other survivors.

Nearby, the U.S. destroyer *Jeffers* fished out of the Mediterranean seven survivors of a C-47 which had crash-landed after being struck by an antiaircraft shell. Rescued were the entire five-man air crew, Maj. C. C. Bowman of the 82nd Airborne Division headquarters who had gone on the flight as an observer, and a paratrooper who had refused to jump.

Another C-47 riddled by gunfire crash-landed behind the American beaches. After a jolting ride on its belly over nearly 200 yards of rough terrain, the C-47 came to a halt after striking a tree. Pulling their way out of the twisted wreckage were Lt. Col. L. G. Freeman, executive officer of the 504th Parachute Infantry Regiment, and 12 other men, all wounded or badly injured.

Yet another C-47 was flying along the coast of southern Sicily, alone and lost. The aircraft was riddled with hundreds of bullet holes, and chunks of the wings and fuselage had been ripped away by shrapnel. In this airplane was a thoroughly angry and grieving commander, Col. Reuben Tucker.

When Tucker's C-47 came under fire over the American beaches, several troopers inside were wounded. Now the pilot became confused. He flew west past Gela along the coast for a considerable distance, then, at the order of Colonel Tucker, reversed his course and headed eastward. In the darkness and confusion, the DZ at Farello airfield was spotted, and Tucker and his stick bailed out. On the ground they were joined by a few planeloads of troopers who had flown in the first serial which had reached the drop zone and jumped without incident.

Rube Tucker counted heads, only a handful of his troopers. Now all he could do was wait and hope that more 504s would somehow make it to the airfield DZ.

Across the Mediterranean from the flaming beaches of Sicily, there was a nervous tapping on the bedroom door of Gen. Maxwell Taylor at an airfield near Kairouan, Tunisia. Turning on a night-light, the 82nd Airborne artillery commander glanced at his watch. It was 2:10 A.M.

Taylor had remained in Tunisia to help dispatch remaining elements of the division to Sicily. After the last of Colonel Rube Tucker's 144 C-47s had disappeared into the night, Taylor went to bed. He intended to rise early for initial reports from Tucker's mass drop behind American lines.

General Taylor opened the door and was confronted by an excited messenger. "Sir," the man blurted out, "the 504s have met disaster. A lot of our planes are returning to airfields here. They're all shot up and they've got a lot of dead and wounded on board."

Knowing that early battlefield reports—especially from a green unit—were often grossly inaccurate, Taylor was not unduly alarmed. But he hurriedly dressed and rushed by jeep to a nearby airfield. Taking a quick look at the scene, he knew that there was a degree of authenticity to the disaster report.

Flak-riddled C-47s, barely able to reach Tunisia, dotted the field. Young paratroopers, lifeless and with parachute packs still in place on chests, were being carried out of the aircraft. These men had spent many grueling months preparing for combat, yet had been killed before firing a shot or even seeing an enemy soldier.

CHAPTER TWELVE

SHOOT-OUT ON HILL 41

It was shortly after midnight of July 12 as Maj. Mark Alexander's parachute battalion was marching through the humid night toward the drop zone north and east of Gela. Weary from their savage fight the day before in which they had knocked out several pillboxes in front of the seaborne 45th Infantry Division, the 505s of the 2nd Battalion only an hour earlier had paused in their march to look on in horror as 23 C-47s carrying fellow paratroopers were shot down by navy and shore antiaircraft guns.

Once an eerie lull had settled over the region following the disaster inflicted upon Col. Rube Tucker's paratrooper flight, Alexander's men resumed their trek toward the west. The men had little to say during the march. They had been fighting and marching for almost 48 hours. Only the rustle of combat gear and the labored breathing of men loaded down with machine gun and mortar components and boxes of ammunition disturbed the tranquillity of the Mediterranean night.

Suddenly the peace was shattered. Out of the darkness to the front, automatic weapons and rifles began pouring fire into the ranks of the marching parachutists. As the troopers scattered for the cover offered by roadside ditches and large boulders, above the rattle of gunfire, Major Alexander, at the head of the column, could hear voices up ahead—American voices. He concluded that he and his men were being confronted by another American force.

"Hold your fire! They're friendlies!" Major Alexander called back to the column of troopers. The parachutists resisted an intense urge to shoot back at their tormentors—whoever they might be.

As suddenly as the firing had begun, it abruptly ended, and each party in the confrontation remained motionless and cloaked in darkness. Alexander, lying in a ditch, shouted out his name and rank and identified his unit.

"We don't believe you!" came back a shout from the 45th Division force.

Later the soldier Alexander was engaging in a shouting match identified himself as a captain in the 45th Division. For more than 20 minutes the parachute major and the Thunderbird captain yelled back and forth at each other, their voices being the only sound in the vicinity.

Eventually the captain became convinced that he was being confronted by American paratroopers, and he "permitted" Major Alexander to approach alone to be authenticated. The captain explained that he and his men, seeing the transport planes shot down by American guns, concluded that Alexander and his men were German paratroopers who had jumped from the flight.

Major Alexander and his troopers continued their march. A short distance north of Gela they were met by a truck convoy which, under the direction of Lt. Col. Charles Billingslea, had set out to meet the battalion. It was 1 A.M. when the fatigued troopers climbed into the trucks.

By dawn the convoy of parachutists reached the headquarters of the 82nd Airborne Division, located a short distance from Biazza Ridge where the 505s under Col. Jim Gavin had fought an epic battle the previous afternoon. Alexander promptly reported to Gen. Matt Ridgway, the division commander. "I have 541 men with me," the major stated.

"Glad to see you," Ridgway replied.

Indeed he was. Alexander's 541 men more than doubled the number under Ridgway's immediate control. Until then, on D-Day plus two, the commanding general had been able to round up only 375 of his more than 5,700 paratroopers who had taken off from Tunisian airfields to parachute into Sicily.

As daylight drifted over the purple hills of Sicily on the twelfth, Capt. Ed Sayre of the 505th Parachute Infantry raised up from his shallow foxhole on embattled Hill 41 on Piano Lupo. A few hours before, Sayre and his paratroopers had driven the Germans from the barren knob after a short but savage fight in the blackness of night.

Sayre glanced around the landscape. What the parachute captain saw sent chills surging along his spine. Hill 41 projected out from American lines like a long extended finger, and during the few hours of darkness after Sayre's men had seized the hill, German tanks had moved in behind and onto the sides of the elevation. The paratroopers and elements of the 1st Infantry Division on the hill were surrounded.

The Germans struck with fury at 7 A.M. to wipe out the American force on Hill 41. Powerful diesel engines echoed across the bleak landscape as a swarm of enemy tanks, trailing towering plumes of dust in their wake, clanked toward the hill from the front. Ed Sayre's paratroopers and the Big Red One Infantry blazed away at the onrushing monsters with rifles and machine guns.

Now the panzers began pouring direct fire from their high-velocity .88s into the ranks of the Americans. Youthful Capt. Bryce Denno, who suddenly found himself commander of the Big Red One battalion the night before when Lieutenant Colonel Crawford was seriously wounded, shouted to an artillery observer in a nearby foxhole, "Get some artillery fire on those damned tanks before they're on top of us!"

An observer for a battery of .155-millimeter guns, the officer hurriedly radioed map coordinates to the big guns and shouted into the mouthpiece, "No time to zero in. They're almost on us. Fire for effect!" It was a risky action but one that had to be taken.

Within minutes the Americans on the beleaguered hill heard the whine of a cluster of large shells approaching from the .155 battery and anticipated the missiles crashing down on the enemy tanks, now but 100 yards away. Instead the rustling noise turned to a roar, much like an express train rushing through a tunnel. Hill 41 erupted into a sheet of flame and explosives as the "friendly" salvo struck the line of American foxholes. Thick clouds of dust and smoke enfolded the hill. Acrid cordite fumes filled nostrils as urgent cries of "Medic!" pierced the haze. Pitiful shrieks and screams from men mutilated by shell fragments rang out over the sun-baked landscape.

In the initial salvo of "shorts," 3 infantrymen of the Big Red One were killed and 12 wounded. Others on the hill cursed the unseen American artillerymen far to the rear and braced for the arrival of more .155 shells into their positions.

Now those on Hill 41 heard another chilling sound: enemy tanks that had slipped in behind the elevation during the night revved motors, ready to assault the hill from the rear. Up ahead of the Americans, German tanks clanked to within 75 yards of their positions.

The Hermann Goering Division was making an all-out effort to wipe out the American force. Due to the caprices of war, an ugly, insignificant little Sicilian hill in a region known as Piano Lupo had suddenly become of utmost importance. The hill happened to sit on the route over which the Wehrmacht was rushing toward the American landing beaches.

Again the beleaguered paratroopers and Big Red One soldiers heard the frightening swishing sound of another salvo of "friendly" .155 shells approaching and hugged the bottom of their foxholes. Hearts beat furiously. Mouths went dry. Perspiration dotted foreheads. But the salvo passed just over the Americans and landed on the intended target—the German iron monsters to the front.

As the explosives rocked the ground all around the enemy tanks, the iron-plated vehicles paused, then began milling about. Still the panzers, though disorganized, kept raking the Americans with point-blank fire from their .88s.

Lt. Col. Arthur Gorham, the commander of the 1st Battalion of the 505th Parachute Infantry, grabbed a rocket launcher and edged his way within range of a menacing Tiger tank which had continued to roll forward. Gorham, out in the open and in full view of enemy tankers, kneeled to take aim at the tank. Gunners in the Tiger spotted the parachute leader and fired an .88 shell at Gorham at point-blank range. Gorham, hard-nosed to the end, fell over dead.

Capt. William Comstock, a medical officer who had seen Gorham being gunned down, ran to the side of the fatally wounded parachutist. An enemy tank shell burst nearby, seriously wounding the battle surgeon who toppled over beside Colonel Gorham's body.

Lt. Dean McCandless, who looked on as first Gorham and then Comstock went down, leaped from his foxhole and dashed through a hail of fire to where the dead Gorham and the critically wounded Comstock were lying. Seeing that the medical captain was still alive, McCandless shouted for Cpl. Thomas Higgins to locate a jeep to evacuate the doctor.

Higgins, traversing a gauntlet of enemy machine gun fire, ran for a quarter of a mile and came upon a 1st Infantry Division soldier in a jeep.

"Give me a hand; I need your jeep," the parachute corporal rasped out while trying to regain his breath from his long run through gunfire. "We've got a badly wounded man out in front of our lines who needs to be evacuated."

"I'm sorry about that," the other replied. "But I'll be goddamned if I'm going to commit suicide driving up onto that hill."

As Higgins pondered his next move, a paratrooper cook in the role of rifleman, Pvt. Bernard Williams, happened along. Higgins quickly outlined the situation, and the two paratroopers took over the jeep and drove it up Hill 41, under fire all the way. There, with the aid of Lieutenant McCandless, they evacuated Captain Comstock and recovered the body of Colonel Gorham.

As the savage fight for Hill 41 raged, the Americans on the embattled elevation received help from an unexpected source. Unseen by the German tanks attacking the hill from the front, several American Sherman tanks slipped up on the enemy force from the flank and poured .75-millimeter shells into the vulnerable sides of the panzers. Four of the enemy tanks were knocked out, and the remaining iron vehicles wheeled around and clanked off to the rear.

In their haste to break off the engagement, the German tanks abandoned their supporting grenadiers, and the Americans on the hill raked the enemy infantrymen with machine gun and rifle fire until the bewildered German foot soldiers fled the scene in the wake of their panzers.

With the strong enemy force to the front driven back—at least for the present—Capt. Ed Sayre's parachutists and Big Red One infantrymen turned their attention to the menacing enemy tanks behind them, from where gunfire had just erupted. The force on the hill was elated to see the source of the sharp cracks: tanks of the U.S. 2nd Armored Division, their crews new to combat, had arrived in the valley and were slugging it out with the veteran tankers of the Hermann Goering Division.

"Well, we've got a grandstand seat," Captain Sayre observed to his men. "We might just as well sit back and observe it."

That they did. As a German tank went up in smoke in the valley behind the hill, the paratroopers in the "balcony" cheered. When an American tank was knocked out, the men groaned. It was a fierce battle, with many tanks strewn about the valley after being hit by the fire of an adversary. Eventually the German tanks made a fighting withdrawal and disappeared toward the north behind a hill mass.

But the Hermann Goering Division refused to quit. Three more times that day tank and grenadier task forces launched frontal attacks against

Hill 41. The assaults, weak and loosely coordinated, were driven back by heavy American artillery fire before they posed a threat to the defenders on the elevation.

The Germans on Piano Lupo were on the run, and American commanders intended to keep them that way. At 4 A.M. the next morning, Capt. Ed Sayre was shaken awake and ordered to jump off with his men to seize a key ridge 3,000 yards to the front. Acting as assault troops for the Big Red One battalion to which the parachutists were attached, Sayre and his men were raked repeatedly by machine gun fire during the advance. But a heavy American artillery barrage on the ridge silenced the machine gun nests, and the paratroopers occupied the objective.

With hardly time to catch their breaths, they received more orders: the infantry battalion and paratroopers were to continue the pursuit and seize the town of Niscemi, an important road junction. Moving forward against only scattered resistance, the combined American force reached a hill overlooking Niscemi.

Declaring that the paratroopers were fresher than his own infantry, the young Big Red One captain, who had suddenly found himself a battalion commander when senior officers were killed or wounded, ordered Captain Sayre and his troopers to attack and capture Niscemi. The 505s promptly jumped off and were not fired on until they entered the outskirts of the town. Sayre's men silenced the enemy machine guns, and a detachment of German infantry departed to the north.

Captain Sayre radioed the acting commander of the 1st Infantry Division battalion: "Niscemi secured."

The straight-leg infantrymen pushed on through the paratroopers and dug in just north of the outskirts. A half hour later Sayre received radioed orders: "You are relieved from 1st Infantry Division. Return to the vicinity of Gela." Gen. Matt Ridgway, commander of the 82nd Airborne, was trying to assemble his scattered division.

Meanwhile, a lanky, curly-haired member of Col. Reuben Tucker's 504th Parachute Regiment was being held under guard near a German regimental headquarters. Pvt. Theodore Bachenheimer, 20 years of age, soft-spoken, polite and carefree in spirit, had parachuted directly onto a fortified German position and was taken prisoner before he could get out of his harness.

So reserved and lacking in outward ferociousness was young Bachenheimer that his comrades back in the States had often speculated if he could endure the rigors of a combat paratrooper. His curly locks and boyish face belied an inner fortitude.

Only eight years before Bachenheimer found himself jumping into Sicily, he had been a bashful schoolboy in Germany where Adolph Hitler's Nazi Party had seized power. Seeking freedom and a more promising life for young Ted, Bachenheimer's parents fled the Third Reich and made their way to the United States. The German-born trooper had taken the oath of American citizenship at Fort Bragg, North Carolina, a few weeks before the 82nd Airborne shipped overseas.

Now it appeared to Bachenheimer that his war was over, minutes after touching down on Hitler's Europe. He was subjected to intensive grilling by skilled and experienced German intelligence officers at the regimental command post, but the calm and collected Bachenheimer withheld from his captors the fact that he had been born in Germany, grew up there and spoke the language fluently. The German interrogators wasted little time on this obviously dull-witted, unimposing American paratrooper.

Bachenheimer waited outside the enemy headquarters for removal to a prisoner-of-war enclosure. He listened unobtrusively through the open door as German battle commanders formulated a plan of attack against American seaborne forces pushing steadily inland. A short time later, after digesting details of the enemy's plan, Bachenheimer noticed that his guard had grown lax and had left to visit a latrine. The parachutist gave a quick glance around, then bolted into the darkness.

A few hours later Bachenheimer made contact with fellow paratroopers, and the information he had learned on German tactical plans while eavesdropping outside the enemy CP was hurried on to higher American headquarters.

In the days ahead, despite his mild appearance and gentle demeanor, Private Bachenheimer became a one-man reconnaissance force. He loved to go on perilous patrols and often, on his own volition, infiltrated behind German lines on Sicily where his mastery of the enemy tongue held him in good stead.

On one occasion Bachenheimer edged up close to a German machine gun post. The enemy crew, in the darkness, could not identify the young private's American uniform and presumed the shadowy figure to be one of their own. Remaining at a discreet distance, Bachenheimer engaged the bored German machine gunners in friendly conversation, joining in a vehement denunciation of Wehrmacht cooking.

When Bachenheimer tired of taunting the enemy machine gun crew and the dark sky was about to dissolve into daylight, he silently removed a grenade from his belt, pulled the pin and tossed the lethal missile at the Germans. His newly made "friends" were blown into pieces. Bachenheimer then returned to his true comrades with the nonchalance of a student reaching home after a senior prom.

Only a few miles from where Private Bachenheimer fled his German captors at the regimental CP, Capt. Pete Suer, a battalion surgeon in the 505s, was in the center of a shoot-out between fellow paratroopers and a force of German grenadiers. Captain Suer, like Bachenheimer, was mild in manner and soft-spoken.

Even comrades in his battalion knew little about Doc Suer's background, as he spoke of it seldom. They did know that he was Jewish, had been a physician in Brooklyn as a civilian, and joined the paratroopers to help bring Nazi Germany to its knees.

Now, as the firefight was at its most intense, Suer spotted several wounded men—American and German—sprawled on the rocklike ground between the adversaries. He raised up from the ground as bullets hissed past his head, vigorously waved a large Red Cross flag, and moved out into no-man's-land where he was in the line of fire from both sides. There he calmly moved from one wounded man to the other without regard to nationality.

Doc Suer was not fired on by the Germans, but each side continued to blast away at the other. The American medical officer, in the center of the hailstorm of automatic weapons and small arms fire, arduously dragged each wounded paratrooper and grenadier to relative safety before he returned to his own position.

Meanwhile, Gen. Matt Ridgway, commander of the 82nd Airborne, was inspecting a position of his men in the vicinity of Ponte Olivo airfield, just west of the high ground of Piano Lupo. The two stars on Ridgway's helmet were glistening in the sun, which attracted the attention of a concealed Italian sniper.

The enemy marksman took aim at the American officer who had suddenly appeared in his rifle sight and squeezed the trigger. Ten feet away from the standing general, Sgt. Thomas Leccese of the 504s felt a sharp, stinging sensation in his hand, followed by relentless painful throbs. A bullet meant for the commander of the 82nd Airborne Division had been off target, striking Sergeant Leccese.

A short time later Leccese was being treated for his painful, but not serious, wound by a parachute medic. "Goddamn, that's strange," the medic observed on looking at Leccese's bleeding hand.

"What's so strange?" a curious Leccese inquired.

"Hell, you've been shot by a wooden bullet."

Enemy snipers on occasion fired wooden bullets, which were outlawed by the Geneva Convention rules of civilized warfare, as a diabolical method of inflicting severe and lasting pain on the victim. Wooden bullets splintered after entering the body and required much additional medical treatment over a long period of time.

After parachuting the night before, Sergeant Leccese was alone and lost. He wandered through the ominous night, hoping to be headed toward the landing beaches. Suddenly the dim silhouette of a farmhouse loomed. He paused for several minutes, listening for voices—German or American. He heard nothing. He saw no sign of the enemy.

Convinced that the farmhouse presented an ideal place to hole up until daylight, Sergeant Leccese, rifle at the ready, cautiously tiptoed onto the rickety old porch. The boards underfoot creaked loudly and sent eerie noises drifting across the night air. The trooper tensed. If the enemy was inside, they certainly would be alerted by this unexpected sound, he thought.

Leccese remained stonelike for nearly five minutes. Only silence prevailed. He slowly pushed open the door and, by the muted rays of the quarter moon, glimpsed around the room. He felt a surge of relief. There was no indication of an enemy's presence. He entered the room, walking softly. Through the open door he could hear the chirping of crickets outside.

The parachute sergeant leaned his rifle against a wall where it would be handy if needed and began walking across the dark room to inspect the rest of the house, hoping to locate a soft bed. Halfway across the room Leccese felt his heart skip a beat; the dim silhouettes of two men suddenly had popped up in front of him. The figures apparently had been sleeping in an adjoining bedroom.

For several moments neither Leccese nor the unknown men moved. At the same split second, Leccese dashed the several feet to where he had leaned his rifle against the wall, and the two shadowy forms bolted for their weapons on the other side of the room. Sergeant Leccese reached his rifle first, grabbed it, whirled and unloaded his clip at the two silhouettes across the room. He heard thuds as the shadowy forms crumpled to the floor.

The parachute sergeant had a sudden surge of fright. Were these two enemy soldiers he had killed—or comrades? It was too dark to tell. He cautiously moved across the room to the slumped figures and exhaled a sigh of relief. By the dim light from the moon seeping through a window, Leccese saw the Wehrmacht insignia on the tunic of each corpse.

Behind the American landing beaches east of Gela on July 12, men of the 1st Infantry Division reached the locale where parachute Capt. Bill Follmer for nearly three days had been directing his company, astride a farmer's mule. A combat surgeon of the Big Red One took a look at Follmer's swollen and discolored ankle, broken on the jump into Sicily, and ordered the company commander back to a hospital ship in the Gulf of Gela.

Captain Follmer returned his Sicilian mule to its owner and with the help of his husky batman started for the shoreline. On the way the two troopers passed the strong point that Follmer's men had captured in a fierce battle only two hours after parachuting to earth. There were many dead Italians sprawled about the fortification, as well as one American paratrooper.

Follmer and his aide moved over to the 82nd Airborne man and saw that he had been shot in the back. Suddenly the captain called out, "Look, he's breathing! He's still alive!" Ashen-faced and his jump suit saturated with blood, the wounded trooper had been lying among the dead Italian soldiers for more than 60 hours.

Shortly afterward a jeep flying a Red Cross flag happened by, and two medics hopped out, tenderly placed the seriously wounded parachutist on a stretcher across the vehicle, and sped off toward an aid station.

Meanwhile that day, a somber Field Marshal Kesselring, Wehrmacht commander in the Mediterranean, flew back to Rome after a conference with General Guzzoni at Enna, headquarters for the Axis Sixth Army in Sicily. All the news from Guzzoni was pessimistic, and the customarily buoyant Kesselring was depressed.

On reaching the Eternal City, Kesselring called on the head of the Italian state, the strutting, bombastic Benito Mussolini. The premier had long expressed the opinion that Sicily could be held against an Allied invasion. Mussolini was visibly shocked to be told bluntly by Kesselring that the island was as good as lost.

The stocky dictator was frozen in silence for a brief period on hearing this totally unexpected news. Then he beat his chest and bellowed, "The occupation of Italy . . . it must not be allowed!" Mussolini now saw the handwriting on the wall. An invasion of mainland Italy would follow an Allied victory in Sicily. Mussolini, in power for 22 years, knew that his days were numbered.

Early that morning of July 12, Col. James Gavin, leader of the 505th Regimental Combat Team, was awakened by the hot rays of the sun beating down on his face as he lay in a shallow foxhole at Biazza Ridge. After he and his men had driven the Hermann Goering Division *kampfgruppe* from the battlefield of the previous day and evening, Gavin moved his CP into a clump of olive trees, climbed wearily into a foxhole, and immediately fell into an exhausted sleep.

Pulling himself sleepily out of the hole, the colonel felt an odd sensation in one leg—it was stiff and extremely sore. He lifted a trouser leg and saw that his shinbone was swollen and red. For the first time Gavin noticed that the material had been torn directly in front of his injury.

Fearing an infection that might remove him from the fight in Sicily, the colonel went to a nearby aid station where sulfa powder was poured on his wound. On the way back to his CP, Gavin concluded that he had been struck by a mortar or artillery shell fragment during the savage fight on Biazza Ridge the day before. Due to the intensity of the struggle and his deep involvement in directing his paratroopers, Gavin had fought for hours and then had fallen into a deep sleep without realizing that he had been wounded.

Later that morning the colonel received orders not to proceed past the Acate River, four miles west of Biazza Ridge. Despite his painful leg wound, Gavin led a small patrol westward as far as the Acate. There he waited for the rest of his troopers who fought at the ridge to catch up with him.

At 8:45 A.M. on July 12, Ponte Olivo airfield, a key facility just west of the high ground at Piano Lupo, was seized by elements of the 1st Infantry Division. Lt. Col. Harold Rippert, leader of the 16th Infantry Regiment, set up his CP in the Italian officers' mess. So rapid had been the flight of the enemy from the airfield that glasses of wine were found in the mess hall which had been filled but abandoned before being consumed.

Shortly after Ponte Olivo was captured, the parachuting war reporter, Beaver Thompson, entered a press facility near Gela. Thompson, who had jumped with the spearheading 505th Regimental Combat Team, was desperate to find a means for sending his eyewitness stories back to the *Chicago Tribune.* He had to return to North Africa with all possible speed.

A soldier at the Gela press facility said to Thompson, "Have you heard? We just took Ponte Olivo. The first American plane is about ready to land there."

"If a plane is coming in, there must be one going out," the bearded correspondent reasoned. He caught a ride to the airfield just in time to see a C-47 glide in for a landing. After touching down, the propellers remained twirling, so Thompson knew that the pilot planned to take off again soon.

Thompson, still in pain from three cracked ribs, a wrenched knee, and gashes in his leg and hand received when he parachuted in the heavy gale, rushed to the C-47 and shouted above the roar of the idling engine, "Where are you heading?"

"Back to North Africa," replied the young Air Corps colonel at the controls.

"Great. Can I go with you?"

"Hop aboard. We can use some company."

Once in the air, the pilot told the reporter that he had flown Colonel Gavin's plane to Sicily the night of the initial parachute strike and recognized Beaver Thompson as one of those aboard.

"How did everything go?" the Air Corps colonel asked cheerfully. "Did we drop you people right on the button?"

"Right on the button, hell!" a forthright Thompson replied evenly. "You dropped us 25 miles from the DZ."

A startled look flushed the pilot's face. "Impossible!" he shot back.

"Maybe it's impossible, but that's what happened," Thompson countered.

The young Air Corps colonel was crestfallen. Moments later he said in a low voice, "Our pilots have been clapping each other on the back for nearly three days for dropping the 505th right on target!" His voice trailed off. He rode the rest of the way to North Africa in stunned silence.

Thompson felt compassion for the Air Corps colonel and his C-47 pilots. They had been handed a complicated mission for which they had neither the training nor the navigational technology to fulfill. In addition, the flight was at night in one of the most intense gales the Mediterranean region had been battered with in months.

At his headquarters outside Gela near dusk on July 12, Gen. George Patton, commander of the invading U.S. Seventh Army, was evaluating the current battlefield situation. He liked what he saw on the situation map. Seventh Army held the key airfields at Ponte Olivo, Comiso and Biscari, and forward ground elements were nearing the final phase line for the beachhead some 20 miles inland.

It was nearing midnight that same day as the beleaguered Gen. Alfredo Guzzoni, commander of Sixth Army, was at his desk in the ancient walled city of Enna, in central Sicily. Off in the distance could be heard the faint purring of airplane engines, not an uncommon sound over the island in recent weeks. The engine noise became louder, turned into a roar, and moments later clusters of bombs were cascading onto Guzzoni's headquarters.

A crescendo of loud explosions tore the fabric of night as bombers of the Northwest African Air Force found their target. Guzzoni's headquarters was in a shambles, and the Sixth Army commander narrowly averted being killed.

The bombing attack left the Italian general, not lacking in personal courage, shaken. It seemed to him to typify the futility of trying to halt the Allied invasion avalanche with the means at his disposal. Distraught and frustrated, an incoherent Guzzoni told aides it was unfortunate that one of the bombs did not land on him so that he could have shared the fate of his men on Sicily.

With the arrival of dawn, General Guzzoni regained his customary verve. But now he could clearly view the situation in Sicily: he knew it was no longer possible to drive Anglo-Americans off the island and that now his forces had to develop tactics of attrition and delay.

Meanwhile, on the morning of July 12, Lt. Col. William Yarborough, commander of the 2nd Battalion of Reuben Tucker's ill-fated 504th Parachute Regimental Combat Team, was marching at a brisk pace across the bleak Sicilian countryside. Yarborough and his stick had jumped far inland during the night to escape the "friendly" gunfire that had devastated Colonel Tucker's armada.

After bailing out and crashing into the concrete-hard ground, Yarborough and his men heard the pealing of church bells nearby. Peering intently through the darkness, the troopers could discern the outline of an ancient walled city just to their front. The church bells, ringing as an antiparatrooper warning, were inside the walls.

Yarborough and most of his stick assembled in the shadows of an olive grove. Six officers and eight enlisted men were accounted for, but two troopers were missing. A hurried council of war was held and a firm conclusion reached: they were lost, surrounded by the foreboding blackness of Sicily. They did know that they were deep behind enemy lines and to reach the landing beaches without being killed or captured would require a great deal of good fortune.

As Colonel Yarborough prepared to move out into the night at the head of his knot of paratroopers, he became aware for the first time that a few of his men were badly wounded, having been hit by shell fragments or bullets before they jumped.

Before departing on a perilous trek cross-country toward the landing beaches, many miles to the south, Colonel Yarborough and his men, gathered under the clump of olive trees, took a solemn vow: "We will not be taken prisoner but, if necessary, will fight to the death."

Early in the afternoon the 504s, perspiring, weary and thirsty, arrived at a farmhouse where a grizzled Sicilian farmer drew water from a well for each man. Colonel Yarborough reached into his pocket and fished out a gold piece. The Sicilian was indignant.

"You Americans came a long way to free me, and I won't take any of your money just for giving you a drink of water," the native protested through an Italian-speaking paratrooper.

After marching for two days and nights, subsisting largely on watermelon and olives, thirsty, foot weary and exhausted, Colonel Yarborough, Lt. John O'Malley, Lt. Louis Fern and the other members of the stick reached the top of a hill where a joyful sight greeted their eyes: the Mediterranean Sea and a coastal road running along its shoreline.

Early elation was tempered by the knowledge that the parachutists did not know what sector of the Mediterranean they had reached. Were the Allies or the Germans in control of this area?

"We can't go on any longer like this," Colonel Yarborough told his men. "We're going to go down to that road in front of us, set up an ambush, and grab the first goddamned vehicle that comes along."

With Yarborough in the lead, the parachutists stealthily slipped down to the coastal road and took up positions in the ditches along both sides.

They had been concealed for only a few minutes when they heard a distant sound: the purr of an approaching vehicle's motor.

The troopers, tightly gripping their weapons, anxiously waited as the hum of the motor became louder and louder. As the vehicle was almost upon them, Yarborough and several other troopers leaped from the ditches and leveled rifles and tommy guns at the two startled occupants.

As the vehicle lurched to a halt, Yarborough lowered his weapon and gave out a sigh of relief. The passenger was an old friend from West Point days, Lt. Col. Chuck Billingslea, who had dropped with Colonel Gavin's 505th Regimental Combat Team as an observer.

Billingslea showed little surprise or emotion on suddenly being confronted by an old friend and a band of paratroopers with weapons pointed at him. "Where in the hell have you been all this time?" Billingslea asked in a matter-of-fact tone.

Yarborough did not respond. He was delighted to be back among his own.

Early on the morning of July 13, Col. James Gavin climbed into a jeep at the assembly area of his parachute force at the Acate River and headed for the airborne objective known as the Y, the complex of concrete fortifications at a road junction south of Niscemi which Captain Ed Sayre and a small band of troopers had captured two days previously. Gavin, on reaching the Y, turned north and drove to the high ground of Piano Lupo.

There the colonel dismounted and walked over the battlefield where Lieutenant Colonel Gorham, Captain Sayre and others of Gavin's troopers had thwarted the western column of the Hermann Goering Panzer Fallschirmjaeger Division. It was not a pleasant sight that unfolded before Colonel Gavin's eyes, but one that brought a lump to his throat and a sickening sensation to the pit of his stomach.

Sprawled about the barren terrain, where they had refused to give an inch to onrushing German tanks, were the bloated bodies of many of Gavin's young paratroopers. They lay where they fell, grotesquely twisted in death. Tiny gas bubbles oozed from hideous, bloody wounds. Thick swarms of Mediterranean flies hovered over the lifeless bodies. Some corpses had turned purple from the unyielding rays of the sun.

Colonel Gavin, laboring mightily to conceal his emotions, turned and headed back to his jeep. In a voice he hoped would not betray his inner feeling, the parachute leader said to his driver, "Head for Gela."

On high ground outside Gela, the 505th Parachute Regiment commander spotted the imposing figure of Gen. George Patton silhouetted against the cloudless blue sky and gazing out over the beehive of activity in the harbor.

Patton was a portrait of sartorial elegance. Three oversized silver stars on his helmet glistened in the bright sunlight, and shirt and riding breeches were immaculate and neatly pressed. Knee-high boots were polished to a gleaming gloss, as befitting an old cavalryman, and on each hip was an ivory-handled revolver.

Gavin halted nearby and, with Garand rifle in hand, approached the Seventh Army commander. Seeing the parachute leader, General Patton's face broke out in a wide grin. "Hello, Gavin," he said in his high-pitched voice. "You and your men did one hell of a goddamned great job!"

Reaching into his back pocket, the tall, silver-haired, ramrod-straight general whipped out a large flask and held it before Gavin. "You look like you could use a drink—here, have one," Patton said.

Gavin, flattered by the praise from a highly regarded battle commander 22 years and 3 grades his senior, reached out for the whiskey flask and took a long drink. Not to take a healthy gulp might appear unappreciative to the ebullient Patton, the parachute colonel thought.

Slim Jim handed the flask back to the general. This dramatic occasion called for more than a simple thank you, Gavin quickly concluded. The young colonel, standing on the breeze-swept hill with the leader of U.S. ground forces in Sicily, launched into a short speech, the thrust being that it was a high honor for Gavin to be drinking out of the same flask with one of history's greatest generals.

CHAPTER THIRTEEN

ATTACK ON PRIMOSOLE BRIDGE

A t several airfields in the vicinity of Rome, 1,817 tough young German *fallschirmjaeger* (paratroopers) were strapping on parachute harnesses as they prepared to board scores of black Junkers transport planes. It was 7 P.M. on July 13, the fourth day since the Anglo-Americans had set foot on Adolf Hitler's Europe.

These members of the elite 1st Parachute Division, wearing their distinctive round steel helmets with cushioned lining designed to absorb heavy blows on landing, gave hurried last-minute inspections to their Schmeisser automatic pistols, MG-42 machine guns and bolt-action rifles. Then they checked them yet again.

The Wehrmacht parachutists, perspiring heavily, waited nervously for the shouted order to get aboard the Junkers. Faces were grim. Jaws set. Eyes narrowed to slits. There was little conversation.

The mission of the German parachute force was to drop behind the lines of Oberst (Colonel) Wilhelm Schmalz's *panzergruppe* (armored group) which was dug in along the Simeto River on the east coast of Sicily, seeking to block the northward drive of Gen. Bernard Montgomery's British Eighth Army toward the key port of Messina. There the *fallschirmjaeger* were to assemble and reinforce Schmalz's already strong defensive line at the southern edge of the Catania plain.

Colonel Schmalz had been ordered by Field Marshal Kesselring to hold the Simeto River line at all costs. A tough, aggressive battle commander, Schmalz intended to do just that.

The reinforcing drop by elements of the 1st Parachute Division was considered by General der Flieger Kurt Student, the "father" of the German airborne service, as a timid move which would have only minimal impact upon the battle situation in Sicily. Two days before, General Student had proposed to Adolph Hitler that both of his airborne divisions be dropped almost onto the Allied seaborne forces as a bold stroke to throw the Anglo-Americans into panic before they became fully established on shore.

General Student was convinced this daring parachute strike would result in the Allies being driven back into the sea, with the help of Axis forces already in Sicily. Hitler listened but was not impressed. The fuehrer was still haunted by the Wehrmacht's parachute and glider attack on the large island of Crete in 1941 when one of four airborne soldiers was killed and nearly half the invading force became casualties, even though the island was wrested from its British defenders.

Student's bold plan to drop both of his divisions onto the seaborne Anglo-Americans was summarily rejected by Hitler. But he approved the employment of a brigade of parachutists to drop behind German lines in Sicily to reinforce the hard-pressed Wehrmacht ground forces.

Now, on the airfields around Rome, shouts rang out: *"Los! Macht das Ihr rein kommt!"* ("Hurry! Get on the planes right now!") Burdened by their heavy combat gear, the German paratroopers waddled to the Junkers troop carriers and climbed on board. Powerful motors revved up, the aircraft spun down runways and lifted off. Rendezvousing over Rome, the Luftwaffe armada of over 100 aircraft set a course for the drop zone south of Catania.

At the same time General Student's German paratroopers were boarding Junkers aircraft around Rome, members of Brig. Gerald Lathbury's British 1st Parachute Brigade were gathered at scattered airfields around Kairouan, Tunisia, preparing to launch Operation Fustian. A total of 1,836 Red Devil paratroopers and 77 gliderborne artillerymen had the mission of dropping and landing seven miles south of Catania to seize and hold the key Primosole bridge in front of the advancing British Eighth Army.

Carrying the British Red Devils into combat would be 135 aircraft, including 105 American C-47s of the 51st Troop Carrier Wing and 11 Albemarles of the Royal Air Force. Two hours after Red Devil paratroopers seized landing zones near Primosole bridge (known to natives as the Sunrise bridge), 11 British Horsa gliders and 8 smaller American Wacos would touch down with the artillerymen and 10 antitank guns.

A short distance to the south of Primosole bridge, the north-south coastal road crossed a smaller river over the Malati bridge. A force of British commandos was to land by sea, move overland under the protective cloak of night, and capture the Malati bridge. With both river spans in friendly hands, Montgomery's 50th Division could pour across and rush northward to seize Catania.

At 7:20 P.M. the first of the Allied troop carrier planes, crammed with grim-faced Red Devils, roared down the runway and lifted into space. One by one, other aircraft followed. Brigadier Lathbury's Parachute Brigade rendezvoused over Tunisia and set a course eastward to Malta, where it would make a sharp turn to the northeast for the final dash to drop zones around Primosole bridge.

As had been forecast, the weather was clear and the wind calm, in direct contrast to climatic conditions four nights previously when parachute elements of the U.S. 82nd Airborne Division and glider forces of the British 1st Air Landing Brigade had been buffeted about in 40-mile-per-hour gales. Down below, the Mediterranean Sea was tranquil, even beautiful, in its clear blue shadings. The first hour of the flight was uneventful.

Yet, had some omnipotent being been hovering over the central Mediterranean region at that moment, he would have observed one of the strangest phenomena of the war—or any war. A force of German paratroopers, flying from Rome, and a brigade of British parachutists, taking off from Tunisia, unknown to each other were winging through the dark skies bound for bail-outs on the *identical* drop zone in Sicily.

By the time the Fustian flight reached Malta, a half-moon beamed through a delicate summer haze, permitting navigators easily to spot the glowing beacon signal on the tiny island. Five miles southeast of Delmara Point on Malta, the flight of Red Devils turned toward the northeast for the final run to Primosole bridge.

Mindful of the two disasters in recent nights when friendly fire raked American and British airborne flights, planners for Operation Fustian had set a course that would be devoid of Allied ships and keep the air armada 10 miles off the east coast of Sicily until it was time to turn sharply inland at the mouth of the Simeto River.

As an additional safeguard to assure that the lumbering, low-flying

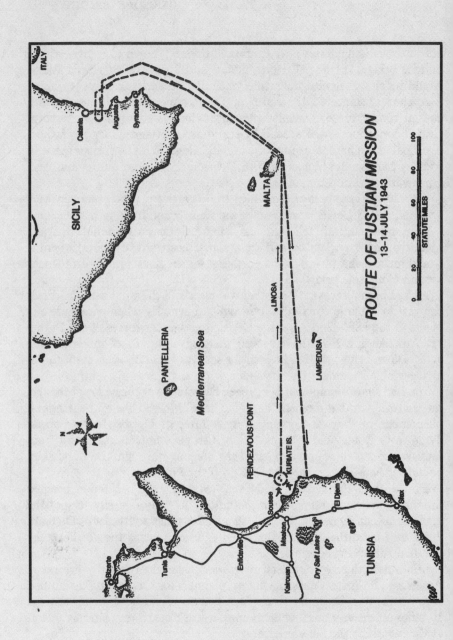

ROUTE OF FUSTIAN MISSION
13–14 JULY 1943

C-47s and Albemarles would not be fired on by nervous Allied gunners, British naval commanders had been notified of the course and time of the Fustian flight and they, in turn, had alerted all Allied vessels in the area of southeast Sicily.

A short distance north of Malta, air crews and Red Devils were startled to discover that they were flying over a convoy of ships knifing through the water toward Sicily. How could this happen? they thought. There were to be no Allied vessels along the flight route. The answer was simple: the flight was far off course.

Deep concern in the dim cabins of the troop carriers turned to alarm as out of the darkness below streams of angry tracer bullets sought out the slow-moving aircraft. There were the sharp reports of antiaircraft shells exploding violently just outside, rocking the airplanes and sending tremors of fear through the occupants. Just as suddenly as the Allied ships had commenced firing, the guns fell silent. Red Devils and air crews breathed loud sighs of relief, hopeful that the friendly fire was an isolated incident triggered by a nervous gunner and would not occur again. The flight burrowed on through the Mediterranean night.

Unknown to the men in the sky armada, more than one Allied gunner on the vessels down below were nervous. Most of them were. Navy and merchant ships off southeast Sicily had just been pounded by Luftwaffe bombers, and as the Fustian flight passed overhead, naval gunners were manning their weapons and anxiously awaiting another German bombing raid. Lookouts on the vessels had been warned to keep a close watch for enemy torpedo bombers. Many did not know what a torpedo bomber looked like.

Nearing a point just southeast of Cape Passero, at the tip of Sicily, the off-course Red Devil flight approached an Allied convoy. Peering up through the moonlit haze, gunners on the vessels could discern the silhouettes of equipment cargo racks under the transport planes which, to many of them, looked like torpedoes under the wings of Luftwaffe bombers. Contrary to instructions, some ships opened fire on their own initiative at the low-flying aircraft which were furiously blinking recognition signal lights and dropping flares.

As if on signal, other ships joined in blasting away at the paratrooper sky train, convinced that the convoy was under attack from the air. Nervous or not, the ship gunners were accurate, although they could hardly miss the lumbering, bulky targets with the blinking lights passing only a few hundred feet overhead. Two C-47s were struck immediately, veered crazily and plunged into the sea, taking all on board to a watery grave.

Two other C-47s began taking frantic evasive action and collided. In a fiery, twisted mass of wreckage, the pair of entangled aircraft and their occupants fell swiftly to the Mediterranean and disappeared from sight. In nine other troop carriers, Red Devils and air crews were riddled by gunfire, leaving many wounded sprawled about the dark, cramped interiors. These nine aircraft, badly damaged and able to continue to fly only through the intense effort and skill of the pilots, turned and limped back to home bases in Tunisia. Six other C-4s without appreciable damage banked away from the curtain of fire and returned to North Africa with all paratroopers still aboard.

The remaining troop carriers pushed on through the intense friendly fire and reached the southeast coast of Sicily, where enemy gunners resumed the barrage of antiaircraft shells and withering fusillades from automatic weapons. Nine paratroop-laden transport planes, lacking armor or self-sealing fuel tanks, were hit and crashed to earth in flames. All had made a partial drop of Red Devils, and four managed to limp out to sea where they crash-landed, and surviving air crew and paratroopers were rescued by passing ships.

Nine out of 10 aircraft flew through the barrage, hugging the ground so closely that tree branches were knocked off and a number of haystacks were sliced in two, leaving straw draped across the windshields. A large number of pilots, dispersed and forced to take violent evasive action by friendly and Axis gunfire, ranged up and down the coastline, seeking a way through the intensive flak barrage. Ten more troop carriers turned and headed back to North Africa with their Red Devils on board; they had just enough fuel remaining to make it to Tunisia.

One C-47, searching up and down the coastline for an opening through the heavy gunfire, was struck by a shell and began to wobble, nearly out of control. The aircrew began to hastily get out a rubber dinghy. The young pilot, a major, circled once again and shouted back, "Put that damned dinghy away. We're going through this time no matter what happens."

The major knifed over the coastline at only 100 feet as machine gun fire and antiaircraft flak sought out the C-47. The plane was pitching and shuddering but pressed onward. Now the aircraft was caught in the ominous glare of an enemy searchlight which clung to the C-47 as the major climbed above 400 feet, throttled back the engine to slow down, and flashed on the green light. The entire stick of Red Devils bailed out. The Air Corps major was not seen again.

The dispersion caused by the intense Axis antiaircraft fire resulted in some troop carriers wandering as far north as Messina, at the northeast tip of Sicily, and as far south as Malta, 80 miles away, in efforts to avoid the flak and locate the drop zones. Four sticks floated to earth on the lower slopes of towering Mount Etna, 22 miles to the north of Primosole bridge, but 39 planeloads came down within a mile of their drop zones.

As the C-47s made 180-degree turns and headed back to North Africa on nearly the same route as that flown to the drop zones, a few were fired on again by Allied ships just off the southern coastline.

Meanwhile, elements of the German 1st Parachute Division, which had taken off from Rome two hours previously, jumped on a drop zone behind the lines of Col. Wilhelm Schmalz's armored battle group. There was the customary confusion of a night drop, and the calm summer air was pierced by the shouts of parachute commanders calling out orders. A rapid assembly was important as the *fallschirmjaeger* were to be into the front lines by dawn.

While trying to locate their units in the darkness, the German paratroopers heard the oncoming roar of a large number of airplanes and, peering upward, were startled to see scores of white parachutes billowing under the dark silhouettes of airplanes. Red Devil paratroopers were jumping almost upon the heads of the German parachutists in the process of assembling.

Confusion was compounded in German ranks over the unexpected appearance of many parachutists floating to earth. The Germans on the ground did not know whether to open fire on the descending chutists as the newcomers might be Wehrmacht reinforcements.

As soon as the Red Devils touched ground, a violent series of chaotic firefights erupted. Neither adversary had been expecting to confront the other. Adding to the confusion were the virtually identical steel helmets worn by the German and British paratroopers which made it impossible to tell friend from foe.

The hand-to-hand battle raged in the blackness. Geometric patterns of white and red tracers laced the sky, and the sharp explosions of hand grenades punctuated the sound and fury. Here and there two shadowy figures grappled to the death in the darkness, followed by loud grunts as a trench knife found its mark in a neck or stomach.

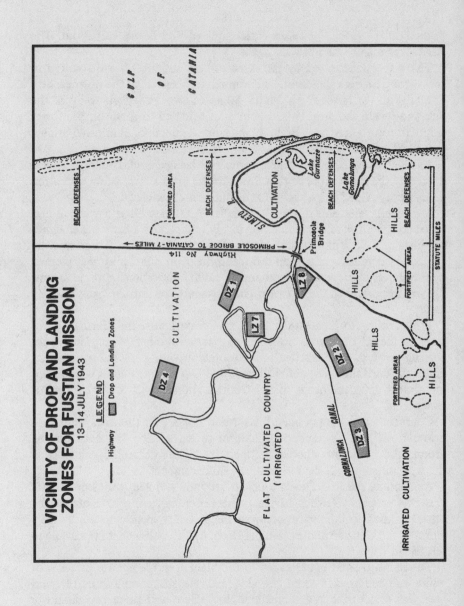

VICINITY OF DROP AND LANDING ZONES FOR FUSTIAN MISSION
13–14 JULY 1943

LEGEND

— Highway

■ Drop and Landing Zones

GULF

OF

CATANIA

BEACH DEFENSES

FORTIFIED AREA

BEACH DEFENSES

SIMETO

CULTIVATION

Lake Gurrauze

Lake Gomolonga

BEACH DEFENSES

HILLS

BEACH DEFENSES

Primosole Bridge

PRIMOSOLE BRIDGE TO CATANIA–7 MILES

Highway No 114

DZ 1

LZ 8

CULTIVATION

HILLS

FORTIFIED AREAS

STATUTE MILES

LZ 7

DZ 4

DZ 2

HILLS

FLAT CULTIVATED COUNTRY
(IRRIGATED)

GORNALUNGA CANAL

DZ 3

FORTIFIED AREAS

HILLS

IRRIGATED CULTIVATION

A Red Devil was cautiously slipping across a field, Sten gun in hand and alert for any sign of an enemy which might mean sudden death. He was glad to have a comrade walking alongside him in the darkness, particularly in the mass confusion. Curious as to his fellow parachutist's unit, he was about to speak when the other asked, *"Hast du meinen Schmeisser gesehen?"* ("Have you found my automatic pistol?")

Startled to learn that he had been walking along with a German soldier, the Red Devil whipped his Sten gun around and squeezed off a burst at his "comrade."

As the furious struggle raged between British and German paratroopers, the glider flight that was to reinforce Brigadier Lathbury's 1st Parachute Brigade with antitank guns and jeeps was approaching the southeast coast of Sicily. The glider force of 77 Red Devil artillerymen had lifted off two hours after Lathbury's men to give the parachutists time to clear landing zones.

Nearing the shoreline, the tug planes and gliders came under intense fire from Axis batteries on land. One glider released early and crashed into the sea with pilots and Red Devils still aboard. Four gliders were shot down and plunged to earth with their occupants. But other tug-and-glider combinations pressed through the hail of fire to reach the landing zones, where the gliders were cut loose and began their descent to earth.

One glider, riddled by machine gun bullets and flak, crashed into the Simeto River, killing or wounding all but one Red Devil. He climbed out of the wreckage, retrieved his weapon, and headed off into the darkness toward Primosole bridge.

A motorless craft crashed into the river bank and, with a rending of twisted metal and ripping of fabric, broke in two. The rear half of the glider sank out of sight in the Simeto, trapping several Red Devils in it. The pilot had been tossed through the windshield of the cockpit and landed 30 feet away on the embankment. His face was a mask of blood, having been slashed by the glass. Other bleeding and mangled glidermen had pulled themselves out of the wreckage and onto the embankment.

Two British parachutists nearby rushed to the site, but there was nothing they could do for the glider pilots and artillerymen. One paratrooper whispered to his comrade, "I'm bloody well glad I got here by parachute and not in one of those bloody gliders!"

Only four Horsa gliders crash-landed close enough to Primosole bridge for their Red Devils and antitank guns to join in the struggle for the river span, but elsewhere over a wide area glider artillerymen were rushing for the bridge as fast as circumstances permitted. Most gliders after grinding to halts were twisted wreckages, so Red Devils had a difficult time getting their antitank guns and jeeps out of the craft. Often this had to be done while under enemy machine gun fire.

In the meantime, a small band of British paratroopers had reached Primosole bridge, quickly driven off an Italian force guarding it, and ripped out explosives from beneath the span. At 2:30 A.M. the bridge had been secured. During the night, other Red Devils reached the Simeto River crossing, and at dawn 240 parachutists and glidermen, under Maj. R. T. H. Lonsdale, were deployed and awaiting the certain counterattack to seize back the vital bridge.

Lonsdale knew his hodgepodge collection of airborne men would be hard pressed to hold the bridge in the face of a full enemy attack supported by tanks and artillery. His 240 men were armed only with personal weapons, two mortars and three antitank guns. There were only a few shells for the mortars and antitank guns.

The Red Devils did not have to wait long for the enemy's appearance. At 6:30 A.M., officers, peering into the distance through binoculars, saw a long convoy of enemy trucks grind to a halt about two miles away on the plain of Catania. Out of the beds jumped several hundred German soldiers, who quicky deployed into a skirmish line and began advancing across the flat ground toward Major Lonsdale's force at Primosole bridge. Several armored cars supported the attacking grenadiers.

Now deadly accurate artillery fire began pounding the Red Devils, and a few glider pilots dug in along the north and south banks of the Simeto River. Even before the German infantrymen reached rifle range, British ranks were dwindling as the heavy artillery fire repeatedly found victims.

Moving steadily forward, the German force was 200 yards away when it began pouring rifle and automatic weapons fire into the British airborne men at the bridge. Outnumbered and outgunned, the Red Devil survivors on the north bank, forced to leave many wounded behind, swam the river and took up defensive positions on the south bank.

Nearly out of ammunition, ranks decimated by enemy fire, physically exhausted, and raked continually with automatic weapons and rifle fire, the handful of airborne men remaining were ordered to fall back to the lower slopes of a nearby hill mass. The oncoming Germans then took over the key Primosole bridge.

As the battered band of Red Devils awaited the final onslaught of the enemy force, a helping hand was received from a totally unexpected source —the British navy. A cruiser offshore began pumping shells toward the bridge. The airborne men heard the swishing sound of a cluster of projectiles overhead and saw the huge shells explode in fiery balls in the center of German positions around Primosole bridge. The ground where the enemy paratroopers and grenadiers had assembled erupted into a sheet of flame, and German bodies were tossed upward before plunging back to earth like limp rag dolls.

Salvo after salvo of six-inch shells pounded the enemy force at the bridge as the thin line of embattled Red Devils broke out in rousing cheers. Now another unexpected development resulted in still more cheering: several British tanks rolled into view and began raking the Germans at the bridge with direct cannon fire.

Confronted with the overwhelming firepower of the unseen British cruiser offshore and the guns of the newly arrived tanks, the surviving Germans at Primosole bridge pulled back in disorder, and by the dark the crucial river span was back in British hands.

During the time the Red Devils had first seized Primosole bridge, a few hours after parachuting into Sicily, a detachment of British commandos stole ashore at Agnone, near the mouth of the Simeto River. The commandos hurried across country in the darkness to their objective, the small Malati bridge. They found it to be lightly defended and drove off the enemy force. Several explosive charges on the bridge were located, ripped out and dropped into the water.

Two hours later, at 5:45 A.M., a strong Italian force that had been rushed to the site attacked the little band of lightly armed commandos and drove them from Malati bridge. Later, after the arrival of reinforcements, the commandos assaulted the river span and recaptured it in a bloody fight.

Back in Tunisia that morning, the U.S. Troop Carrier Command began adding up preliminary figures on the cost of seizing Primosole bridge. A total of 135 C-47s, with American pilots and crews, had taken off from Tunisia. Of that number, 11 were shot down with the loss of most Red Devils and air crews, 49 were severely damaged by friendly and enemy gunfire, with many on board killed or wounded, and 47 had bullet and shrapnel holes.

Not all the losses were in the sky. The battleground around the Primosole bridge was strewn with the bodies of fighting men—British, German and Italian.

CHAPTER FOURTEEN

CHARGE AT TUMMINELLO PASS

E arly on July 13, the man with the ultimate responsibility for Operation Husky, Gen. Dwight Eisenhower, boarded a British destroyer, the HMS *Petard,* at Malta. The supreme commander was anxious to get ashore in Sicily to see for himself conditions there. The *Petard* sailed along coastal waters of the island, only a short distance from the beaches, a locale in which several Allied vessels had been sunk by the Luftwaffe.

Despite the protest of aides, Eisenhower insisted on going ashore in the Canadian sector personally to congratulate the 1st Canadian Division under young, inexperienced Maj. Gen. Guy Simonds. The Canadians were seeing their first action, and Eisenhower wanted to welcome them into the Allied command.

Nearing the beach on a DUKW amphibious vehicle, the supreme commander's course took him past 100 Canadian soldiers frolicking in the surf during a brief respite from the front lines. Recognizing Eisenhower as he passed only a few yards away, the Canadians stood up in the water and gave the supreme commander a rousing and prolonged cheer.

Eisenhower acknowledged the acclamation with a wave of his hand and the broad, infectious smile for which he had become known throughout the Allied world.

Not far from where Eisenhower waded ashore through the surf, British Gen. Bernard Montgomery was being driven to the front in an open staff car on this stiflingly hot midsummer day. As he approached a slow-moving truck, the driver recognized Montgomery, leaned out of his vehicle with one foot on the running board, and made a sweeping, bowing gesture with the top hat he was wearing. Except for the hat, the British soldier was totally naked.

General Montgomery acknowledged the unorthodox salute with a wave and a smile.

The Eighth Army commander, whose troops in North Africa and now in Sicily had long been fighting in sweltering weather, had been tolerant of his men's combat attire. But that night, recalling the incident along the road with the truck driver, he issued his only directive of the war with regard to battle dress. It was short and to the point: "Top hats will not be worn in Eighth Army."

Now that Anglo-American forces were firmly established in Sicily, a directive for a coordinated offensive to drive the Axis off the island was handed down by Gen. Harold Alexander, the British commander of Fifteenth Army Group. Gen. Bernard Montgomery's battle-tested Eighth Army was to attack northward across the Catania plain and reach Messina, the escape port for Axis forces on Sicily in the northeast tip of the island. Gen. George Patton's largely inexperienced U.S. Seventh Army was to "clean up" the western two-thirds of Sicily.

Patton ordered his II Corps, commanded by Gen. Omar Bradley, to attack due north in the center of Sicily to reach the coast on the left of the British Eighth Army. To clean up the far western portion of the island, Patton hurriedly formed a provisional corps under Maj. Gen. Geoffrey Keyes. Elements in the provisional corps were the 82nd Airborne Division (less the 325th Glider Infantry Regiment and the attached 509th Parachute Infantry Battalion, both in reserve in Tunisia), the 3rd Infantry and 2nd Armored divisions, and two battalions of Lt. Col. William O. Darby's Rangers.

Spearheading the advance of the 82nd Airborne would be what was left of Col. Reuben Tucker's 504th Parachute Infantry Regiment. Alone and in small groups, 504s had been making their way to the regimental assembly area. Tucker had assembled three battalions and support troops of his command in the vicinity of Agrigento, west of Gela, and now was straining at the leash to attack.

On the morning of July 18, General Keyes's new provisional corps jumped off toward the northwest. The 504 paratroopers, unlike the armored and conventional infantry outfits in the corps who landed by sea with a large assortment of rolling stock, had principally their feet to move them forward. Tucker's men launched the attack with only three or four ancient Italian trucks to carry heavy equipment, ammunition and rations, but soon the available transportation began steadily to multiply.

As the men of the 504th plodded along the coastline, perspiring profusely in the scorching heat and burdened under the load of battle gear each had to carry, Sicilian farmers on the route became upset when their donkeys, horses, mules, carts, wheelbarrows, buggies and wagons began mysteriously to disappear. In the drab villages and towns, paratroopers "requisitioned" aged and battered motorcycles with solemn assurances to the protesting Sicilian owners that General Eisenhower himself would see to it that the cycle owners were compensated.

Soon the advancing columns of the 504th Parachute Infantry Regiment took on the appearance of a Gypsy caravan, so profuse in their ranks had assorted farm animals and conveyances become. But these nonauthorized additions could carry only the heaviest accoutrements of war. Mile after mile the marching parachutists wheezed along, oozing sweat and gasping for breath.

Armed resistance along the route was varied, usually depending upon the fighting spirit of local commanders. Most German units, including the elite Hermann Goering and 15th Panzer divisions, had been pulled back to the northeast to help defend the key port of Messina, as had been a number of mobile Italian divisions. Facing the advancing 82nd Airborne were principally static Italian coastal divisions that had, in effect, been abandoned by the Axis Sixth Army due to lack of transportation.

Morale in these static Italian divisions, never good, had hit rock bottom. Few members had ever been enthused over their roles as participants in "Mussolini's war." In the ranks were many Sicilians, whose primary ambition was to get out of the army and return to their humble farms and villages.

Often, as men of the 82nd Airborne approached an Italian position and prepared for a fight, the Americans were greeted with broad smiles and calls of *"Avete una cigaretta?"* ("Do you have a cigarette?") Some officers already had suitcases packed for the trek to a prisoner-of-war enclosure.

As the rapid-time march of American paratroopers across the island continued, floods of Italian prisoners became a major problem. Soon leading elements of 504s would merely point down the road to the rear, and ragtag groups of new Italian POWs marched off cheerfully into what they hoped would be a safe and relatively comfortable stint in confinement.

One group of Italian soldiers, natives of Sicily, protested with wounded feelings because the paratroopers would not take charge of them. "Get the hell out of here," an American told them. "Go home. Go anyplace. We've got a war to fight!"

On occasion, advancing paratroopers were fired on by an Italian garrison as "a matter of honor." Having satisfied that honor, white flags of surrender were lifted. But "honorable" shells and bullets were often lethal and took a toll among the airborne men.

At the point of the marching columns, Lt. Col. William Yarborough, commanding officer of the 2nd Battalion of the 504th Parachute Infantry, was climbing into a three-quarter-ton truck, one of the handful of regulation vehicles in the regiment. With Yarborough were a driver and an Italian-speaking trooper being taken along as an interpreter.

It was Yarborough's intention to reconnoiter ahead of his marching men. Driving off in a thick cloud of dust, the battalion commander and his two companions rolled on into the barren countryside. They saw no sign of the enemy, so periodically Yarborough would motion to the slightly apprehensive driver and say, "Keep going."

The truck passed over a low rise in the road, and the three Americans tensed. They had driven into the midst of about 100 Italian soldiers. The enemy force was as startled to suddenly be confronted by three armed American paratroopers as Yarborough and his men were to see the Italians.

Before the shocked driver could bring the truck to a halt, he had driven in among the enemy force, which quickly leveled automatic weapons and rifles at the unexpected intruders. Staring at the muzzles of scores of guns, the Americans were powerless to take action. There was only one course available to them—remain seated and motionless in the halted truck.

The leader of the Italian force promptly approached Colonel Yarborough and began excitedly talking and gesturing wildly with both hands. "All I can make out is that he's worried as hell about his honor," the Italian-speaking American said to Yarborough.

Knowing that the only way he and his two troopers, many miles in front of the main body of the 82nd Airborne, could escape from their dire predicament was to bluff their way out of it, the parachute colonel said to his interpreter, "Tell him that the entire 82nd Airborne Division—12,000 men—is right behind us and is moving up rapidly. Tell him that I demand he surrender his men promptly to us before there is much bloodshed."

Colonel Yarborough and his men knew that was only partially true. Elements of the 504th Parachute Infantry Regiment were moving forward but were many miles to the rear, and since they were traveling by foot, donkey cart and mule, it would be a considerable length of time before the main body of paratroopers reached the site.

Yarborough's surrender demand was relayed to the Italian commander. A startled look came over the enemy officer's face, and he launched into another long tirade and soon was wringing his hands, apparently in despair.

"What's he yapping about now?" Yarborough asked his interpreter.

"Can't make out most of it, he's talking so fast. But I believe it's his honor again."

"Tell him he can surrender with the highest honor," the colonel directed. "He's not surrendering to just us three but to the 12,000 American paratroopers with us."

A fleeting curious look flashed across the interpreter's face. What 12,000 American paratroopers? he was thinking.

The Italian officer silently mulled over the proposal. Then, with a sigh and a resigned wave of the arm, he said, "All right, I hereby surrender my men to the United States 82nd Airborne Division."

The American colonel and his two troopers labored to conceal their inner surge of relief. "It's the only sensible thing to do," Yarborough assured the distraught Italian.

Immediately taking charge of the highly delicate and potentially explosive situation, Colonel Yarborough, through his interpreter, ordered the 100 Italians to throw all pistols, automatic weapons and rifles into the bed of the three-quarter-ton truck. The enemy force promptly complied. Three heavy machine guns, set up nearby and ready for action, were ordered dismantled and the parts and ammunition scattered about.

With the Italian force disarmed, the three American paratroopers and their captives began the wait for the promised appearance of a large body of the 82nd Airborne Division. The minutes ticked by. Yarborough and his men periodically sneaked furtive glances up the road in the direction from which their fellow paratroopers would appear—if they appeared.

As time dragged by, the three Americans sensed that the Italians were growing increasingly surly. These were not Sicilian soldiers wanting only to get back to their farms, but men from northern Italy who were not certain that they wanted to spend the balance of the war in a POW camp.

"These bastards are starting to get mean," the interpreter whispered to Colonel Yarborough.

"What're they saying?"

"From what I can pick up, they think they've been 'had.' "

One hour passed. Then two hours. Then three. The Americans were growing increasingly apprehensive. "I think these Eyties are getting ready to jump us," the colonel whispered to his two companions.

Sullen mutterings among the Italians increased. The three paratroopers now withdrew from the center of their prisoners and set up a "defensive line" 30 yards away and, for the first time, unlimbered their weapons in the event the large number of Italians rushed them.

Now the situation evolved into a staring contest. The Americans gazed intently at their prisoners, and the Italians' eyes seldom left a fixed position on the paratroopers. As the sun began to disappear into the western horizon, one of the paratroopers half-shouted to the other two, "Look back there! Here come our guys!"

Off in the distance a company of 504s was marching steadily in the direction of the confrontation site. "Well, it's not 12,000 men, but they'll do!" a trooper observed with a sigh of relief, summing up the feelings of the three. As the company of paratroopers, exhausted from a 30-mile march that day arrived, Colonel Yarborough glanced in the direction of the Italian officer. The enemy's face was aglow with visible relief. He had surrendered with honor to the 82nd Airborne Division, not to three isolated paratroopers.

The Italian prisoners were taken in tow by a detail of All-Americans and marched to the rear. Colonel Yarborough and his men continued on their way.

Meanwhile, Gen. George Patton, commander of the U.S. Seventh Army, was meeting with reporters at his headquarters outside Gela. Always buoyant and optimistic, the sartorially splendid Patton was in fine fettle.

"We're kicking the Krauts' and Spaghetti Benders' asses all over Sicily," the audacious commander began. One hand rested on the ivory-handled revolver on his hip. "But don't sell the enemy short," Patton cautioned. "The Krauts are always tough, and the Italian troops, most of whom are

rom northern Italy, have often fought very desperately. To sell the enemy
short would be an injustice to the fighting spirit of our own men."

As the 82nd Airborne on Sicily continued its push to the northwest, Lt.
John O'Malley was trudging along near the head of a column of troopers,
foot weary and tired from constant marching and occasional fighting. He
was mindful that his posterior was sore. Two days previously an ME-109
fighter plane suddenly had swooped down and sent long bursts from its
flaming machine guns at the marching column of 504s.

Caught out in the open, the 504s made a frantic dash for the nearest
cover and landed pell-mell in cactus hedges that lined both sides of the
road. Yelps of pain rang out above the chatter of the Luftwaffe fighter's
guns. As the enemy aircraft gained elevation from its strafing run, banked
and fled for its home base, the paratroopers scrambled out of their cactus
beds. None was seriously injured, but faces were contorted with pain from
pricks of angry cactus needles.

Lieutenant O'Malley had landed on his posterior. For the previous two
days, at each rest stop O'Malley lowered his trousers and, to the accompa-
niment of a chorus of jibes from the troopers, proceeded to dig cactus
needles out of his buttocks.

Now, as dawn was breaking over the purple hills of Sicily, O'Malley and
the troopers were approaching a terrain feature identified on maps as Tumminello Pass. An eerielike ground fog shrouded the passage. High hills,
majestic in their early morning splendor, stood guard on each side of the
pass.

Suddenly the quiet that had hovered over the barren landscape was
shattered as an enemy .77-millimeter gun, concealed in the thick fog of
Tumminello Pass, began plastering the paratroopers with shells fired at
point-blank range. So close was the tormenting enemy gun that the sharp
crack of missiles exploding around them could be heard by the 504s before
the report of the muzzle blast reached their ears.

As the ambushed parachutists scrambled frantically for what little cover
was available on the barren flatlands, a heavy fusillade of automatic weapons and rifle fire poured into the ranks of the Americans from enemy
troops positioned in the hills to either side of the pass.

As soon as the firing erupted, Lieutenant O'Malley dashed behind a
large boulder and began firing his Garand rifle in the direction of the
unseen enemy. Pausing briefly, he glanced around to see that his comrades
had instinctively deployed into a defensive line, and a few were blasting

away at the yawning, fog-shrouded Tumminello Pass and the hills to either side.

Looking toward his right, O'Malley saw that his battalion commander, Lieutenant Colonel Yarborough, had taken cover behind a hefty-sized rock and was squeezing off rounds from his Garand at the concealed enemy force. New to combat and finding themselves suddenly ambushed, many troopers were not firing in the direction of the opposing positions.

Above the din of battle, Colonel Yarborough called out repeatedly along the line of parachutists, "Start firing! Let 'em have it! Fire away!" Soon each airborne man was blasting away in the direction of the enemy, which caused a noticeable reduction in the automatic weapons fire raking the paratroopers.

As the cacophony from the shoot-out echoed through the barren hills, Lieutenant O'Malley detected a muzzle flash from an enemy machine gun at the mouth of a cave in the face of the elevation alongside the pass. He kept peering at the cave to make certain of what he saw. Again the flash of gunfire from the mouth of the opening as angry bullets hissed into American positions.

The lieutenant reached into the bandoleer of .30-caliber AP (armor-piercing) bullets he had borrowed two days previously from an American tank unit—without the knowledge of the tankers. Taking careful aim, O'Malley fired a round of AP into the cave, then another, and a third and a fourth. He kept peppering away at the opening on the side of the hill until he finally expended his "borrowed" ammunition. His one-man war on the enemy machine gun nest was successful. Not another muzzle flash was seen from the cave.

Once Colonel Yarborough had galvanized all troopers into firing weapons, he ordered Lt. Hoss Drew to work his platoon around to the flank and attack the enemy force from that position. Pulling themselves along on their stomachs, with weapons cradled across arms, Drew and his troopers, under the protective curtain of fire from comrades, reached a point 100 yards to the side.

Yarborough, O'Malley and others lying down covering small arms fire heard Lieutenant Drew shout above the din of battle: "Fix bayonets! Fix bayonets!" It was a chilling order. Even tough paratroopers did not relish the thought of closing with a determined enemy at bayonet range. Soon the ominous clinking of razor-sharp bayonets being attached to the tip of rifle barrels drifted across the landscape.

Moments later Lieutenant Drew called out, "Charge!" His platoon scrambled to their feet, bayonets glistening in the sun, and began running toward enemy positions. As they dashed forward, most were shouting unintelligible words at the top of their voices.

The sight of American paratroopers charging their lines with the nasty-looking bayonets ready for action had a demoralizing impact on the enemy force arrayed around Tumminello Pass. Drew and his men were only half-way to the defile, its fog now dissipated by the sun's rays, when a white flag appeared among the rocky crevices where the opposing force was entrenched. Another white flag followed. And a third. Soon the entire enemy position was awash with white flags.

As the Americans held their fire but leveled their guns as a precautionary measure against treachery, scores of the enemy force began emerging from their places of concealment. The troopers were startled to see that they had been opposed by Italians. So intense had been the fighting that Colonel Yarborough and others thought they were facing customarily tenacious German troops.

The parachute colonel waved the remainder of his men forward to accept the surrender. Tired and hungry as his troopers were, following a 10-hour march and a fierce firefight, Yarborough ordered his men to dig in at the entrance to the pass in preparation for an expected counterattack.

As the troopers finished the task, a jeep was spotted far off in the distance, heading for Tumminello Pass from the direction Yarborough's men had recently advanced. Garbed in thick clouds of dust, the vehicle carried a driver and a passenger. It ground to a halt near the troopers' defensive line and out hopped Gen. Matthew Ridgway. Striding briskly toward Yarborough who had gone out to meet him, Ridgway, without preliminaries, asked sternly, "Yarborough, what in the hell is going on around here?"

"Sir, we ran into a pretty good-sized force of Eyties and had a hard scrap before we overran them," the battalion commander replied. "We had quite a few casualties."

Ridgway made no immediate response. Yarborough was irritated. He thought at least the 82nd Airborne commander could have had a few words of praise for the job his men had done after being ambushed.

The stern-faced general quickly glanced along the line of paratrooper foxholes. He reddened with anger. "Goddamn it, Colonel," Ridgway exploded, "what're you doing sitting here on your ass? Get on through that pass and dig in on the other side before the enemy pours in here and you have to capture the pass a second time!"

With that, the general turned on his heel, climbed back into the jeep, and sped off in the direction from which he had just arrived.

Now it was Yarborough's turn to get red-faced with resentment. Out of hearing of his men, he ranted and raved against the commanding general of his division. But an order was an order. Amidst an avalanche of curses and grumbling, the exhausted paratroopers put on their combat gear and trudged to the far side of Tumminello Pass where they again dug in.

As the ball of fire that was the Mediterranean sun began to sink, tranquillity reigned over Tumminello Pass. The expected enemy counterattack never materialized. Thirty-year-old Bill Yarborough, after a meal of sorts, rested on the rock-hard ground next to a large cactus bush and reflected upon his encounter with General Ridgway a few hours previously.

The battalion commander soon concluded that, in this instance, the airborne division's commanding general was tactically correct. Indeed his paratrooper force should have been moved promptly to the far side of the pass, Yarborough now realized.

"I've got a lot to learn yet about command," the parachute officer mused to himself. "But Ridgway still could have said a few words of praise for my men."

Moments later an exhausted Bill Yarborough fell asleep.

CHAPTER FIFTEEN

EXPEDITION IN A LEAKING FISHING BOAT

A s members of the 82nd Airborne Division were preparing to jump off for the grueling 150-mile march to help sweep the Axis out of western Sicily, the British warship HMS *Romney* was plowing through coastal waters just offshore from Pachino, at the southeast tip of the island. The ship was engaged in supporting General Bernard Montgomery's Eighth Army in its attack northward toward Messina. It was July 16.

Suddenly a lookout on the *Romney* shouted, "Something in the water out there! Looks like a man!" As others responded to the call, the lookout pointed to what appeared to be a floating corpse.

The ship's skipper ordered the craft steered alongside the object bobbing about in the swells, and the body was hauled aboard. The corpse was clothed in the garb of a U.S. paratrooper. An officer removed the man's dogtags and other identification and saw that he was Capt. Herbert G. Kaufman. It was also apparent that the parachutist had died from a jagged wound in the neck.

Navy Lt. W. E. Halbert, commanding officer of the *Romney,* ordered all personal possessions removed from Captain Kaufman's remains; then, in accordance with standard procedures in wartime deaths at sea, burial services were held on shipboard, and the American's body was committed to the deep.

This was the Captain Kaufman who had been jumpmaster for his C-47 when it approached the fireswept coast of Sicily at midnight on July 9. He had been standing in the door when hit by a shell fragment and tumbled out the opening. His aircraft had been over the sea at the time, and some of his stick, seeing the jumpmaster apparently bail out, followed him through the door, parachuted into the Mediterranean, and drowned.

Meanwhile, foot-weary troopers of the 82nd Airborne had pushed on until they reached St. Margherita, nearly 100 miles northwest of their jump-off line at Agrigento, where they were halted by General Patton. The green 2nd "Hell on Wheels" Armored Division under Maj. Gen. Hugh Gaffey, a component of the provisional corps, dashed northward and on July 22 slammed into the large coastal city of Palermo which fell like an overripe fruit.

Col. Rube Tucker's 504th Parachute Infantry headed north and seized Alcamo and Castellammare del Golfo, two good-sized cities west of Palermo in the northwest tip of the triangular-shaped island. Col. Jim Gavin's 505s were given the mission of capturing Trapani, located on the coast west of Alcamo, the last major town in western Sicily to be held by the Axis.

On July 24, two days after Palermo fell, Gavin's paratroopers were approaching the eastern outskirts of Trapani when they heard a familiar sound—the whine of incoming artillery rounds. As explosions rocked the ground around leading elements of the 505th Regiment, enemy troops positioned on a 2,500-foot-high mountain, which guarded the approaches to Trapani, sent a fusillade of automatic weapons and rifle fire into the ranks of the parachutists.

The 82nd Airborne men quickly dashed for cover and called in their own supporting artillery, which pounded the port of Trapani as well as Italian defenders on the towering mountain. The 505s, despite great fatigue from marching almost constantly for five days and nights, attacked both the heavily fortified mountain and the adjacent city of Trapani, and within a few hours had seized both places.

The All-Americans, although pounded periodically by Italian artillery for three hours, sustained only one casualty—a bazooka man received a burn while firing his weapon. Enemy infantry offered only token resistance.

When the commander of the Italian garrison in Trapani, Adm. Alberto Manfredi, his honor satisfied, surrendered the port to General Ridgway of the 82nd Airborne, 5,000 enemy soldiers were taken into captivity.

Trapani was the end of the line for the paratroopers in the cleanup of western Sicily. They had completed a speed march of 150 tortuous miles under a scorching sun, with occasional stiff enemy resistance, in only six days. They had crossed some of the most difficult terrain in Europe, and when they reached their objectives, many 82nd Airborne men had worn the soles of jump boots through to their feet.

As the two parachute regiments in western Sicily awaited new orders, Colonel Tucker's 504th Regiment, garrisoned in scattered towns around his headquarters, was plagued by an epidemic of cut telephone wires. These lines provided communication between elements of the division, so intelligence officers promptly stamped the damage as the work of trained and skilled German and Italian saboteurs.

Colonel Tucker ordered that details of paratroopers be secreted near telephone lines about the countryside with the mission of nabbing the saboteurs in the act. Pfc. James McNamara and his close friend, Pfc. Joseph Hart, were among the pairs assigned to the task.

McNamara and Hart secreted themselves in a grove of olive trees, and a few hours later two Sicilian men drove up in a donkey cart to a nearby telephone line. The Americans looked on as one of the men began to wind telephone wire over his arm. McNamara leaped from his hiding place and shouted in his best Italian, *"Alto!"* ("Halt!")

The frightened Sicilian broke out in a run, and McNamara fired shots over the fleeing man's head. Grinding to a halt, the native threw his arms into the air. The paratrooper approached the shabbily dressed peasant who was shaking violently, expecting to be shot on the spot. One look at the pitiful, quaking figure assured McNamara and Hart that this was not a trained, sinister saboteur but merely a poverty-stricken native pilfering a few yards of wire which he hoped to sell or barter.

The two troopers called regimental headquarters, and a warrant officer was sent to the site. Hart and McNamara gave the new arrival a quick rundown on the situation, and the warrant officer telephoned Colonel Tucker, reporting the apprehension of a "saboteur."

Now a large number of excited and worried Sicilians, men and women, had heard the commotion and gathered around. The warrant officer hung up the telephone and said to Hart and McNamara, "Colonel Tucker said to shoot the saboteur."

McNamara and Hart had no intention of shooting an unarmed native whose offense was one of petty theft. They were convinced Colonel Tucker did not fully understand the situation.

"If you want him shot, shoot him yourself," McNamara said to the warrant officer. "I'm sure as hell not going to do it."

The warrant officer pulled out his .45 Colt. Sensing what was about to occur, the Sicilian peasants who had gathered about began a loud chorus of weeping, wailing, screaming and hollering. At this crucial point the village priest happened by, and he vigorously protested the apparent imminent execution of the peasant who was caught stealing the telephone wire.

The Sicilian priest insisted on talking to the regimental Catholic chaplain. Soon Capt. Edwin J. Kozak was on the line from Colonel Tucker's headquarters. Father Kozak was held in high regard by troopers of the 82nd Airborne. A forceful man, Kozak had always spoken up to generals when he felt they were not acting in the best interests of the men in matters not related to combat operations.

"This is not a saboteur," the Sicilian priest explained to Captain Kozak. "He's just a poor, ignorant peasant who was taking some telephone wire. Now your men have been ordered to shoot him."

"Put the warrant officer on the line," Father Kozak rasped.

When the warrant officer picked up the receiver, the chaplain stated firmly, "Don't harm this Sicilian. Bring him in here promptly—alive!"

At regimental headquarters, Colonel Tucker took one look at the nondescript, quaking saboteur and canceled the order to shoot him. After receiving a stern warning, the Sicilian was quietly released.

Some 200 miles to the northeast, on the Italian mainland, Pvt. Bill Grisez, Pvt. John Rinkovsky, and a handful of other 82nd Airborne men were pacing like caged tigers behind the barbed wire of a German prisoner-of-war camp at Naples. Grisez and his comrades had parachuted into Sicily with Colonel Gavin's combat team, had landed directly among German troops in a fortified position, and after a short firefight were taken prisoner.

At the POW camp, the principal meal was barley soup which the hungry Americans consumed even though worms were occasionally detected wiggling in it. It was barley soup or nothing.

Having conquered the far western portion of mountainous Sicily, commanders in the 82nd Airborne Division discovered they had a major problem on their hands. As American forces advanced, Fascist government officials fled, leaving scores of occupied towns and their citizens existing in chaotic conditions. It was the practice for Allied Military Government (AMGOT) to follow in the wake of combat troops and administer occupied towns. But the sweep through western Sicily had been so rapid, AMGOT was left far behind—at Gela or Scoglitti or even North Africa.

This resulted in leaders of 82nd Airborne combat units having to substitute temporarily as governmental functionaries. One of these "instant mayors" was Lt. Col. William Yarborough, commander of the 2nd Battalion of the 504th Parachute Infantry, who had recently led his men in the bitter fight at Tumminello Pass. He took over as "mayor" of Alcamo, a role for which he had had no specific training but which he performed with typical American know-how and ingenuity.

As in other towns overrun by the 82nd Airborne, there were tremendous civil problems. Colonel Yarborough set the price of bread, adjudicated civil disputes, and performed other governmental functions for 10 days, which forestalled total anarchy. Overnight the parachute leader had become a combination mayor, judge, chief of police, goodwill ambassador and chaplain without portfolio.

While working in his office one day, Yarborough was puzzled on hearing a rumbling noise in the basement of the building. Taking two troopers along, he descended the steps to the lower level and discovered three anti-Fascists operating a small hand-fed press. The Sicilians turned white with fear. They were convinced that they were in serious trouble for printing their personal political views.

Colonel Yarborough's manner soon convinced them that they were not facing imprisonment, after which they began to talk freely. "All during the reign of Mussolini we have been turning out literature opposing him and his actions to keep the underground movement alive," a Sicilian stated. "We knew then we faced certain imprisonment or execution if detected."

Then the swarthy native asked Yarborough, somewhat timidly as if expecting a certain refusal, "Is it possible for us to continue?"

"Hell, yes," replied the American colonel. "In our country we have a free press and free speech. That is the heritage of free men. Now you have that privilege, too. Print any damned thing you want."

A few hours later the streets of Alcamo were flooded with a blitz of white leaflets produced by the three Sicilians in their basement. Walking through the town on official business, Colonel Yarborough was handed one of the leaflets by a native woman, her face flushed with excitement. The parachute leader's eye caught the large headline: VIVA AMERICANOS!

Later Yarborough received word that a Sicilian woman was in a prison at Castellammare after being found guilty by the Fascist government of political opposition and sentenced to 20 years without receiving a trial. The mayor was outraged.

"Get over to Castellammare pronto and tell whoever is in charge of that prison that I want this woman released, and released immediately," Yarborough instructed one of his officers. "And tell him if he does any foot-dragging on this, that I am personally coming after his ass!"

Two hours later the imprisoned woman was free again. She had never learned the nature of her "crime."

On the heels of a steady stream of reports on appalling conditions at area civilian prisons, Colonel Yarborough visited one to see for himself. An elderly jailer showed him records of a large number of inmates who had been charged by the Fascist government with "crimes against the state." Few had received trials.

"Won't you please speak a few words to these men?" the old jailer pleaded.

Taking an interpreter along, Yarborough entered the courtyard of the prison and was shocked by conditions there. They were even worse than he had been told. These political prisoners had been existing in putrid squalor, clothes in tattered rags, many with no shoes, all on the verge of starvation.

Faces pressed against bars and emaciated arms dangling through them, the hollow-eyed inmates stared at the American officer with a mixture of hope and fear. Yarborough struggled to keep the emotion and deep compassion he felt inside out of his voice as he began speaking, pausing periodically for the interpreter to translate his words.

"American justice has come to Sicily," the colonel began. "Each of you will have your case examined promptly by our officials. Those of you who were jailed solely on political charges will be freed, and those of you who were jailed for violation of criminal law will be given an early and fair trial."

There were several moments of total silence. Then, as though the Messiah had just returned to earth, cheers rocked the ancient jail, and tears ran down the craggy faces—tears of joy and hope.

Meanwhile, Col. Jim Gavin, who had led the initial parachute strike on Sicily, was at his command post at Trapani, going through a large stack of personal letters and official communications that had accumulated during the past two weeks. As with other All-Americans, Gavin had arrived at Trapani exhausted from his two-week ordeal of relentless marching and fighting. Along with the physical exertion and battle anxieties the colonel had shared with his men, he had been carrying the heavy burden of a commander responsible for the success of a crucial mission. After a shower, change of clothing and a few filling nutritional meals, he was again his normal buoyant self.

Official business taken care of, Gavin took pen in hand and wrote a letter to his preteen daughter Barbara back in Washington, D.C. The tone of the message subconsciously reflected the gnawing inner anguish that tore at his fiber over the loss of so many of "my boys," an invisible load the colonel had to endure alone:

> When this war ends, I think I would like to be a curate in an out-of-the way pastorate with nothing to do but care for the flowers and meditate on the wickedness of the world. I have had more than enough excitement and danger to do for a lifetime.

Shortly after the parachute elements and support troops of the 82nd Airborne Division completed cleaning up the far western portion of Sicily, the fact that supply lines for American forces had become overextended received the attention of Seventh Army headquarters. More than two weeks after the invasion, supplies were still coming ashore at the small port of Gela, which not only lacked the capacity to unload major tonnage but was some 150 miles from Seventh Army units in northwest Sicily.

Trapani, which had been captured by the 505th Parachute Infantry Regiment, had excellent harbor facilities and could serve as a crucially needed port. There was one major obstacle to its immediate use by Seventh Army: the tiny Egadi Islands, lying a few miles offshore from Trapani, were garrisoned by enemy troops. On the Egadis were several batteries of coast and field artillery which could play havoc with Allied shipping attempting to enter Trapani harbor.

The islands, named Levanzo, Marittimo and Favignana, had to be taken, so the U.S. Navy was mounting an amphibious operation for that purpose.

Learning of navy plans for seizure of the Egadis, two 82nd Airborne Division lieutenant colonels, Robert Wienecke and George Lynch, proposed to General Ridgway that the two officers sail to the Egadis and negotiate a peaceful surrender with the enemy commander. Wienecke and Lynch considered the mounting naval operation wasteful in time, manpower and ships.

Listening to the proposal, Ridgway responded, "Damned good idea. But I don't want you two to go. Let a junior officer take some men and do the job."

First Lt. Ivan F. Woods, a tall young Texan and executive officer of M Company of Lt. Col. Cannonball Krause's battalion of the 505th Parachute Regiment, was given the assignment. Woods reported to a division operations officer and was told that while there were enemy troops and artillery on the Egadis, intelligence did not know precisely where they were positioned or how many of them there were. The paratrooper force would also have to furnish its own vessel, as none would be available from navy units.

Lieutenant Woods hastily rounded up 28 paratroopers and headed for the docks at Trapani. There, after considerable haggling with a fisherman, Woods negotiated the rental of a battered, leaking wooden boat barely 20 feet in length and secured the services of the Sicilian owner to operate the craft.

With Woods, his 28 parachutists and the fisherman crammed into the boat, a course was set for the nearest island of Levanzo. Landing at the docks, the parachute detachment leaped out with weapons at the ready. Woods deployed his men to search the small piece of land but soon learned there was no enemy force on the island.

The troopers climbed back aboard the small vessel, which tilted and threatened to capsize when one side or the other held too many men, and headed for the next island, Marittimo. There the landing procedure was repeated, but again no enemy troops were found.

"Okay, head for the big island," Lieutenant Woods ordered the fisherman when all paratroopers had scrambled back into the boat. That island was Favignana. Woods and his men knew that if the two smaller islands held no enemy troops, they had to be congregated on Favignana. There the impending showdown loomed. With memories of the bloody clash at Biazza Ridge still fresh in their minds, the grim-faced All-Americans steeled themselves for battle.

Woods and his small force, with tommy guns and rifles poised for immediate action, edged up to the fishing docks at Favignana. The only sounds were the gentle lapping of the surf on the beaches and the monotonous throbbing put-put-put of the wheezing old boat motor. Had the enemy garrison spotted the approach of the boat crammed with American soldiers and now was lying in wait to open a fusillade of automatic weapons fire?

The 505s scrambled up onto the dock. Not a shot was fired or an enemy soldier seen. Woods and his men moved cautiously down the only street of the little harbor town, and despite the sudden, unexpected arrival of alien soldiers wearing baggy jump suits, few Egadi citizens paid attention to them.

Interrogating natives through an interpreter, Woods learned that the headquarters for the Italian garrison on the island was located in a farmhouse a mile inland and that most of the troops were located in that area.

"Ask how many Italian soldiers there are," the lieutenant told his interpreter.

"They say there are hundreds of them" was the reply.

In approach-march formation and weapons at the ready, the 29 paratroopers moved out toward the farmhouse. Nearing the enemy headquarters without being fired on, the troopers spotted an Italian colonel emerging from the structure. Lieutenant Woods and an interpreter went forward to meet him.

The Italian identified himself as commander of the garrison on Favignana. Militarily correct but affable, the enemy colonel explained that the Egadi Islands had been out of communication with the mainland for several days. He said that this lack of communication with higher levels of the Axis command indicated to him that the Allies were rapidly overrunning Sicily.

Lieutenant Woods assured the Italian that that indeed was the case, and he urged the Favignana garrison to surrender to avoid needless bloodshed. "If you do not, we will have to bring down heavy air attacks and naval shelling on you," the parachute officer warned. Actually, Woods had neither air nor naval units available for the purpose but reasoned that the Italian colonel did not know that fact.

"There is only a four-day supply of food on Favignana for my troops and the civilian population," the enemy officer observed. "I see no reason to die for a lost cause."

Woods was relieved to hear that the Italian was anxious to surrender his garrison. But only later would the lieutenant learn that on the approach of the 29 American paratroopers in the leaking fishing boat, the Italian colonel had ordered the destruction of a battery of .75-millimeter guns, four battalions of .76s and four batteries of naval .152-millimeter coastal guns. The latter guarded the approach to Trapani harbor.

Now the Italian commander's concern turned to his soldier's honor. He said he would surrender the garrison but only to an American officer of senior rank. This left Lieutenant Woods in a dilemma: he could either order his 28 troopers to fight the much larger enemy force or return to the mainland to secure a high-ranking officer to accept the Favignana surrender. Woods chose the latter course.

Leaving his troopers near the farmhouse with orders to "be on the alert but don't do anything to provoke the Eyties," the lieutenant climbed into the leaking fishing boat and returned to Trapani. He hurried to division headquarters and hastily briefed officers there on the "Mexican standoff" on Favignana between his 28 parachutists and several hundred Italian troops. He asked for a senior officer to return with him to accept the enemy surrender.

"Hell, I'll go," General Ridgway responded. He gathered up some personal gear, strapped on his .45 Colt and accompanied Lieutenant Woods to the creaking fishing boat. Arriving at the Favignana docks, Ridgway and Woods marched briskly to the farmhouse headquarters, where the Italian colonel came forward to meet them. Spotting the two stars of major general's rank on Ridgway's collar, a fleeting trace of relief swept across the enemy colonel's face. His soldier's honor would remain unsullied.

Smartly saluting Ridgway, the Italian handed the American general his ceremonial sword, indicating honorable capitulation to a worthy foe. The 82nd Airborne commander returned the salute, accepted the steel blade, and after a brief conversation left for the mainland.

Lieutenant Woods and his 28 troopers set about disarming the Italian garrison. A head count revealed that 437 enemy soldiers had surrendered. Returning the POWs to Sicily was a tedious and time-consuming task. The wheezing, huffing old fishing boat for the next several hours shuttled batches of Italians from Favignana to the docks at Trapani.

Lieutenant Woods accompanied one of the last groups of prisoners being ferried to Sicily. As the boat chugged along, there was a sudden loud explosion, and the ancient little fishing craft seemed to rise slightly out of the water. It had struck a floating mine. There was a concerned murmur from the Italians, and Woods wondered if all aboard were destined for a grave on the bottom of the Mediterranean Sea. But the old fishing boat was more sturdy than it appeared; after its initial shudders from the explosion, it put-putted on into Trapani harbor.

As Lieutenant Woods leaped onto the dock, his potentially perilous mission accomplished without the loss of a man, a curious thought flashed through his mind: after the heavy combat he had survived at Biazza Ridge and elsewhere in Sicily, it would have been ironic had he been killed in action by drowning in a native fishing boat.

The scorching days of July melted into a stifling Mediterranean August, and the 82nd Airborne received orders to return to North Africa to prepare for another mission. As the paratroopers, now battle-tested veterans, climbed into C-47s for the flight to Tunisia, they were proud that they had measured up in their first major test against a strong, tenacious and experienced foe. The Wehrmacht's elite Hermann Goering Panzer Fallschirmjaeger Division had made an all-out effort to reach the landing beaches and smash invading seaborne forces at the water's edge. But standing in the way of the onrushing German panzers and refusing to give an inch were young men of steel wills and stout hearts, wearing the baggy jump suits and ankle-high boots of the American paratrooper.

Proud were the survivors of the Sicilian holocaust; yet in their minds' eyes the youthful, cheerful, exuberant faces of close friends, who had given their last full measure of devotion for God and country, appeared and reappeared like ghostly apparitions. These gallant young men of the All-American division fell at such obscure and undistinguished places as Biazza Ridge . . . the Y . . . Tumminello Pass . . . Piano Lupo . . . Vittoria . . . Santa Croce Camerina . . . Ponte Dirillo . . . Niscemi . . . Biscari . . . and countless locales in between and in the shell-punctured skies over the foreboding landscape that was Sicily. Places where these Americans died, and their heroic achievements, would soon be forgotten by an indifferent public, but to the surviving warriors of the 82nd Airborne Division these places and heroics would forever remain hallowed.

Now, at scattered airfields around Trapani, the revving of powerful C-47 motors echoed across the bleak landscape. One by one the aircraft sped down runways and lifted off. Soon the sky armada was winging toward North Africa, leaving Sicily behind. Few All-Americans looked back.

EPILOGUE

During late July and early August 1943, Allied generals were convinced that they were driving Axis forces back into the northeast tip of Sicily through a series of brilliant tactical strokes. Actually, when the Hermann Goering Division failed to smash the seaborne landings, a decision had been reached at the highest Axis levels to abandon the island.

Consequently, Axis forces conducted a masterful rearguard action while moving battle-tested troops, weapons and rolling stock into the port of Messina for evacuation to the Italian mainland, two miles across the Strait of Messina.

Northeast Sicily, with its rugged mountain masses and deep defiles, was ideal for an orderly Axis withdrawal. Pursuing Anglo-American armies under General Montgomery and General Patton were virtually canalized to the coastal roads where small bands of tenacious German soldiers made the Allies pay dearly for each foot of ground purchased.

Beginning the night of August 10–11 under Generalleutnant Hans Hube, who left an arm on a frozen Russian battleground, Operation Lehrgang evacuated 39,569 German troops (including nearly 4,500 wounded), 47 tanks, 94 large guns, 2,000 tons of ammunition and fuel, and more than 15,000 tons of equipment and supplies.

Without being fired on, a motorized raft carried the last detachment of Italian soldiers across the narrow strait at noon on August 16, just as

General Patton's leading elements entered Messina. This completed the transfer of 62,182 Italian soldiers, 41 artillery pieces, 227 vehicles, 1,000 tons of ammunition and fuel—and 14 mules.

The evacuation by sea of a powerful Axis force and most of its weapons and equipment, under almost total Anglo-American sea and air domination, was a feat in some ways more brilliant than the British army's withdrawal from Dunkirk in 1940. Three first-rate German divisions and four Italian divisions had made a clean getaway.

After a five-week campaign, the Allies, who eventually committed 467,000 troops, suffered 20,000 casualties. German losses were placed at 12,000 killed or captured and many thousands wounded. Italian casualties included 147,000 killed, wounded or captured.

The tragedy of the shooting down of 23 troop carrier planes of Colonel Tucker's 504th Parachute Infantry Regiment by friendly fire obscured for a time the significant contribution to victory in Sicily made by Anglo-American airborne forces.

Years after Sicily, Gen. Matt Ridgway, commander of the 82nd Airborne Division, pointed out, "No one knows who fired the first shot [at Colonel Tucker's flight], and probably no one will ever know. Nervous and excited gunners, who had been under heavy attack by the Luftwaffe, forgot friendly planes were to pass over. A few opened fire at the C-47 flight and the firing was contagious."

Once Sicily had been secured, the chorus of criticism of the Anglo-American airborne mission increased to a crescendo, most of it seeking to blame someone else or another branch of the service for the shortcomings in the operations. Much of the denunciation was nationalistic in nature.

Gen. Frederick A. M. Browning, the British airborne advisor to the Allied supreme commander, who played a major role in planning the parachute and glider strikes, was vitriolic in his remarks concerning the American Troop Carrier Command for dropping Col. James Gavin's reinforced parachute regiment over a 60-mile stretch of southeast Sicily. Browning, by implication, absolved himself of culpability.

British Air Marshal Arthur Tedder, air advisor to Gen. Dwight Eisenhower, was strongly critical of the flight plan for the ill-fated reinforcing mission that took Colonel Tucker's C-47s over many miles of American beaches bristling with weapons.

Lt. Col. William Yarborough, commander of the 504th Parachute Infantry Regiment battalion that suffered heavy losses from friendly fire and who later became a three-star general, was stridently vocal in condemning a faulty flight plan for the tragedy, so outspoken that he was removed from his command. To this day (1984) Yarborough maintains a faulty plan drawn up by those not conversant with airborne operations was responsible for the 23 C-47s being shot down and the loss of more than 300 paratroopers and many Air Corps crews.

Despite the heavy verbal salvos fired in the wake of the Sicily campaign, three of the four airborne missions in Operation Husky were acclaimed by Allied and German battle commanders once the fog of war had dissipated. Gen. Bernard Montgomery said that the seizure of the Ponte Grande bridge outside Syracuse by gliderborne Red Devils speeded by seven days the northward advance of his Eighth Army.

Italian commanders, after the war, were even more emphatic. An Italian general said that "the key to the English success in getting ashore was the failure of our troops to blow the Ponte Grande bridge," a failure resulting from its seizure by British glider troops.

Gen. George Patton, commander of the U.S. Seventh Army, had praise for the results achieved by Colonel Gavin's 505th Regimental Combat Team. Never one to issue laudatory remarks unless such was deserved, Patton stated, "Despite the original miscarriage, Colonel Gavin's initial parachute assault speeded our ground advance by 48 hours."

Gen. Kurt Student, "father" of German airborne forces, said after the war, "It is my opinion that had it not been for the Allied airborne forces blocking the Hermann Goering Division from reaching the beachhead, that division would have driven the initial seaborne forces back into the sea."

Adolph Hitler, the German fuehrer and commander in chief of the Wehrmacht, indirectly added his voice to those acknowledging the overall success of Allied airborne operations in Sicily. Hitler had grown sour on parachute and glider forces since heavy losses incurred in the 1941 capture of the island of Crete by German airborne formations. After Sicily, the fuehrer urged General Student to expand his parachute and glider forces. Too late, responded Student. The Allies controlled the sky.

Field Marshal Kesselring, commander of Wehrmacht forces in the Mediterranean, said after the war, "The American paratroopers effected an extraordinary delay in the movement of our own troops and caused large losses."

Although Allied Supreme Commander Dwight Eisenhower expressed skepticism as to the future deployment of large airborne formations (a position he was later to reverse), at the conclusion of Operation Husky he wrote in longhand: "Our losses were inexcusably high, with blame about equally divided among the several services, and with a large measure falling on me because of my failure to make better provisions against misunderstandings, particularly in the follow-up operations. . . . But in spite of all this the airborne troops contributed markedly to success, in both the American and British sectors."

Years later, Gen. Matt. Ridgway placed the airborne assault on Sicily in perspective: "Deplorable as was the loss of life which occurred, I believe that the lessons learned could have been driven home in no other way, and that these lessons provided a sound basis for the belief that recurrences could be avoided. The losses were part of the inevitable price of war in human life."

PRINCIPAL INTERVIEWS AND CONTACTS

82ND AIRBORNE DIVISION:

Col. Mark J. Alexander (Ret.), Eugene G. Bennett, Buffalo Boy Canoe, Sam DeCrenzo, Willard R. Follmer, Lt. Gen. James M. Gavin (Ret.), Louis A. Hauptfleisch, Col. Alfred W. Ireland (Ret.), Lt. Col. Walter B. Kroener (Ret.), Laurence Maxton, James H. McNamara, Maj. John J. O'Malley (Ret.), Gen. Matthew B. Ridgway (Ret.), Charles Sammon, Col. Edwin M. Sayre (Ret.), John J. Schwartz, Lt. Col. Mack C. Shelley (Ret.), Billy L. Tackett, Hugh A. Tracy, Richard Wagner, Col. Warren R. Williams (Ret.), Ivan Woods, Lt. Gen. William P. Yarborough (Ret.), Harvey J. Zeigler.

509TH PARACHUTE INFANTRY BATTALION:

Col. Carlos C. Alden (Ret.), Lt. Col. Archie Birkner (Ret.), Charles H. Doyle, Lt. Col. Hoyt Livingston (Ret.), Kenneth R. Shaker, Ernest T. Siegel, Solomon Weber.

COMBAT CORRESPONDENT:

John H. "Beaver" Thompson *(Chicago Tribune).*

U.S. NAVY (GELA TASK FORCE):

Harry C. Taylor.

AMERICAN CIVILIANS:

Barbara Fauntleroy, Patrick Freni, Thomas Lecesse, Jr., Norma Yarborough.

BIBLIOGRAPHY

BOOKS

Ambrose, Stephen E., *The Supreme Commander: The War Years of General Dwight D. Eisenhower.* New York: Doubleday, 1970.

Bauer, Eddy, *Encyclopedia of World War II.* New York: Marshall Cavendish Corp., 1970.

Bekker, Cajus, *The Luftwaffe War Diaries.* New York: Doubleday, 1969.

Bradley, Omar, *A Soldier's Story.* New York: Henry Holt & Co., 1951.

British Air Ministry, *By Air to Battle.* London: 1945.

Brown, Anthony Cave, *Bodyguard of Lies.* New York: Harper & Row, 1975.

Butcher, Harry C., *My Three Years with Eisenhower.* New York: Simon & Schuster, 1946.

Carter, Ross, *Those Devils in Baggy Pants.* New York: Appleton-Century-Crofts, 1951.

Chatterton, George, *Wings of Pegasus.* London: McDonald, 1962.

Dank, Milton, *The Glider Gang.* New York: J. B. Lippincott, 1977.

Dawson W. Forrest, *Saga of the All American.* Privately Printed, 1946.

Devlin, Gerard M., *Paratrooper!* New York: St. Martin's Press, 1979.

Eisenhower, Dwight D., *Crusade in Europe.* New York: Doubleday, 1948.

Garland, A. N. and Smyth, H. M., *Sicily.* Washington: Chief of Military History, 1965.

Gavin, James M., *On to Berlin: Battles of an Airborne Commander.* New York: Viking, 1978.

Gregory, Barry, and Batchelor, John, *Airborne Warfare.* London: Phoebus, 1979.

Irving, David, *The War Between the Generals.* New York: Congon & Lattes, 1981.

Kietel, Wilhelm, Field Marshal, *The Memoirs of Field Marshal Kietel.* New York: Stein & Day, 1965.

Killen, John, *A History of the Luftwaffe.* New York: Doubleday, 1968.

Lewin, Ronald, *Ultra Goes to War.* New York: McGraw-Hill, 1978.

Liddell Hart, B. H., *History of the Second World War.* New York: Putnam's Sons, 1971.

Masters, John, *Road Past Mandalay.* New York: Harper, 1961.

Montgomery, Field Marshal Bernard, *Memoirs.* London: Collins, 1958.

Morison, Samuel Elliott, *Sicily and Salerno.* Boston: Little Brown & Co., 1954.

Mrazak, James E., *The Glider War.* New York: St. Martin's Press, 1977.

Patton, George S., Jr., *War As I Knew It.* Boston: Houghton Mifflin Co., 1947.

Ridgway, Matthew B., *Soldier: The Memoirs of Matthew B. Ridgway.* New York: Harper, 1956.

Senger und Etterlin, Fridolin von, *Neither Fear Nor Hope.* New York: Putnam's, 1964.

Summersby, Kay, *Eisenhower Was My Boss.* New York: Prentice-Hall, 1948.

Taylor, Maxwell D., *Swords and Plowshares.* New York: W. W. Norton & Co., 1972.

Tregaskis, Richard, *Invasion Diary.* New York: Random House, 1944.

Warren, John C., *Airborne Operations-Mediterranean.* Maxwell AFB: Air Force, 1956.

Winterbotham, F. W., *The Ultra Secret.* New York: Harper & Row, 1974.

Yarborough, William P., *Bailout Over North Africa.* Williamstown, N.J.: Phillips Publications, 1979.

PAMPHLETS

Davies, Howard P., *British Parachute Forces.* New York: Arco, 1974.

Davis, Brian L., *German Parachute Forces.* New York: Arco, 1974.

Andrews, John C., *Airborne Album.* Williamstown, N.J.: Phillips Publications, 1982.

MISCELLANEOUS

Allied Force Headquarters (Algiers) Intelligence Summary (June 16–July 14, 1943).

Life, Time, Saturday Evening Post magazines.

Chicago Tribune newspaper files.

INDEX

Acate River, 71, 183, 187
Adams, Pvt. Harlan, 85, 86, 89
Afrika Korps, 6, 18, 34
Agrigento (Sicily), 202, 212
Alcamo (Sicily), 212, 215
Alden, Capt. Carlos C., 34
Aletti Hotel, 37, 107
Alexander, Gen. Harold R., 17, 202
Alexander, Maj. Mark J., 8, 67–68, 83, 126–27, 128, 129, 130, 173–74
Alexandria (North Africa), 25
Algeria (North Africa), 154
Algiers (North Africa), 13, 16, 21, 24, 25, 28, 37, 47, 107
Allen, Maj. Gen. Terry, 150, 151
Allied Force Headquarters, 13, 16, 21, 24, 37, 107
Ancon (ship), 101, 102, 150
Anderson, Lt. C. A., 109
Andrews, Lt. H. N., 42

Apana River, 50, 53
Arabs, 7
Augusta (Sicily), 46–47, 54
Avola (Sicily), 82, 88, 89, 90, 91, 92
Axman, Sgt. Julius, 74

Bachenheimer, Pvt. Theodore, 178–79, 180
Baillie, Hugh, 107
Balkans, 9, 21, 29, 64
Ballinger, Maj. Thomas, 48
Batcheller, Lt. Col. Herbert, 139
Bay of Algiers, 37
Beatty (warship), 170
Beirut (Lebanon), 25
Bellerophon (insignia), 16
Benghazi (North Africa), 25
Bennett, Pfc. Eugene G., 73, 74
Berlin (Germany), 2, 4, 10, 21, 22, 25

Biazza Ridge, 137–49, 159, 160, 174, 183, 218, 221
Billingslea, Lt. Col. Charles, 58, 139, 174, 187
Biscari (Sicily), 121, 135, 221
Biviere Pond, 96
Bizerte (Tunisia), 24, 25
Boise (warship), 108, 109
Boston (USA), 138
Bowman, Maj. C. C., 170
Bradley, Lt. Gen. Omar N., 101, 102, 146, 148, 150–51, 160, 202
Brassell, Lieutenant, 83
Brooke, Gen. Alan, 37
Brooklyn (USA), 180
Browning, Maj. Gen. Frederick A. M., 15, 19, 20–21, 34, 152, 223

Caltagirone (Sicily), 75, 109, 110, 151
Canoe, Sgt. Buffalo Boy, 68–70, 71
Cape Murro de Porco (radio station), 51
Cape Passero, 43, 45, 47, 193
Casablanca (North Africa), 1, 37
Carabinieri (police), 150
Cary, Capt. R. W., 109
Castellammare del Golfo (Sicily), 212, 216
Catania (Sicily), 18, 19, 189, 190–91, 198, 202
Chappel, Trooper Henry, 97
Chatterton, Col. George, 19, 20, 35, 36, 45, 47
Chicago (USA), 21
Chicago *Tribune,* 56, 66, 184
Chinago, Michael, 103

Christopher S. Shales (ship), 156
Churchill, Winston, 36–37
Clark, Lt. George, 96
Clark, Maj. Gen. Mark W., 154
Clausewitz, von Karl, 16
Clee, Lt. Robert, 127
Colosseum (Rome), 124
Comstock, Capt. William, 176–77
Conrath, Generalleutnant Paul, 10, 74, 75, 109, 123, 151
Corsica, 82, 126
Crawford, Lt. Col. Joseph, 117, 133, 175
Crete, 2, 190, 224
Comiso airfield, 185
Cunningham, Adm. Andrew B., 30, 36

Darby, Lt. Col. William O., 103, 150, 202
De Crenzo, S. Sgt. Sam, 155, 165–66
Delaware, University of, 76
Delmara Point, 191
Denno, Capt. Bruce F., 133, 175
Down, Brigadier Eric, 15
Drew, Lt. Hoss, 208, 209
Dunkirk (France), 223

Eaton, Lt. Peter J., 121
Egadi Islands, 217, 218, 219
Eisenhower, Gen. Dwight D., 13–14, 15, 16, 17, 19, 22, 23, 24, 26, 28–29, 30, 31, 36, 43, 106, 107, 152, 201, 203, 223, 224
ENIGMA (German code) 22, 23
England, 16, 17, 154

Enna (Sicily), 10, 25, 75, 100, 151, 182, 185

Fadello, Col. Emilio, 16
Farello airfield, 153, 157, 160, 165, 171
Fascists, 214–15, 216
Favignana island, 217, 218, 219, 220
Fern, Lt. Louis, 158, 161, 186
Foley, Pvt. Philip, 138
Follmer, Capt. W. R. "Bill," 93–94, 95, 96, 102, 126, 182
Fort Bragg (North Carolina), 4, 157, 179
France, 9, 37
Frascati (Italy), 10, 21, 29
Freeland, Sgt. Harold, 127
Freeman, Lt. Col. Leslie G., 171

Gaffey, Maj. Gen. Hugh, 212
Galland, Gen. Adolph, 125–26
Galpin, Sgt. D. P., 50
Games, Pvt. Robert, 98, 99
Gavin, Barbara, 217
Gavin, Sgt. Jack E., 56
Gavin, Col. James M., 1–2, 3, 4, 8, 12, 13, 17, 18, 21, 22–23, 32, 33, 34, 35, 36, 38, 39, 55–56, 57, 58, 59, 60, 61, 63, 64, 65, 66–67, 74, 76–77, 79, 99, 100, 106–7, 110, 124, 130, 131, 135–49, 153, 155, 159, 160, 174, 183, 184, 187, 188, 216–17, 223
Gela (Sicily), 12, 17, 18, 32, 55, 67, 73, 74, 75, 82, 94, 96, 99–100, 102, 103, 104, 108, 109, 110, 116, 120, 123, 130–31, 133, 136, 137, 150, 151, 153, 156, 157, 160, 171, 173, 182, 184, 202, 206, 215, 217
Geneva Convention, 181
Gerbini airfield, 108
Gillette, S. Sgt. Robert W., 67
Goebbels, Josef, 4
Goering, Reichsmarschall Hermann, 125–26
Gorham, Lt. Col. Arthur "Hardnose," 110, 111, 112–13, 114, 115, 116, 117, 119, 131, 132, 150, 176–77, 187
Gort, Gen. Lord, 29, 36
Grisez, Pvt. Bill, 214
Greece, 8, 9, 21, 24, 29
Guadalcanal, 37
Gulf of Cadiz, 9
Gulf of Gela, 101, 102, 103, 135, 156, 157, 158, 160, 170, 182
Guzzoni, Generale Alfredo, 10, 11, 25, 100, 101, 135, 182, 185

Hackett, Brigadier H. W., 15
Hagen, Maj. Walter, 139, 141–42
Haifi (North Africa), 25
Halbert, Lt. W. E., 211
Hardin, Lt. Col. Harrison, Jr., 129
Hart, Pfc. Joseph, 169, 213
Hearn, Sgt. Carl, 98
Herkness, Sgt. Frank, 76–83, 85, 89–90, 92
Hewitt, Adm. H. Kent, 24, 25
Hicks, Brigadier P. H. W., 15, 17, 18, 40, 51–52, 103
Higgins, Cpl. Thomas, 176–77
Hill "41," 132–34, 174–75, 177–78
Hitler, Adolph, 5, 6, 7, 8–11, 16,

22, 25, 34, 76, 123, 125, 135, 179, 189, 190, 224
Hollywood (USA), 73
Homs (North Africa), 12
Hopkinson, Maj. Gen. G. F., 15–16, 19–20, 41–42, 43, 48, 106
Hourigan, Father Frank, 104
Hube, Generalleutnant Hans, 222
Huelva (Spain), 9
Huss, Pete, 37–38

International News Service, 37
Ireland, Capt. Alfred W., 56, 59, 63, 142, 145–49
Italian army, 7

Janney, Lt. Richard, 98
Jeffers (warship), 170

Kairouan (Tunisia), 12, 15, 18, 21, 31, 33, 35, 40, 55, 59, 77, 124, 125, 153, 171, 190
Kaufman, Capt. Robert G., 68, 211
Kean, Brig. Gen. William B., Jr., 151
Keerans, Brig. Gen. Charles, 6–7, 57, 154, 160
Kesselring, Generalfeldmarschall Albert, 10, 14, 21–23, 29, 75, 109, 150, 151, 182–83, 189–90, 224
Keyes, Maj. Gen. Geoffrey, 202
Kietel, Generalfeldmarschall Wilhelm, 22
Kirk, Rear Adm. Alan G., 101
Kouns, Lt. Col. Charles W., 119
Kozak, Chaplain Edwin J., 214

Krause, Lt. Col. Edward "Cannonball," 137, 139, 218
Kroener, Lt. Walter B., 94, 96–97
Kronheim, Lt. Al, 131
Kyle, Flight Officer Morris, 42
Kuehl, Chaplain Delbert A., 169–70

Lathbury, Brigadier Gerald, 15, 18, 190, 191, 197
Leccese, Sgt. Thomas, 180–81
Lee, Brig. Gen. William H., 154–55
Levanzo island, 217, 218
Lewis, Lt. C. G., 109
Licata (Sicily), 101, 103
Linosa island, 59–60
London, 37
Lonsdale, Maj. R. T. H., 198
Low Countries, 2
Luftwaffe, 16, 17–18, 29, 88, 108, 109, 125, 140, 153, 156–57, 190, 193, 201, 207, 223
Lynch, Lt. Col. George, 217

Maddalena Peninsula, 51
Magee, Sgt. John, 158
Malati Bridge, 191, 199
Malta, 12, 13, 28, 29, 36, 43–45, 60, 74, 106, 155, 191–93, 195, 201
Manfredi, Adm. Alberto, 212
Marina di Raguso (Sicily), 129
Marittimo island, 217, 218
Marshall, Gen. George C., 31, 37, 63
Martin, Capt. William, 9
May, Lt. Robert, 142

McCandless, Lt. Dean, 176–77
McCormick, Col. Cedric, 107
McGinity, Capt. James, 72
McNamara, Pfc. James M., 168–69, 213–14
Menzies, Stewart, 9
Messina (Sicily), 18, 189, 195, 202, 203, 211, 222
MI–6 (British intelligence), 9
Middleton, Maj. Gen. Troy H., 71, 135, 146
Miller, Lt. Arthur, 129–30
Mississippi (USA), 72
Monrovia (ship), 29
Montgomery, Gen. Bernard L., 13, 17, 18, 19, 25, 36, 40, 45, 104, 106, 201–2, 211, 222
Mosquito (airplanes), 12–13
Mountbatten, Lord Louis, 36
Mount Etna, 195
Murone, Corporal, 140
Mussolini, Benito, 25, 182–83, 203, 215

Naples (Italy), 214
Nazi Party, 4–5, 11, 18, 21, 179, 180
Niscemi (Sicily), 109, 110, 113, 121, 122, 136, 178, 221
North Africa, 2, 5–8, 10, 15, 18, 25, 28, 30, 34, 72, 83, 101, 125, 154, 184, 194, 202, 215, 221
Northwest African Air Force, 185
Norton, Capt. John, 127–28

Oberbefehlshaber Sued, 10
Oberkommando der Wehrmacht, 8, 10, 21–22

Objective Y, 110, 116, 122, 187, 221
O'Malley, Lt. John, 157–59, 161, 186, 207–8
O'Mara, Pvt. Lawrence, 104
Operation Fustian, 18, 190, 191
Operation Husky, 9, 15, 16–17, 29, 31, 37, 38, 224, 225
Operation Husky One, 18, 55
Operation Husky Two, 18
Operation Ladbroke, 18, 40, 50, 53
Operation Lehrgang (German), 222
Operation Mincemeat, 9
Operation Torch, 154
Operation Trojan Horse, 9
Oran (Algeria), 25
Ott, Lt. James C., 122–23
Oujda (French Morocco), 1, 6, 8, 15

Paccassi, Flight Officer J. G., 170
Pachino peninsula, 103, 211
Palermo (Sicily), 64, 212
Palestine, 15
Pappas, Lt. Anthony J., 21
Patton, Lt. Gen. George S., Jr., 13, 17, 25, 26, 29, 55, 103, 106, 152, 160, 185, 188, 202, 206, 222–23, 224
Pegasus (insignia), 16
Petard (warship), 201
Piano Lupo, 17, 82, 88, 99, 110, 113, 114, 116, 119, 121, 127, 131, 133, 136, 150, 174, 176, 178, 180, 183, 187, 221

Piazza Maritime Augusta-Syracusa, 46, 47, 51, 54
Ponte Dirillo (bridge), 71, 135, 221
Ponte Grande (bridge), 17, 19, 35, 40, 41, 48, 50–53, 103, 224
Ponte Olivio airfield, 13, 180, 183–84
Porto Empedocle (Sicily), 101
Port Said (North Africa), 25
Primasole bridge, 18, 191, 195, 197–200

Radio Rome, 124
Ramsey, Adm. Bertram, 24, 103
Red Cross, 34, 91–92, 180
Ridgway, Maj. Gen. Matthew B., 1–4, 6–8, 20–21, 25–26, 55, 117, 126, 151–53, 154–55, 160, 174, 178, 180, 209–10, 212, 217–18, 220, 223–25
Rinkovsky, Pfc. John, 214
Rippert, Lt. Col. Harold, 183
Robinson, Sgt. James, 97
Rome (Italy), 10, 14, 21, 29, 124, 150, 189, 190, 191
Rommel, Generalfeldmarschall Erwin, 6, 18, 34
Romney (warship), 211
Rosenthal, Pvt. Leonard, 99
Roosevelt, President Franklin D., 37
Rossi, Generale Enrico, 51, 52
Rowan (ship), 153, 156
Royal Air Force, 12, 14
Rozman, Private, 161, 164
Russell, Lt. Clyde R., 126–27, 128
Russia, 11, 83

Ryder, Lt. Col. William T., 56–58, 66–67, 139

Sammon, Lt. Charles E., 83, 84, 88–91
San Dominico Hotel, 14
Santa Croce Camerina (Sicily), 68, 135, 221
Santa Spina (Sicily), 151
Sardinia, 8, 22, 24, 29, 37, 64, 82, 126
Savannah (warship), 108–9, 116
Sayre, Capt. Edwin M., 110–113, 115–19, 131, 133–34, 174–75, 177–78, 187
Scambelluri, Trooper Mike, 85–87, 89
Schmalz, Col. Wilhelm, 189, 195
Scoglitti (Sicily), 75, 151, 160, 215
Senger, Generalleutnant Fridolin von, 11, 16, 135–36
Shaker, Lt. Kenneth R., 125
Shelley, Capt. Mack C., 166–68
Siegel, Lt. Ernest, 125
Simeto River, 18, 190, 197–99
Simonds, Maj. Gen. Guy, 201
Sprinkle, Lt. Norman, 128
Stein, Lt. Lester, 128
Ste. Margherita (Sicily), 212
Strait of Messina, 18, 22
Student, General der Fleiger Kurt, 190, 224
Suer, Capt. Pete, 180
Sunrise Bridge, 191
Swingler, Lt. Harold H., 148
Syracuse (Sicily), 13, 17, 20, 35, 41, 43, 45, 51, 53, 54, 55, 64, 82, 99, 103

Tackett, Pvt. Billy J., 72–73
Taormina (Sicily), 14
Taylor, Signalman Harrry C., 156
Taylor, Brig. Gen. Maxwell D., 6, 154
Tedder, Air Marshal Arthur, 223
Thomas, Lt. F. E., 121
Thompson, John H. "Beaver," 56–58, 60, 65–67, 144–45, 184
Trapani (Sicily), 212–13, 216–18, 220–21
Tregaskis, Richard, 37–38, 107
Tripoli (North Africa), 25
True, Radioman Edward J., 109
Truscott, Maj. Gen. Lucien K., 24
Tucker, Col. Reuben H., 3, 18, 32, 124, 152, 153, 155, 157, 170–71, 178, 185, 203, 213, 214, 223
Tumminello Pass, 207–10, 215, 221
Tunisia, 3, 6, 8, 13, 15, 19, 26, 36, 38, 45, 57, 59, 76, 154, 160, 171, 191, 194, 199, 202, 221

ULTRA (Allied decoder), 14, 22–23, 142
United Press, 107
United States Army, 7, 33

United States Navy, 139

Vandervoort, Maj. Benjamin H., 56, 63–65
Vittoria (Sicily), 25, 110, 136

Wagner, Pfc. Richard, 161–65
War Department (U.S.), 31
Washington, D.C., 6, 217
Weber, Sgt. Solomon, 125
Weschler, Lt. Ben L., 137–39
West Point, 2, 187
Wienecke, Lt. Col. Robert, 217
Williams, Pvt. Bernard, 177
Williams, Lt. Col. Warren R., 155, 165
Wilson, Flight Officer Robert, 47
Withers, Lt. Louis, 50–51
Wood, Sergeant, 81–82
Woods, Lt. Ivan F., 218–21

Yarborough, Lt. Col. William P., 154–55, 157–59, 161, 166, 185–86, 204–10, 215–16, 223
Yardley, Lt. Col. Doyle R., 6
Youks les Bains airfield, 56

Ziegler, Lt. Harvey J., 140